PRIVACY LAW
IN A NUTSHELL

By

JOHN T. SOMA
Professor of Law
University of Denver Sturm College of Law
Executive Director—Privacy Foundation

STEPHEN D. RYNERSON
Holme, Roberts & Owen
Denver, Colorado

Mat #40613565

Nutshell Series, In a Nutshell, the Nutshell Logo and West Group are trademarks registered in the U.S. Patent and Trademark Office.

© 2008 Thomson/West
      610 Opperman Drive
      St. Paul, MN 55123
      1–800–313–9378

Printed in the United States of America

ISBN: 978–0–314–18134–3

ACKNOWLEDGEMENT

We owe thanks to those who have helped us on this Nutshell. University of Denver law student John "Zach" Courson assisted us in the final draft by suggesting numerous changes, as well as organizing and tracking the normal plethora of last minute changes. Law students Adam Aldrich and Kathleen Ott also assisted in the final editing. Given the breadth of the privacy subject, law students David Bashford, John Cadkin, Laura Chartrand, Sean Clemmensen, Amanda Farnsworth, Howard Carter Gilmer, Kendell Gracey, Kyle Green, Dave Howell, Abe Kean, and Molly Young provided excellent initial research on various privacy topics.

The technology aspects of various chapters were much improved by comments from computer consultant Robert T. Voorhees, Littleton, Colorado, and Diane Bales, Administrative Assistant to the Privacy Foundation was also extremely helpful through the entire process of writing this Nutshell.

JTS
SDR

*

OUTLINE

OUTLINE

OUTLINE

OUTLINE

TABLE OF CASES

References are to Pages

TABLE OF CASES

PRIVACY LAW
IN A NUTSHELL

*

CHAPTER ONE

INTRODUCTION

Imagine someone listening to your personal telephone conversation with your mother, a computer recording what you purchased from the grocery store, or a surveillance camera watching every turn of the page as you flip through a magazine at a newsstand. These seemingly harmless activities undertaken by each individual involve the transfer and recording of information. We live in a world where information is the foundation of modern society. Federal, state, and local governments, as well as intergovernmental organizations, assemble near-limitless amounts of personal information concerning individuals' birth, marriage, divorce, property, court proceedings, driving records, political activities and affiliations, criminal transgressions, professional licensing, travel, and countless other activities. Private businesses also gather personal information for marketing purposes, to prepare credit histories, or to sell to various other entities, both private and public. This collection of personal information by its very nature implicates the concept of privacy—a concept of central importance in today's technological world.

Before venturing into the complex and difficult task of defining privacy one must understand why the topic is important and why privacy law is one of the most exciting developing fields of legal study. Professor Roger Clarke, a pioneer in the field of privacy and information technology, describes individual privacy as consisting of four dimensions: the psychological, the sociological, the economic, and the political. Psychologically, people need private space to preserve a sense of individual identity. Sociologically, people require the opportunity to connect and interact with others, but without the continual threat of being observed. These dimensions of privacy have long been recognized. Indeed, as the Eighteenth Century British philosopher Jeremy Bentham wrote in describing his vision of the ultimate prison (the "Panopticon"), "the most important point [is] that the persons to be inspected should always feel themselves as if under inspection. . . . "[1] More recently, the economic and political dimensions have come to be recognized as critically important as well. Economically, people must be able to plan and innovate without their efforts being subject to continual scrutiny by others who might seek to appropriate their ideas. Politically, if representative governments are to be functional, people need to be able to think, argue, and act without fear of their identities being exposed. For a free political system to function successfully people must be able to vote without the fear of retribution from others who hold a different viewpoint. Individuals must have privacy in their choice to engage in

1. JEREMY BENTHAM, PANOPTICON OR THE INSPECTION HOUSE, Letter V (1787), *available at* http://www.johnkeane.net/pdf_docs/teaching_sources/bentham/bentham.pdf.

the political process, as well as in their decision of what causes to support. All four of these dimensions inform the study of the law of privacy.

It is vital that both lawyers and the public in general become familiar with the study of privacy law. First, with the increasing rapidity of technological advancement and ever-greater exchanges of information, traditional, and largely unquestioned, notions of privacy are being challenged as never before. Through the collection, manipulation, and dissemination of personal information, commercial and government entities are gaining more influence over individual autonomy and decision making. As members of a democratic society we have the choice, through studying and understanding privacy laws, to shape the kind of society we desire as we move ever deeper into the Information Age. Second, and flowing in large part from the first trend, public concern over invasions of privacy has grown tremendously in the last few decades. Privacy concerns appear with increasing frequency on the legislative agendas of Congress and state legislatures, and garner increased media attention with each subsequent revelation about theft or misuse of personal information. Third, at the nexus of the first two trends, we find an increasing amount of litigation which implicates privacy law, either directly or indirectly. Lawyers are faced with drafting privacy policies for businesses, litigating privacy issues, and helping a variety of industries and government agencies conform to ever more complex and pervasive privacy regulations.

Most law students will receive only tangential schooling on the subject of privacy law. Criminal procedure discusses the constitutional limits on where police can go and what evidence the police can collect in criminal investigations under Fourth Amendment searches and seizures; reproductive, sexual and family privacy is deemed a subset of First and Fourteenth Amendment jurisprudence; and privacy in cyberspace is often treated as a subset of intellectual property, trade law or communications law. None of these particular courses, however, are aimed at providing students with a systemic framework through which broader debates about privacy issues can be examined. As a result, privacy problems are often not well articulated and we, who are being affected by privacy intrusions, are faced with the lack of a convincing account of what is at risk when privacy is threatened and what exactly the law must do to solve these problems. Rather than using a narrow, topical framework that isolates specific sub-types of privacy protection, privacy law is best understood by first approaching it from a broad conceptual perspective before moving to an examination of particular sub-topics.

In this Nutshell, we will divide the study of privacy into four parts. First, we begin by examining the history of privacy law. More specifically, we explore the definitions of privacy from a wide array of jurists, philosophers, legal scholars, psychologists, economists and sociologists. This is followed by a discussion of the historical trends in privacy including: a general discussion of the development of international privacy rights, the European Union's view on privacy, the United States' view on privacy, the Organization for Economic Cooperation and Development ("OECD") guidelines, and the collection, retention, accuracy and use of privacy information. The first part concludes with a discussion of the technological impact on privacy.

Second, we have selected representative examples of court decisions, federal statutes/legislation, agency decisions, state constitutions and statutes, and professional ethical rules. These authorities are the root of claims brought on behalf of those who demand privacy against government officials, business entities, and private individuals in the United States.

Third, we provide an overview of international privacy law for comparison with the United States' standards and views on privacy. Canada, the European Union, South Korea, China, India, and Japan are all analyzed. Notwithstanding the philosopher Ayn Rand's observation that, "[c]ivilization is the progress toward a society of privacy,"[2] privacy does not have a universal meaning that is the same across all cultures. Indeed, the significance of privacy in a particular nation depends on the social importance attached to the context in which privacy concerns are raised. Also in this chapter, we review legal developments, business perspectives, and worker/customer concerns regarding transborder privacy data flows. Transborder data flows include the transfer of data containing personal or sensitive

2.   AYN RAND, THE FOUNTAINHEAD 683 (Signet ed. 1996) (1943).

information from an entity in one nation to an entity in another. This is an area of both increasing economic significance and regulation around the world.

Finally, we explore a variety of current and developing challenges to privacy. This chapter focuses primarily on the challenges new technologies pose to the legal concepts discussed in earlier chapters.

This Nutshell is by and large not structured around traditional legal categories such as torts or constitutional law. Rather, it provides an overview of legal theories, principles, doctrines, statutes, rules, policies, and international norms and customs, which define and inform the term "privacy," as well as where the challenges to individual privacy are likely to be in the future based upon developing technologies. The broad structure of this book is intended to allow individuals to develop a legal and logical framework to understand potential implications for privacy concerns in a variety of contexts.

CHAPTER TWO
HISTORY AND DEFINITIONS

I. A BRIEF HISTORY OF PRIVACY

Constitutional scholar William Beaney remarked in an article shortly after the U.S. Supreme Court's landmark privacy decision in *Griswold v. Connecticut*, "even the most strenuous advocate of a right to privacy must confess that there are serious problems of defining the essence and scope of this right."[1] Indeed, the only certainty in defining privacy is that it is a concept that is highly malleable depending on the experience, interests, and agenda of the person interpreting it and the socio-political context the definition is offered in. For most individuals, however, privacy's definition does not depend on some philosophical underpinning, but rather is a simple, even intuitive concept. This Nutshell does not provide an exhaustive list of philosophical definitions of privacy; however, it does use some of the common philosophical positions to illustrate the fluidity and complexity of this concept. By declining to endorse any of the particular definitions, we attempt to provide an objective and comprehensive

1. William M. Beaney, *The Right to Privacy and American Law*, 31 LAW & CONTEMP. PROBS. 253, 255 (1966).

account of what exactly "privacy" is to certain individuals.

A.   Historical Evolution of Privacy

Although not defined explicitly as "privacy," it is clear that some idea of an individual need for separateness from the public sphere has existed since the mythic era of the earliest human civilizations. In the Sumerian *Epic of Gilgamesh*, composed over four thousand years ago, the human, but immortal, Utnapishtim lives as a hermit and does not reveal his identity to his visitor, Gilgamesh, until the wandering king has explained the reason for his trip to Utnapishtim's home. In the Old Testament of the Bible one of the signs that humans have learned the distinction between good and evil is that Adam and Eve make clothing for themselves to conceal their nakedness.

More formally, privacy concerns appear in the Code of Hammurabi, one of the earliest legal texts. Drafted in the Babylonian Empire in approximately 1760 B.C.E., paragraph 21 of the Code made it a crime to break a hole through the wall of another's house. Privacy concerns are also reflected in the Laws of Manu, codified in India in approximately 200 B.C.E. That text included a provision under which if an individual deposited goods or money with a storehouse in secret, the custodian was obliged to likewise return such goods or money to the owner in secret.

In Greek and Roman societies, philosophers increasingly recognized the significance of the distinction between the private and public realm. At his trial for corrupting the youth of Athens, one of the accusations Socrates defended himself against was the claim that if his teachings were not illegitimate then he should have entered the realm of politics and spoken publicly instead of privately instructing students. Socrates rebuked his accusers, stating that to openly declare his teachings would have simply incited the public against him even sooner and "he who will fight for the right, if he would live even for a brief space, must have a private station and not a public one."[2] Meanwhile, the Roman Stoic philosopher Epictetus explained that logic dictated that human thoughts are inherently private—even the threat of imprisonment or death could never force an individual to truly disclose what his or her thoughts were.

Over the ensuing centuries, one can see the slow but steady movement toward the recognition of what most Twenty–First Century Americans would call "privacy." In 1361, the Justices of the Peace Act in England provided for the arrest of peeping toms and eavesdroppers. At his trial in 1535 for allegedly denying the legitimacy of Henry VIII's status as head of the Church of England, Thomas More rejected the suggestion that his silence in the face of the charges against him could be sufficient evidence to support a conviction. Echoing Epictetus'

2. 2 PLATO, THE DIALOGUES OF PLATO 125 (Benjamin Jowett trans., Macmillan & Co. 3d ed. 1892)

observations from more than a thousand years earlier, More stated, "[F]or this my taciturnity and silence neither your law nor any law in the world is able justly and rightly to punish me, unless you may besides lay to my charge either some word or some fact in deed."[3]

As Europe moved into the era of the Enlightenment, the distinction between public and private spheres became ever more important as people sought to limit the increasing powers of government. In the late Seventeenth Century, John Locke, one of the most influential political philosophers in history, emphasized the point repeatedly in his works that the state must necessarily be restrained from invading the property or person of its citizens. As he explained, "Though the earth ... be common to all men, yet every man has a 'property' in his own 'person.' This nobody has any right to but himself."[4] In 1765, British Lord Camden, striking down a warrant to enter a house and seize papers wrote, "We can safely say there is no law in this country to justify the defendants in what they have done; if there was, it would destroy all the comforts of society, for papers are often the dearest property any man can have."[5] In 1776, the Swedish Parliament enacted the Access to Public Records Act, which required that all government-held informa-

3.   ERNEST EDWIN REYNOLDS, THE TRIAL OF ST. THOMAS MORE 84 (1964).

4.   JOHN LOCKE, TWO TREATISES OF GOVERNMENT 204 (George Routledge & Sons 2d ed. 1887).

5.   Entick v. Carrington, 95 Eng. Rep. 807, 817 (C.P. 1765).

tion be used for legitimate purposes. In 1789, the French Declaration of the Rights of Man and the Citizen declared, "No one should be disturbed on account of his opinions, even religious, provided their manifestation does not upset the public order established by law."[6]

These are just some examples of the origins of the idea of privacy. Although privacy as a concept existed, it did not receive formal acknowledgment in the American legal community as a protectable "right" until the publication of Samuel D. Warren and Louis D. Brandeis's' "The Right to Privacy."

B.   The Modern Era: Warren and Brandeis's "The Right to be Let Alone"

As far back as 1834, the U.S. Supreme Court stated that a "defendant asks nothing—wants nothing, but to be let alone until it can be shown that he has violated the rights of another." *Wheaton v. Peters*, 33 U.S. 591, 634 (1834). It was here where the American legal system first acknowledged an individual interest in being let alone; however, the context was different from how Warren or Brandeis used it. Equally, the "right to be let alone" first appeared in T.M. Cooley's *A Treatise on the Law of Torts* as part of the phrase the "right to enjoy life and be let alone." Although Cooley coined the term, it did not receive widespread recognition until Warren and Brandeis's article.

6.   Déclaration de Droits de l'Homme ét du Citoyen, art. X (Fr. 1789).

Much debate surrounds the motivation of Warren and Brandeis to write an article devoted to the topic of privacy. Some scholars speculate it was a response to the increased sensationalism of the press in general or, perhaps more cynically, in reaction to media attention focused on the lavish social parties the Warren family was known for hosting in the 1880s. Whatever their motivation for writing the article, its impact was, and continues to be, undeniable. The article's key phrase, "the right to be let alone," continues to dominate privacy discourse, not just in the U.S. legal system, but abroad as well. Warren and Brandeis stated, "Gradually the scope of these legal rights broadened; and now the right to life has come to mean the right to enjoy life,—*the right to be let alone*; the right to liberty secures the exercise of extensive civil privileges; and the term 'property' has grown to comprise every form of possession—intangible, as well as tangible."[7] Almost forty years later, Brandeis echoed this "right to be let alone" in his dissent in *Olmstead v. United States*, 277 U.S. 438, 478 (1928):

> The makers of our Constitution undertook to secure conditions favorable to the pursuit of happiness. They recognized the significance of man's spiritual nature, of his feelings, and of his intellect. They knew that only a part of the pain, pleasure and satisfactions of life are to be found in material things. They sought to protect Americans in their beliefs, their thoughts, their emo-

7. Samuel Warren & Louis Brandeis, *The Right to Privacy*, 4 HARV. L. REV. 193, 193 (1890).

tions and their sensations. They conferred, as against the Government, *the right to be let alone*—the most comprehensive of rights, and the right most valued by civilized men. To protect that right, every unjustifiable intrusion by the Government upon the privacy of the individual, whatever the means employed, must be deemed a violation of the Fourth Amendment. And the use, as evidence in a criminal proceeding, of facts ascertained by such intrusion must be deemed a violation of the Fifth.

Though the "right to be let alone" has become a catch-all definition of privacy today, the specific definition lies in its context. Warren and Brandeis used the term in proposing a new tort: the invasion of privacy. The invasion of privacy was a more profound harm than mere injury to reputation, one that damaged a person's sense of his or her own independence, distinctiveness, dignity, and honor The "right to be let alone" is the freedom from unwanted intrusions into the person. Warren and Brandeis's "right to be let alone" is not a concept developed out of a constitutional right, but in tort.

Warren and Brandeis did not demand the recognition of an absolute right to privacy, in part because the word privacy does not appear in the U.S. Constitution. Rather they sought to ground privacy in the common law right to life, a right enunciated in the Declaration of Independence, and formally recognized by the Fifth Amendment to the Constitution. Warren and Brandeis, recognizing this potential inconsistency, articulated six limitations on the right to privacy. First, the right to privacy generally permits publication of public material. Matters of general or public interest do not facilitate an unwarranted invasion of individual privacy—the very event Warren and Brandeis sought to protect. Second, "the right to privacy does not prohibit the communication of any matter, though in its nature private, when the publication is made under circumstances which would render it a privileged communication according to the law of slander and libel."[8] "Circumstances" entail courts of justice, legislative bodies, municipal assemblies, or any public body formed as a voluntary association. Third, there must be special damages suffered by the invasion of privacy through oral publication. Like the elements of many present day laws, an individual must have suffered a specific redressable personal damage. Fourth, the right to privacy terminates upon the publication of the facts by the individual, or with consent of the individual. If an individual chooses to publish any facts detrimental to his or her person or consents thereto, no action will lie in tort. Fifth, according to the authors, truth is not a defense. Sixth, the lack of "malice" in the publisher is not a defense. The intent of the individual publishing materials intruding on someone's privacy is irrelevant because privacy is to be protected, rather than a particular state of mind punished. These six limitations serve to provide some limits on a concept revolutionary for its time. As

8. *Id.* at 216.

commentators have pointed out, "the right to be let alone" of Warren and Brandeis, although revolutionary in its impact, was in many ways simply the logical culmination of earlier work and, as some would argue, it suffers a number of significant defects.

Critics suggest the "right to be let alone" is fundamentally flawed in two respects: it is either too broad or too narrow. "Too broad" means the definition counts as violations of privacy things that intuitively are not; while "too narrow" fails to count as violations of privacy things that intuitively are. Professor Judith Thomson of M.I.T. illustrates the problem of a broad definition with the following example: "If I hit Jones on the head with a brick I have not let him alone. Yet, while hitting Jones on the head with a brick is surely violating some right of Jones's, doing it should surely not turn out to violate his right to privacy. Else, where is this to end? Is every violation of a right a violation of the right to privacy."[9] Conversely, Thomson's example of a too narrow definition is: "The police might say, 'We grant that we used a special X-ray device on Smith, we grant we trained an amplifying device on him so as to be able to hear everything he said; but we let him strictly alone, we didn't even go near him—our devices operate at a distance.' "[10] Although their definition is open to criticism, whether one is a critic or advocate of Warren and Brandeis's

9. Judith Jarvis Thomson, *The Right to Privacy*, 4 PHIL. & PUB. AFF. 295 (1975).

10. *Id.*

definition, it is undeniable that their article opened the floodgates to privacy as a legitimate legal concern and continues to be at the heart of a variety of different philosophical definitions.

II. DEFINITIONS

As the idea of privacy has become more important to human societies over the past century or so, philosophers and other scholars have increasingly wrestled with the difficult question of what, exactly, is "privacy?" Below we discuss a few of the major schools of thought on the subject and their disagreements with each other.

A. Conceptual vs. Interpretive Ways to View Privacy

Privacy definitions can be analyzed two different ways: interpretively and conceptually. Interpretively viewing privacy concentrates on examining the evolution of privacy jurisprudence in the common law and the courts' explorations of the concept—particularly Brandeis's dissent in *Olmstead* and forward. A purely conceptual analysis focuses on the search for a privacy definition whose foundation rests on general philosophical grounds and hence, can be used to evaluate and make sense of privacy debates arising not just from a particular legal tradition, but within any political or legal system. In this Nutshell, privacy is approached with both interpretive and conceptual analysis in an effort to provide an explanation of the numerous definitions currently pervading privacy discourse.

B. Anti–Reductionism/Limited Access to Self vs. Reductionism

Conceptual analysis of privacy leads to a variety of different philosophical definitions. Several scholars define privacy broadly as limited access to the self or "anti-reductionism." Anti-reductionists assert that a diverse set of invasions of, or interferences with, an individual should be understood under the basic heading of privacy. Even within the anti-reductionist camp, definitions differ as to what interferences include. For most, interferences with personal information, secrecy, repose, reserve, bodily integrity, anonymity, solitude, seclusion, and decisions are treated as separate dimensions of privacy. While at first glance it appears privacy as limited access is identical to the "right to be let alone" because solitude appears in both definitions, limited access definitions are a more complex formulation of that right. Anti-reductionists acknowledge that privacy extends beyond simply being apart from others. Under this view, individuals are afforded much greater privacy protection because the definitions are extremely expansive.

E.L. Godkin, a contemporary of Warren and Brandeis who was trained as an attorney and later became an influential magazine editor, was the first theorist to advance privacy as a limited access theory by observing that "nothing is better worthy of legal protection than private life, or, in other words, the right of every man to keep his affairs to himself, and to decide for himself to what extent they shall be the subject of public observation and discussion."[11] Godkin's definition did not expressly provide for limited access. As a result, later anti-reductionist theorists sought to advance a more concise definition of accessibility. Legal philosopher Anita Allen stated that, "a degree of inaccessibility is an important necessary condition for the apt application of privacy."[12] Perhaps the most compelling limited access definition of privacy is advanced by Professor Ruth Gavison. Gavison believes an individual's interest in privacy is related to accessibility to others. Accessibility in Gavison's theory is parsed into three facets: "the extent to which we are known to others, the extent to which others have physical access to us, and the extent to which we are the subject of others' attention."[13] Privacy in this view is not understood as a psychological state or as a form of control over personal information; rather it is a combination of three separate and irreducible elements: secrecy, anonymity, and solitude. A violation of any one of these elements infringes upon accessibility and is a violation of privacy. Many anti-reductionists characterize the primary virtue of their approach to analyzing priva-

11. E.L. Godkin, *Libel and its Legal Remedy*, 12 J. OF SOC. SCI. 69, 80 (1880).

12. ANITA L. ALLEN, UNEASY ACCESS: PRIVACY FOR WOMEN IN A FREE SOCIETY 10 (1988).

13. Ruth Gavison, *Privacy and the Limits of Law*, 89 YALE L.J. 421, 422–24 (1980).

cy as being that it is relatively unconstrained by narrow cultural and legal issues and thus promotes a more universal view of privacy.

Some critics accuse limited access definitions of over-emphasizing a form of individual control over access to the self as opposed to a state of existence. As explained by Professor David O'Brien, the weakness of the limited access definition is that, "privacy is not identical with control over access to oneself, because not all privacy is chosen ... some privacy is accidental, compulsory, or even involuntary."[14] Limited access definitions also fail to articulate what violations of access implicate privacy. Although limited access theorists or anti-reductionists can catalog a variety of interferences with privacy, their definition provides no guidance as to the degree of access necessary to constitute a violation of these accessibility interferences.

Reductionists believe the more expansive conceptions of privacy are vague, ambiguous, or indeterminate. Motivated by views of what ought to be protected from intrusion through the recognition of rights, reductionists assert that privacy can be reduced to other concepts and rights. An argument in favor of this theory is that it affords greater protection of privacy rights within existing legal frameworks than anti-reductionist theory. By viewing "privacy" as being the sum of a broad collection of already acknowledged rights, a violation of "priva-

14. DAVID M. O'BRIEN, PRIVACY, LAW, AND PUBLIC POLICY 15 (1979).

cy" is actually the violation of another right, which is clearly redressable.

Professor Thomson, the most well known of reductionists, has studied numerous cases which are usually considered to represent violations of the right to privacy, and concluded that all of the cases can be sufficiently and equally explained in terms of violations of liberty, property rights or rights over the person. As she states, the "right to privacy is everywhere overlapped by other rights."[15] In a sense, a privacy violation is better understood as a violation of a more basic right. Legal decisions that implicate remedies for privacy violations can be analyzed most effectively and consistently by reference to some other corresponding violation of a basic right, not "privacy" as a standalone right. It would be an error, however, to conclude that Thomson and other reductionists are trying to eliminate the right to privacy. Rather, reductionists conclude from this analysis that the protection of privacy can be better accomplished by ensuring basic rights are not violated. Many reductionists would argue that the advantage to this approach is that by relying on extensions of more concretely established rights the validity of a "right to privacy" is bolstered.

Critics of reductionism suggest that by conceding the non-existence of a true "right to privacy" and, instead, attempting to derive it from a cluster of other rights, the reductionists are undermining the

15.   Judith Jarvis Thomson, *The Right to Privacy*, PHILOSOPHICAL DIMENSIONS OF PRIVACY 284 (Ferdinand David Schoeman ed. 1984).

overall goal of protecting privacy. In this view, deriving a privacy remedy as a result of some other right's violation obscures the extent of current legal protection for privacy *qua* privacy. Reductionism is also criticized as giving the erroneous impression that the concern with privacy is a modern, and particularly Western, phenomenon. By treating privacy only as a label for selected aspects of other basic rights, reductionism is seen as threatening to undermine belief in the distinctness and importance of privacy for privacy's sake, as well as exposing privacy protections to the risk of being eroded by collateral changes in the law governing the underlying rights reductionists are otherwise trying to ground their definition on.

C.   Control vs. Condition Definitions of Privacy

Legal scholars debate whether privacy is best understood as a capacity for control or description of a condition. A number of theorists conceive of privacy as a form of control over personal information. Control definitions associate privacy with an individual's control over access to some characteristic of the self. Professor Charles Fried of Harvard Law School stated that privacy "is not simply an absence of information about us in the minds of others; rather it is the control we have over information about ourselves."[16] It is irrelevant whether the information is a general fact or a detailed ac-

16.   Charles Fried, *Privacy*, 77 YALE L.J. 475, 482 (1968).

count; if the person seeks control over the information, it is private information that should be protected. Under this definition of privacy, the emphasis is on guarding as private all information over which individuals want to preserve control.

"Informational privacy," a term coined by political scientist Dr. Alan Westin, is an example of a control definition of privacy. Informational privacy is the interest an individual has in managing the handling of his or her own personal information. In other words, "privacy" is not a first principle, but rather is a function of the claim and ability of a party to determine why, when, how, and to what extent information about it is shared with others. From this definition, Westin concludes that personal information would be best thought of as a form of property right.[17] Control over information is ownership in the information.

Advocates of conditional privacy definitions are the staunchest critics of control definitions and informational privacy. Scholars argue control definitions are too narrow because they exclude those aspects of privacy that are not informational, *e.g.*, a right to make determinations about reproduction or how one's children should be raised. Proponents of the control definition rebut this point by noting that it can encompass protection of all information over which individuals want to preserve control. The *facts* of such things as reproductive decisions and child rearing are clearly informational in nature; individuals may seek to retain control over

17. *See* ALAN F. WESTIN, PRIVACY AND FREEDOM 324 (1967).

those facts and thereby protect the underlying decisions and activities. As with most legal theories, however, it is vulnerable to attack on the basis of a word's meaning. Theorists relying on control definitions often fail to define what is meant by "control" over information, and the word can plainly range from extremely narrow to extremely broad. Legal philosopher Tom Gerety has pointed out that the most popular definition used by control theorists "includes *all* control over *all* information about oneself, one's group, one's institutions. Surely privacy should come, in law as in life, to much less than this."[18] Even if one were to limit the definition of "control" to the exertion of management power over specific information, the concept is still arguably overbroad because individuals lose control over "information" in manners not involving anything most people would consider an invasion of privacy. For example, if an individual is observed walking down a public street and then enters a particular building, the information that the individual visited that particular building is now beyond his or her control because it is known to the observer. Other critics argue control is not a necessary condition for the existence of informational privacy because a person can lose control over information but still retain privacy.

"Condition" definitions define privacy as a condition or state of affairs in which it is possible to describe changes that may be considered losses of

18. Tom Gerety, *Redefining Privacy*, 12 Harv. C.R.-C.L. L. Rev. 233, 262–63 (1977).

privacy. If the condition changes, that alteration in the state of affairs is seen as a diminution of an individual's privacy. A loss of privacy in this view is contingent on a change in the conditions of the privacy definition. This approach obviously simplifies the process of finding a privacy violation because one no longer needs to focus on normative arguments. Instead the question of whether "privacy" has been lost becomes a pure question of fact. The aim of condition definitions is to explain what a "loss of privacy" consists of, without addressing either the circumstances that led up to that loss or otherwise attaching any particular legal, moral, or political significance to the change in condition.

While some theorists suggest limited access definitions are a subset of control definitions, these definitions are not identical to control definitions because privacy is often accidental or involuntary. Indeed, limited access definitions are better viewed as an example of condition definitions. Limited access definitions define privacy as a condition of limited access to one or more aspects of a person; therefore, the loss of privacy is recognized as a loss of inaccessibility. Two prominent limited access theorists discussed above, Anita Allen and Ruth Gavison, define privacy with a set of conditions—Allen's relies on accessibility, while Gavison's focuses on solitude, secrecy, and anonymity. A violation of these conditions results in a corresponding privacy loss, but a "loss" depends on the asserted condition. This inevitably leads to the question: what are the conditions for a privacy loss? Conditions are those dictated by whoever is articulating the definition. As a result, condition definitions ultimately become particularized to each individual. While offering opportunities for flexibility in policy-making, this approach also makes it difficult for two different individuals to determine whether they are actually advocating the same scope for "privacy."

D. Privacy as Intimacy and Sociological Perspective

A more recent privacy definition that has drawn increasing interest argues that "intimacy" properly defines what information or matters are private. Many of these theorists stress the significance of developing various interpersonal relationships with others. This theory views privacy as consisting of some form of limited access or control, and it locates the value of privacy in the development of personal relationships. Charles Fried, also a control definition theorist, argues that privacy has inherent value because privacy is essential for one's development as an individual, with a moral and social personality, able to form intimate relationships involving respect, love, friendship, and trust. Privacy as intimacy allows one to define oneself and freely choose which social relationships to develop. Justifications for defining privacy as intimacy vary. In the view of Professor Jeffrey Rosen of George Washington University Law School, "when intimate information is removed from its original context and revealed to strangers, we are vulnerable to being misjudged on the basis of our most embarrassing, and therefore most memorable, tastes and preferences."[19] While intimacy is a narrow concept, it is classified as a sociological perspective because intimacy affects how social relationships are developed. Privacy allows us to vary our behavior with different people so that we may maintain and control our various social relationships.

Critics claim intimacy definitions merely serve to privilege embarrassing or otherwise awkward information individuals want to keep away from others. Philosopher Jeffrey Reiman provides an example of this inadequacy. Reiman observes that individuals reveal information to psychoanalysts that they would not reveal to close friends or family members, but the same individuals would not say that they had intimate relationships with their psychoanalysts. As an intimacy theorist himself, Reiman argues that the definition may be nuanced by placing greater emphasis on qualitative aspects of intimacy.[20] Yet this attempt to bolster the theory of privacy as intimacy reveals that it can also be too narrow a definition. The theory centers almost exclusively on interpersonal relationships and the feelings produced by them; minimizing by omission concerns about the confidentiality of financial information, political activity, and other subjects frequently considered "private." As Professor Julie Cohen noted

19. JEFFREY ROSEN, THE UNWANTED GAZE 9 (2001).

20. *See* Jeffrey H. Reiman, *Privacy, Intimacy, and Personhood*, PHILOSOPHICAL DIMENSIONS OF PRIVACY 304–06 (Ferdinand David Schoeman ed., 1984).

in further critiquing the intimacy definition of privacy, for many modern individuals economic concerns are paramount in their daily lives, not preserving or deepening their intimate associations.[21] The intimacy definition can also be criticized for arguably discarding the notion that an individual may have a privacy interest in his or her internal thoughts or acts taken in solitude because of its emphasis on person-to-person communications.

E. Economic Perspective on Privacy

While most theorists believe privacy is an important democratic right that the state has some duty to protect through regulatory policy, scholars arguing from an economic perspective believe privacy is better protected through individual responses and market-based mechanisms. One of the most well-known advocates of the economic perspective on privacy is Judge Richard Posner of the U.S. Court of Appeals for the Seventh Circuit. For Posner, many approaches to defining privacy lead to economically inefficient results. The emphasis in defining privacy should instead be on identifying those circumstances in which access to information diminishes its economic value.[22] Where shielding information maximizes economic gain, the information should be protected; conversely, where the dissemination of information maximizes these gains,

21. *See* Julie E. Cohen, *Privacy, Ideology, and Technology: A Response to Jeffery Rosen*, 89 Geo. L.J. 2029, 2031–32 (2001).

22. Richard A. Posner, The Economics of Justice 232–35 (1981).

the information should not be protected from public exposure. While this approach to defining privacy has the virtue of prioritizing objective criteria, thus making it easier to establish what constitutes "privacy" and the loss thereof, it does have two major weaknesses. First, as Professor Cohen has noted, it is clear that a free market is able to find some means of wringing value from almost any piece of information. While the fact that any given individual prefers a particular brand of toothpaste is nearly valueless in isolation, when this information is aggregated from millions of individuals, it can be worth vast sums to businesses interested in marketing toothpaste or complimentary goods. Balancing those relative interests across literally billions of transactions every day in the United States is in practice impossible. Second, as has been explored at length above, the concept of "privacy" (however defined) has a strong psychological component, which is not easily susceptible to quantification in market transactions.

F. The Feminist Critique of Privacy

Many feminist theorists believe privacy is used as a shield to conceal domination, degradation, and abuse of women and others who are viewed as being outside the power structure of modern societies. Professor Catharine MacKinnon of the University of Michigan Law School believes privacy can be dangerous for women because it is used to conceal repression and physical harm of women in the domestic sphere, while discouraging intervention by state actors. She suggests traditional concepts of privacy should be abandoned because they have at root been developed to privilege those with power over those without power.[23] The challenge for feminists is drawing the appropriate line between government invasions of privacy and protecting the notion of privacy without letting this protection lead to the abuse of women in the private domestic realm. A critique of the view espoused by Professor MacKinnon and related theorists is that they have fundamentally misapprehended the definitions of privacy other modern theorists have been working on. In most of the other theories discussed here, individuals can only unilaterally privilege information concerning themselves; where two or more individuals are involved ordinarily each of them is considered to be free to separately determine whether information is shielded.

G. Problems with Philosophical Definitions of Privacy

Despite the insight and understanding these philosophical definitions bring to privacy discourse, as with all theories, there is an inherent criticism. Most definitions successfully enhance our ability to understand the moral basis for privacy; however, few of these definitions account for the privacy issues that have developed in the wake of information technology advancements or offer specific guid-

23. *See generally* CATHARINE MACKINNON, TOWARD A FEMINIST THEORY OF THE STATE (1989).

ance on questions of public policy. Philosophical definitions are, in the end, shaped as much by these developments as they influence our view of these developments. As a result, modern expectations of privacy may not be satisfied unless a new philosophy of privacy develops which accounts for technological advancements. Professor Helen Nissenbaum, a Senior Fellow at the Information Law Institute, argues philosophical definitions bring with them the implication that privacy is an interest we need to defend in the private sphere alone and that privacy in public information makes no sense at all. Put another way, Professor Nissenbaum explains, "these theories lack mechanisms to deal with conflicts involving privacy in public and have generally not taken up hard questions about surveillance in nonintimate realms."[24] For example, data warehousing companies often explain that their collection of personal information has no troubling implications for personal privacy because the information has been drawn from the public domain, thus no individual's expectation of privacy was violated. This is exactly the question philosophical theories largely fail to confront: when is such surveillance in public acceptable and when is it an invasion of privacy? Answering this question is part of the ultimate challenge of privacy law as it seeks to convert esoteric theories into legal concepts. The other part to that challenge is conforming those

24. Helen Nissenbaum, *Protecting Privacy in an Information Age: The Problem of Privacy in Public, available at* http://www.onlineethics.dnsalias.com/CMS/computers/compessays/nisspriv acy.aspx (last visited Mar. 15, 2008).

legal concepts to the practical realities of day-to-day human existence and real life expectations of privacy. The next section considers the primary way the U.S. legal system has sought to reconcile the elegant philosophies of privacy and the messy facts of the real life—tort law.

III. TORT HISTORY

A right to privacy or its ensuing definition differs greatly from how the law of privacy is applied in the legal world. Although privacy is an important value, it is not protected without some sort of enforcement mechanism or redressability. In the U.S. legal system, torts, civil wrongs that will support an action for damages, are the broadest means of protecting against breaches of privacy.[25] Most people acknowledge Warren and Brandeis's article as first articulating a privacy tort. The identification and elaboration of four major privacy torts followed, and is best understood by examining William Prosser's categories individually: appropriation, false light, intrusion, and disclosure.

25. Privacy rights may also be established by contracts and statutes. Constitutional protections exist as well and will be discussed at length below. Each of these methods is typically narrower than the protections of tort law. Contracts typically only provide protection to the actual parties to the agreements. U.S. Statutes most often guard only specific pieces of information held by individuals or entities that fall within narrowly drafted criteria. The U.S. Constitution and most state constitutions only cover privacy violations by state actors. By way of comparison, the European Union has a broad privacy Directive, with many supplemental Directives and rules.

A. Appropriation

The longest recognized privacy tort, appropriation is the act of appropriating an individual's name or likeness for the appropriator's advantage. Violations of this right often involve a defendant's use of a person's name on a product label or in advertising a product or service without consent. The rationale of this tort is to prevent unjust enrichment by the theft of "goodwill" associated with a particular individual's identity and to prevent the psychological discomfort that can result from unexpectedly becoming an object of public attention. The first signs of appropriation are found in the cases *Roberson v. Rochester Folding Box Co.,* 64 N.E. 442 (1902), and *Pavesich v. New England Life Ins. Co.,* 50 S.E. 68 (1905).

In *Roberson*, a picture of a young woman was printed on a flier advertising a baking flour company, which used the picture without permission or compensation. The woman's family claimed the unwanted attention caused her severe embarrassment and humiliation. The New York Court of Appeals surveyed a number of earlier cases which dealt with possible appropriations of people's likenesses and concluded:

An examination of the authorities leads us to the conclusion that the so-called "right to privacy" has not as yet found an abiding place in our jurisprudence, and as we view it, the doctrine cannot now be incorporated without doing violence to settled principles of law by which the profession and the public have long been guided.

64 N.E. at 447. In a sharply worded dissent, Justice Gray disagreed. Drawing on what can be recognized as reductionist and control theories of privacy, Justice Gray concluded, "I think that this plaintiff has the same property in the right to be protected against the use of her face for defendant's commercial purposes as she would have, if they were publishing her literary compositions." 64 N.E. at 450.

Three years later, the Georgia Supreme Court, expressly rejecting the majority decision from *Roberson*, reached an opposite conclusion in *Pavesich*. In *Pavesich*, an insurance company used a man's picture to sell insurance without his authorization. After reviewing the history of efforts to litigate questions of privacy law and quoting at length from Judge Gray's dissent, the Georgia court explained:

The knowledge that one's features and form are being used for such a purpose and displayed in such places as such advertisements are often liable to be found brings not only the person of an extremely sensitive nature, but even the individual of ordinary sensibility, to a realization that his liberty has been taken away from him, and, as long as the advertiser uses him for these purposes, he can not be otherwise than conscious of the fact that he is, for the time being, under the control of another, that he is no longer free, and that he is in reality a slave without hope of freedom, held to service by a merciless master;

and if a man of true instincts, or even of ordinary sensibilities, no one can be more conscious of his complete enthrallment than he is.

So thoroughly satisfied are we that the law recognizes within proper limits, as a legal right, the right of privacy, and that the publication of one's picture without his consent by another as an advertisement, for the mere purpose of increasingly the profits and gains of the advertiser, is an invasion of this right, that we venture to predict that the day will come when the American bar will marvel that a contrary view was ever entertained by judges of eminence and ability....

50 S.E. at 80–81. While *Pavesich* laid the ground for the tort of appropriation and acknowledged a right to privacy, it also recognized the tension that this right could have with other long-established principles of both contract law and free speech. *See* 50 S.E. at 72, 74. This tension has led to the development of affirmative defenses to the tort.

The most common defense, and one necessarily implicated by the First Amendment to the U.S. Constitution, is that the subject's personality is of public interest. News agencies can use the name, likeness or identity of an individual in news stories, even though they have a commercial motive in publishing, broadcasting, or distributing the information. In most jurisdictions, a news organization must show the material published was "newsworthy." Almost any information about a well-known public figure or a public official will be considered newsworthy, as well as any person's recent involvement in criminal behavior. As with each privacy tort, a right against appropriation can be waived by either explicit or implied consent. A final defense to appropriation is that the individual is not identifiable. This defense is rarely raised because, logically, the person who could bring the claim will rarely learn their likeness has been improperly appropriated.

B. False Light

False light concerns placing an individual in a "false light" in the eyes of the public, typically by publicly misrepresenting statements as being attributed to the individual. These misrepresentative statements are usually highly offensive to the person or otherwise may expose them to danger of retribution by other parties that have learned of the statements. At first glance, this appears similar to defamation, and some commentators have indeed suggested that courts are migrating away from what would otherwise be difficult defamation cases into the more lenient realm of the false light tort. This is inconsistent with the purpose behind false light. A successful defamation action requires that the information be false; whereas in a privacy action for false light, the information is usually accurate or non-falsifiable, but creates a misleading impression about the alleged speaker. According to § 652D of the *Restatement (Second) of Torts*, false light occurs when the publication by the actor would be highly offensive to a reasonable person and the actor undertook the publication with knowledge or a reckless disregard as to the falsity of the publicized matter and the false light in which the other would be placed.

False light tort violations emerged in *Hinish v. Meier & Frank Co.*, 113 P.2d 438 (1941), where the plaintiff's name was falsely signed to a telegram to the governor urging defeat of certain legislation. The Oregon Supreme Court found, based on an extension of the appropriation tort, that the defendants had taken the plaintiff's name "and whatever influence he may have possessed, and injected them into a political controversy in which . . . he had no interest." 113 P.2d at 448. Interestingly, unlike Judge Gray and the *Pavesich* court, the *Hinish* court reached this conclusion based on explicitly anti-reductionist grounds in reaction to technological advancements:

> [W]e deem it unnecessary to search for a right of property, or a contract, or a relation of confidence. The question is whether a right of privacy, distinct and of itself and not incidental to some other long recognized right, is to be accepted by the courts and a violation of the right held actionable. . . .
>
> Our consideration of the subject leads us to the conclusion that natural justice and the needs of the society in which we live should prevail over objections based upon the novelty of the asserted cause of action. It is time that fictions be aban-

doned and the real character of the injury be frankly avowed. When Brandeis and Warren wrote in 1890, it was the unseemly intrusions of a portion of the press into the privacy of the home that was emphasized as the main source of evil; since then motion pictures and the radio have been perfected and have taken their places among our great industries, while instantaneous photography today accomplishes miracles scarcely dreamed of fifty years ago. Thus, the potentialities for this character of wrong are now greatly multiplied. A decision against the right of privacy would be nothing less than an invitation to those so inclined who control these instrumentalities of communication, information and education, to put them to base uses, with complete immunity, and without regard to the hurt done to the sensibilities of individuals whose private affairs might be exploited, whether out of malice or for selfish purposes.

113 P.2d at 446–47.

There are several defenses to a false light tort claim. False light is the only privacy tort that allows accuracy as a defense. If the public statement was correctly attributed to the plaintiff, then there is, by definition, no false light claim. Other defenses include that the individual was not identified, the conduct was not offensive to a reasonable person, and consent to the use of the individual's name. Whether the tort of false light will eventually evolve from its privacy roots into a watered down defamation tort remains to be seen. For now it continues to be important to view the two concepts separately, with false light being a true privacy tort.

C. Disclosure

Disclosure (sometimes called "wrongful publication of private facts") is the act of publicizing embarrassing facts about an individual which were otherwise not widely known. For example, sexual relations, contents of personal letters, family quarrels, medical treatment, and photographs of a person in their home have all been classified as "private facts" by courts. One can break down this tort into four elements: dissemination of (1) true information; (2) offensive to a reasonable person; (3) not of public concern; and (4) so intimate that publication outrages the public's sense of decency.

The first signs of the disclosure tort appeared in *Melvin v. Reid*, 297 P. 91 (1931). The plaintiff was a former prostitute who, following a trial and acquittal on murder charges, had reformed herself and had taken up "an exemplary, virtuous, honorable, and righteous life," and whose criminal past was not widely known. 297 P. at 91. The defendants produced a motion picture based on the plaintiff's earlier life in which they used her real name and advertised the film as being a true account of the plaintiff's life. Following a review of the law of other states, the California court concluded that while the defendants were entitled to produce a film based on the facts of the plaintiff's life, the use of the plaintiff's real name was "not justified by any standard of morals or ethics known to us...." 297 P. at 93. The court specifically declined to say that it was devising a new tort, instead basing its decision on the California state constitution's protection of the right of "pursuing and obtaining safety and happiness." *Id*. Relying in part on *Melvin*, the Florida Supreme Court formally recognized a tort of disclosure in *Cason v. Baskin*, 20 So.2d 243 (1945).

Disclosure is the privacy tort that most closely butts up against the First Amendment's guarantee of freedom of speech and press. In *Cox Broadcasting Corp. v. Cohn*, 420 U.S. 469 (1975), a television station obtained details about the rape and murder of a seventeen year-old girl from court records and subsequently broadcast her name and other truthful information about her. The victim's father, claiming his privacy was invaded by the use of his daughter's name, sued the station pursuant to a Georgia statute banning the release of rape victims' names and also in tort for wrongful disclosure of private facts. In a decision that effectively overruled the prototypical disclosure case, *Melvin v. Reid*, the U.S. Supreme Court held that, given the information had been obtained from official court records, the First and Fourteenth Amendments precluded a claim based on the tort of disclosure. 420 U.S. at 492–96. The Court concluded by observing:

> If there are privacy interests to be protected in judicial proceedings, the States must respond by means which avoid public documentation or other exposure of private information. Their political

institutions must weigh the interests in privacy with the interests of the public to know and of the press to publish. Once true information is disclosed in public court documents open to public inspection, the press cannot be sanctioned for publishing it.

420 U.S. at 496. The decision in *Cox Broadcasting* significantly limited the growth of the disclosure tort and, to some extent, has forced it into a hybridization with the tort of intrusion discussed below.

Although most courts had presumed newsworthiness and use of information from public records were defenses to the tort of disclosure, the *Cox Broadcasting* ruling made clear that these defenses were not merely prudential, but constitutionally required. Consequently, newsworthiness is generally an extremely successful defense because courts have broadly construed what information is of legitimate public concern. Furthermore, because courts have recognized that certain individuals are hypersensitive, a requirement that the disclosure outrage community notions of decency or be patently offensive to a reasonable person has been required since the earliest cases. *See, e.g., Cason*, 20 So.2d at 251 ("The protection afforded by the law to this right must be restricted to 'ordinary sensibilities,' and cannot extend to supersensitiveness or agoraphobia."). Finally, courts have long taken into account a plaintiff's character as a public figure when determining whether the disclosure was tortious.

D. Intrusion

Appropriation, false light, and disclosure are all torts that require publicity; intrusion, on the other hand, is unwanted information gathering in someone's private space. Intrusion is the act of invading an individual's private affairs or solitude. Legal wrongdoing occurs at the time of the intrusion, not at publication as in the other three torts. Intrusion on an individual's solitude encompasses not only physical intrusion into their presence, but also audio and visual intrusions via artificial means.

Identifying the exact point at which the tort of intrusion formed is difficult given that many of the cases that first explored this tort concerned facts that would suggest other types of privacy torts or perhaps not even be recognized as privacy torts at all under modern jurisprudence. One of the early cases which stands out as recognizing the key distinction of the harm flowing from the intrusion itself, rather than the publication, is *Rhodes v. Graham*, 37 S.W.2d 46 (Ky. 1931). In *Rhodes*, the defendants tapped the telephone lines of the plaintiffs and made recordings of their conversations. There was no indication that the defendants publicized the contents of the recordings or otherwise disseminated them beyond the circle of conspirators involved in the wiretapping. Citing Warren and Brandeis' article and analogizing the situation to that of the common law trespass tort of eavesdropping, the Kentucky Court of Appeals concluded:

The evil incident to the invasion of the privacy of the telephone is as great as that occasioned by unwarranted publicity in newspapers and by other means of a man's private affairs for which courts have granted the injured person redress. Whenever a telephone line is tapped the privacy of those talking over the line is invaded and conversations, wholly proper and confidential, may be overheard.

37 S.W.2d at 47.

It also bears mention that intrusion differs from the tort of disclosure in that it extends protection even over public figures whose personal affairs might otherwise be considered sufficiently newsworthy to merit publication. In *Galella v. Onassis*, 487 F.2d 986 (2d Cir. 1973), a freelance photographer followed Jacqueline Kennedy Onassis for purposes of photographing her at inopportune times, but claimed he was permitted to do so because she was a public figure. The Second Circuit thought differently stating, "[t]here is no constitutional right to assault, harass, or unceasingly shadow or distress public figures." 487 F.2d at 991.

The primary defense to a claim of intrusion is that the alleged tortfeasor's conduct actually took place in a public space. Claims generally will not lie for intrusive actions in public spaces, with the exception of harassment, but in such situations other non-privacy torts, *e.g.*, assault, battery, or intentional infliction of emotional distress, are more likely to be invoked. Freedom from intrusion can also be waived by either explicit or implied consent. A narrower defense occurs through recognition of a right for individuals pursuing news stories to go on property with law enforcement and fire officials. In *Florida Publishing Co. v. Fletcher*, 340 So.2d 914 (Fla. 1976), a newspaper photographer accompanying fire investigators took a picture of a silhouette left on a floor by a girl's body who had been trapped in the fire. The girl's mother sued, claiming trespass and an invasion of privacy. The Florida Supreme Court did not find there was a trespass or invasion of privacy because the fire was a disaster of public interest and it was customary for journalists to accompany public officials to the scene of disasters. 340 So.2d at 915. Ultimately, the tort of intrusion frequently disappears in a sea of reductionism because it is a rare occasion that a putative commission of the tort will not be accompanied by other, better-established, torts relating to the protection of person and property.

IV. TODAY'S PRIVACY LANDSCAPE

Examining the development of privacy definitions allows one to understand how flexible the concept of "privacy" is. Our review so far has focused primarily on U.S. law. In an increasingly global economy, it is important to become familiar with the international privacy environment in comparison to the generally held U.S. view of privacy. The issues individuals consider private are formed by culture and history, and vary across cultures and historical eras. Equally, technological advancement is both an endogenous and exogenous driver of change in expectations regarding privacy. There is also a common denominator underlying both cultural and technological concerns regarding privacy: the commoditization of information and, by necessary implication, privacy. Successful privacy laws must be reactive to both social and technological reality, while simultaneously facilitating and restraining the use of personal information in market transactions. This precarious troika describes the modern state of privacy.

A. Privacy and Globalization

A majority of countries throughout the world recognize some form of a right to privacy in their constitutions.[26] These provisions include at least rights of inviolability of the home and secrecy of communications. Newer constitutions, including those of South Africa and Hungary, include specific rights to access and control over one's personal information. In countries including the United States, where no explicit right to privacy is found in

26. In 2006, the US-based Electronic Privacy Information Center and the UK-based Privacy International have completed the most comprehensive survey of global privacy to date. The survey, titled "The Privacy & Human Rights Report," tracked developments in 70 countries, assessing the state of surveillance and privacy. The purpose of the report is to recognize countries where privacy protection is of high priority and those countries whose privacy efforts have lagged behind in privacy protection. Report, *Privacy and Human Rights 2006: An International Survey of Privacy Laws and Developments, available at* http://www. privacyinternational.org.

the Constitution, the right is often implied through other provisions. In the 1960s, protecting personal information became an increasing concern because of the digitization of personal information and the increased reliance by both public and private entities on the collection, use, storage, and exchange of personal information. In the early 1970s, countries began adopting laws to protect the privacy of information within their countries and, by the late 1980s, most advanced industrial countries had adopted some form of privacy law.[27] There is a general shift towards the development and adoption of comprehensive privacy laws that establish a mechanism for protection. These laws vary with particular governments, with some advocating more stringent laws like the European Union and others placing less importance on privacy including, perhaps surprisingly, the United States.

1. *The European Union's view on privacy*

All European countries recognize privacy as a human right through the Convention for the Pro-

27. Major national laws in order of their passage include: Swedish Data Act (1973); U.S. Privacy Act (1974); German Data Protection Act (1977); Canadian Privacy Act (1977); French Law on Informatics and Liberties (1978); Norwegian Personal Data Registers Act (1978); Danish Private Registers Act (1978); Austrian Data Protection Act (1978); Luxembourg's Data Protection Act (1979); Iceland's Act on the Systematic recording of personal Data (1981); New Zealand's Official Information Act (1982); British Data Protection Act (1984); Finish Personal Data File Act (1987); Irish Data Protection Act (1988); Australian Privacy Act (1988); Japanese Personal Data Protection Act (1988); and the Netherlands's Data protection Act (1988).

tection of Human Rights and Fundamental Freedoms (discussed further in Chapter 4 on international privacy). Due to Europe's historically greater distrust of corporations than in the United States, European privacy law has focused most heavily on protecting consumers' personal information from being improperly collected or misused by commercial entities.

In most European nations personal information cannot be collected without consumers' permission and they have the right to review the data and correct inaccuracies; companies that process data must register their activities with the government; and personal information cannot be shared by companies or across borders without express permission. Even intrusions into privacy that most Americans take for granted, including employers monitoring their employees' private communications or checkout clerks requesting addresses and telephone numbers from patrons, are restricted in many European countries. To a large extent, these rights stem from the E.U. Directive on Data Protection of 1995 ("Data Protection Directive"). The Directive's purpose is to provide for analogous protections for personal information throughout the European Community.

Central to the Data Protection Directive is enforceability. The European Union wants to ensure that individuals have rights enshrined in explicit rules, and that they can go to a governmental authority that can act on their behalf to assist in the preservation of those rights. Indeed, the Data

Protection Directive is in many ways a classical example of "positive law"—it creates broad obligations for private entities to protect the personal information of individuals and strongly proscribes how such information, once collected, can be used or disseminated.

2. *The United States' view on privacy*

In the United States, privacy is most often equated with liberty from an intrusive government. Traditionally, Americans have been, if not necessarily trusting of the business sector, then at least not highly skeptical of it; instead reserving their deepest distrust for the institutions of government, and particularly the Federal government. Illustrative of the United States' position on privacy is a statement from Senator George McGovern: "One way to attack a nation such as the United States which depends heavily on information and communications is to restrain the flow of information—cutting off contact between the headquarters and the overseas branches of a multinational firm; taxing telecommunications crossing borders; building information walls around a nation." Thus, the United States has mainly focused not so much on the protection of personal privacy in day-to-day affairs, but instead at the point where individuals most directly come into conflict with government—criminal law.

When the United States has addressed privacy concerns beyond the criminal context, it most often has sought to do so in a manner that would have the least possible impact on economic activity beyond what was perceived as being necessary to address a particular immediate concern. The United States uses what is typically called a "sectoral approach" that relies on a mix of legislation and self-regulation. The United States avoids general data protection rules in favor of specific laws governing, for example, video rental records and information collected during certain types of financial transactions. A variety of mechanisms enable enforcement, but there is a strong bias toward self regulation, where companies and industry bodies establish codes of practice. In most day-to-day situations in the United States, unlike in the European Union, the default position will be that either no privacy protection applies beyond the privacy torts (not all of which are even recognized in every state), or a limited amount of protection flowing from contractual agreements.

3. *The OECD Guidelines and international harmonization on privacy*

In 1977, the Organization for Economic Cooperation and Development ("OECD") convened an international conference to discuss the problems of "transborder data flows"—the ability to manage the international movement of personal information. Over 300 representatives from various governments, private industry, and intergovernmental organizations determined that national legislation on privacy of personal data should be harmonized. In an effort to mitigate what it feared might be an overly restrictive approach to the subject, the United States government formed an interagency task force that drafted the proposed guidelines, and in 1980 the OECD adopted guidelines that included most of the United States' proposals.

The OECD guidelines include eight principles which have become the touchstone of modern privacy law in the international context.[28]

1. The Collection Limitation Principle: "There should be limits to the collection of personal data and any such data should be obtained by lawful and fair means and, where appropriate, with the knowledge or consent of the data subject."

2. The Data Quality Principle: "Personal data should be relevant to the purposes for which they are to be used, and, to the extent necessary for those purposes, should be accurate, complete and kept up-to-date."

3. The Purpose Specification Principle: "The purposes for which personal data are collected should be specified not later than at the time of data collection and the subsequent use limited to the fulfillment of those purposes or such others as are not incompatible with

28. Organization for Economic Cooperation and Development, OECD Guidelines on the Protection of Privacy and Transborder Flows of Personal Data, *available at* http://www.cdt.org/privacy/guide/basic/oecdguidelines.html (last visited April 15, 2007).

those purposes and as are specified on each
occasion of change of purpose."

4. The Use Limitation Principle: "Personal data
    should not be disclosed, made available or
    otherwise used for purposes other than those
    specified in accordance with Paragraph 9 ex-
    cept: a) with the consent of the data subject;
    or b) by the authority of law." Paragraph 9
    refers to the purpose specification principle.

5. The Security Safeguards Principle: "Personal
    data should be protected by reasonable securi-
    ty safeguards against such risks as loss or
    unauthorized access, destruction, use, modifi-
    cation or disclosure of data."

6. The Openness Principle: "There should be a
    general policy of openness about develop-
    ments, practices and policies with respect to
    personal data. Means should be readily avail-
    able of establishing the existence and nature
    of personal data, and the main purposes of
    their use, as well as the identity and usual
    residence of the data controller."

7. The Individual Participation Principle: "An
    individual should have the right: a) to obtain
    from a data controller, or otherwise, confir-
    mation of whether or not the data controller
    has data relating to him; b) to have communi-
    cated to him, data relating to him within a
    reasonable time; at a charge, if any, that is
    not excessive; in a reasonable manner; and in
    a form that is readily intelligible to him; c) to

be given reasons if a request made under subparagraphs (a) and (b) is denied, and to be able to challenge such denial; and d) to challenge data relating to him and, if the challenge is successful to have the data erased, rectified, completed or amended."

8. The Accountability Principle: "A data controller should be accountable for complying with measures which give effect to the principles stated above."

Although several countries recommended the Guidelines be adopted as a legally enforceable treaty, that proposal was rejected. Adherence was completely voluntary, but in the years following the adoption of the Guidelines many nations enacted legislation or regulations that in some manner tracked them. The most notable example of this is the E.U.-U.S. Safe Harbor, which seeks to reconcile the European and American approaches to privacy described above.

Following the announcement of the Data Protection Directive in 1995 there was considerable apprehension about the state of U.S. privacy law on the part of both E.U. regulators and U.S. businesses with European presences. Because of the lack of an overarching U.S. privacy law it was believed that when the Directive formally took effect in 1998 E.U. privacy authorities would find that the United States was failing to provide adequate legal protection for personal information. This would have required shutting down the transfer of personal information from the European Union to the United States, impacting billions of dollars of trade in services in precisely the manner Senator McGovern had expressed fear over decades earlier.

A compromise between the parties was reached based on the OECD Guidelines and a hybrid approach to enforcement. This compromise became memorialized as the "Safe Harbor," which is analyzed at length in Chapter 4. Briefly, the Safe Harbor incorporates the OECD Guidelines as regulations administered primarily by the Federal Trade Commission. U.S. businesses voluntarily certify that they will comply with provisions of the Safe Harbor and are thereby allowed to continue receiving data transfers from the European Union. The precise means of complying with the Safe Harbor are left to the discretion of the businesses registering with it, but the Federal Trade Commission, under its authority to punish deceptive trade practices, enforces compliance with those standards once enunciated.

B. Privacy and Technology

Whether altering the definitions of privacy or causing greater collection, retention, and use of personal information, technology challenges and reshapes privacy law and policy on a daily basis. Indeed, courts recognized almost as a matter of course when adopting the privacy torts that technological advancements have altered traditional expectations of privacy. These advancements assist the aggregation, storage, and analysis of immense amounts of information about people; breed an extraordinary capacity to track and monitor people; and permit access to, communication, and publication of this information at ever greater volumes and speeds.

Specific fields of technological development that impact privacy will be discussed in Chapter 5, but it is useful to first contemplate the point that, as the U.K. Royal Academy of Engineering suggests, all information technologies can be divided into three major categories. "Connection" technologies are those which affect how organizations transfer information both internally and externally, whether to or from other organizations or individuals. While improvements in connection technologies lower transaction costs while permitting broader distribution of goods and services, they also lead to greater collection and retransmission of personal information. "Processing" technologies are addressed to the problems of how organizations internally handle information. Effectively, they represent the ability to add value to the raw data collected and moved through connection technologies. "Disconnection" technologies are means to control access to personal information. These may be employed by parties utilizing connection and/or processing technologies to shield already collected information in their possession, or by parties that wish to prevent the collection/processing of their information in the first place. It is useful to keep these three categories of technology in mind while reviewing efforts to protect privacy, as they give context to regulatory schemes.

C. Privacy and Economics

It is unquestionable that "information," broadly construed, has had value for as long as sentient life has existed on Earth. Having exclusive knowledge of the location of a prime hunting ground was a survival advantage over other tribes. Knowing the healing properties of particular herbs conferred status and a position of power over others who lacked this information. As civilization advanced, information became more easily quantified in value, whether as drachmas, shekels, or wen, but the type of information still largely concerned the exterior world—what trade goods were available where, what the physical properties of certain materials were, and so forth.

The revolution that has happened over the past century or so, and most particularly in the post-World War II era, is the economic significance of personal information, *i.e.*, information unique to a particular individual. While personal information was always an exploitable resource, for example to be able to curry favor with a particular noble, it was rarely worth systematically collecting because the vast majority of people lived at bare subsistence levels.

The development of mass production flowing from the Industrial Revolution and the corresponding rise of living standards began to alter this equation. As the average person gained disposable income and leisure time, they became more appealing subjects for marketing purposes. This drove the development of marketing into a science, as manufacturers, distributors, and retailers increasingly sought to understand the consumer preferences of the general public. While the ability to predict the specific preferences of a specific individual remained elusive, marketers discovered that preferences were generally tied to more easily quantified demographic data: sex, age, race, education level, and income were all found to be valuable predictors of the buying habits of individuals. Given the high cost of collecting, storing, and processing this information manually, however, marketers were constrained to conducting surveys of limited numbers of individuals, and long-term storage of the raw data was out of the question except for particularly valuable information.

The invention and refinement of computers and computer networking solved the marketers' problem. Personal information equivalent to trillions of hardcopy pages of text is now stored and routinely transmitted at minimal cost. Driver's license and motor vehicle records, voter registration lists, medical records, court records, credit card activity indices, financial transfers, and personalized shopping data collected from "loyalty cards" join traditional demographic information in these databases. Each of these datapoints enables companies to predict future behavior and consumer preferences on an increasingly individualized level. Indeed, not only is information used that has been directly collected, but interpolation from that information is increasingly possible as well. For example, purchasing a house in one neighborhood as compared to another will trigger different direct marketing based on census tract information. As computer processing power continues to grow, the marketers' need for additional personal information to provide more datapoints likewise increases.

This process is, of course, value neutral in and of itself. Humans, by nature, are consumers and generally aspire to do so in a manner that best satisfies their wants and needs, and marketers do not specifically aspire to compromise individual privacy. As Professor Cohen has noted, the "colonization of private spaces by cookies, web bugs, smart microchips, and self-enforcing licenses is an entirely predictable consequence of the market-driven search for more and better information. If information is money, there is no reason to expect that the desire for more information should stop politely at the residential doorstep or its virtual equivalent."[29] Ironically, if, as political philosopher Chris Sciabarra has suggested, capitalism was the driving force in developing the modern concept of privacy by enabling people "to produce, earn, and keep the product of their efforts, and to acquire private estates within which to pursue private joys,"[30] it may also pose the most pervasive threat to privacy.

29. Julie E. Cohen, *Privacy, Ideology, and Technology: A Response to Jeffery Rosen*, 89 GEO. L.J. 2029, 2041 (2001).

30. Chris Matthew Sciabarra, *Privacy and Civilization*, THE FREE RADICAL, at 6 (Sept.-Oct. 2003).

CHAPTER THREE
U.S. LEGAL BASIS OF PRIVACY

I. U.S. CONSTITUTION

Constitutional privacy is generally understood to mean the right of persons to be free from unwanted and unwarranted governmental intrusions. These rights or "autonomy interests" have been found to include reproductive freedom; family relationships; sexuality; personal autonomy; decisions about dying and death; and informational privacy. Constitutional privacy also embraces the right of the individual not to have certain private information gathered, preserved, or disseminated by the government. Constitutional law accordingly restricts intrusions into certain areas or communications.

As was discussed at length in Chapter 2, there are many different philosophical approaches to defining privacy. In U.S. constitutional law, however, scholars find that there are two primary definitions that courts concern themselves with: (1) individual privacy or autonomy; and (2) data privacy or control of information. As Professor Raymond Nimmer of the University of Houston Law Center explains, the "autonomy" definition refers "to the ability of an individual to prevent others from knowing, discovering, or disclosing sensitive generally confidential information pertaining the private life of the individual or to recover damages from their having done so...." The "control" definition refers to "what right an individual has to prevent or control another party's use of data that is personally identifiable to the individual, but was lawfully obtained by the other party."

A. Privacy and Autonomy

Neither the U.S. Constitution nor any of its amendments specifically mentions the right to privacy. The First, Third, Fourth, and Fifth Amendments all contain some privacy components. The First Amendment guarantees freedom in both religious and political matters, including the freedom of association. In his famous *Commentaries on the Constitution of the United States*, Justice Joseph Story noted that these freedoms were intended to secure the rights of "private sentiment" and "private judgment." The Third Amendment protects the privacy of the home in peacetime from soldiers seeking quarters without the owner's consent. Justice Story explained that that the purpose of this provision was "to secure the perfect enjoyment of that great right, of the [English] common law, that a man's house shall be his own castle, privileged against all civil and military intrusion." The Fourth Amendment prohibits intrusions into dwellings, specifically providing that persons have the right to be secure in their persons, houses, papers, and effects, against unreasonable searches and seizures. Judge Thomas Cooley likewise considered this an extension of the common law principle that "a man's house is his castle" and that in this castle, persons were to be free from "the prying eyes of the government." The Fifth Amendment, by prohibiting compulsory self-incrimination and thereby guaranteeing the right to silence, protects the privacy of one's thoughts. This can be seen as an affirmation of Sir Thomas More's remark to his prosecutors two centuries earlier that silence cannot be taken as an admission of guilt.

Arguably, privacy was always highly valued by American society; however, the U.S. Supreme Court did not specifically recognize an independent right to privacy until the latter half of the Twentieth Century. In the landmark privacy case, *Griswold v. Connecticut*, 381 U.S. 479 (1965) Justice Goldberg, joined by Chief Justice Warren and Justice Brennan (in their concurring opinion) found the Ninth Amendment to be the source of the right to privacy, starting a line of privacy cases that continue to dominate all analysis of individual privacy rights vis-à-vis Federal and state governments.

1. *Griswold v. Connecticut*

Sixty years after Georgia became the first state to recognize a right to privacy,[1] the Supreme Court announced in *Griswold* an independent right to

1. Pavesich v. New England Life Ins. Co., 50 S.E. 68 (Ga. 1905).

privacy under the U.S. Constitution. The Supreme Court declared unconstitutional a Connecticut law that prohibited the use and distribution of contraceptives. The state law also made it a crime to assist, abet, or counsel a violation of the law. The Supreme Court, in an opinion by Justice Douglas, found that the right to privacy was a fundamental right. Choosing to avoid questions of substantive due process (a form of constitutional jurisprudence which many courts consider discredited), the Court expressly rejected the proposition that the right was derivable from the due process clause of the Fourteenth Amendment. Instead, the Court found that privacy was implicit in many of the specific provisions of the Bill of Rights, including the First, Third, Fourth, and Fifth Amendments.

> The forgoing cases suggest that specific guarantees in the Bill of Rights have penumbras, formed by emanations from those guarantees that help give them life and substance. Various guarantees create zones of privacy.... We have had many controversies over these penumbral rights of privacy and repose. These cases bear witness that the right of privacy which presses for recognition here is a legitimate one.

381 U.S. at 484–85.

In a concurring opinion, Justice Goldberg, joined by Chief Justice Warren and Justice Brennan, suggested that the Ninth Amendment could be a source of authority to protect privacy rights absent an express textual reference to the concept. Meanwhile, Justices Harlan and White, concurring in the judgment, postulated in separate concurrences that if there was a right to privacy that protected individuals against action by state governments it would be independently derived from the Fourteenth Amendment.

In the dissenting opinion, Justices Black and Stewart argued that there was no right to privacy mentioned in the Constitution and that they believed the Court was at risk of following in the steps of the substantive due process decisions by enforcing values that had no textual basis in the Constitution.

The *Griswold* court's approach has been heavily criticized and, while its conclusion that a constitutional right to privacy exists has been influential, its legal analysis has not been followed by subsequent cases. Constitutional scholars note that the penumbral approach is ultimately a form of substantive due process analysis. Regardless of criticism, however, numerous subsequent U.S. Supreme Court cases have extended the right of privacy first established in *Griswold*.

2. *Roe v. Wade*

Roe v. Wade, 410 U.S. 113 (1973), is best known for recognizing a constitutional right to abortion. But this conclusion flowed from the Court's analysis of a right to privacy. In an effort to avoid the fractured concurrences of *Griswold*, Justice Blackmun's opinion paved over the question of where precisely a right to privacy could be found in the Constitution:

> This right to privacy, whether it be founded in the Fourteenth Amendment's conception of personal liberty and restrictions upon state action, as we feel it is, or, . . . in the Ninth Amendment's reservation of rights to the people, is broad enough to encompass a woman's decision whether or not to terminate her pregnancy.

410 U.S. at 153. Ultimately, however, the *Roe* Court concluded that regardless of its origin, the right to privacy was protectable via the Fourteenth Amendment's due process clause.

3. *Bowers v. Hardwick*

In *Bowers v. Hardwick*, 478 U.S. 186 (1986), the Supreme Court upheld a state sodomy law that criminalized private homosexual activity between consenting adults. Justice White, writing the majority opinion, stated that the fundamental right to privacy in the Court's earlier decisions did not have "any resemblance to the claimed constitutional right of homosexuals to engage in acts of sodomy." 478 U.S. at 190. Elaborating on this point, Justice White explained that homosexual activity could not be considered a fundamental right because it was not part of the United States' history and traditions and it was not a form of individual liberty that must be defended in the democratic process, thus the statute would be upheld. The majority rebuffed the defendants' privacy argument, suggesting that *Gris-wold* and *Roe*, among other cases, did not actually create a broad right to privacy but rather were to be viewed as part of a line of cases dealing with limitations on government interference with child rearing.

The four dissenting Justices, however, sharply argued that a right of privacy was at issue in the case:

> This case is no more about "a fundamental right to engage in homosexual sodomy," . . . than *Stanley v. Georgia*, 394 U.S. 557 (1969), was about a fundamental right to watch obscene movies, or *Katz v. United States*, 389 U.S. 347 (1967), was about a fundamental right to place interstate bets from a telephone booth. Rather, this case is about "the most comprehensive of rights and the right most valued by civilized men," namely, "the right to be let alone." *Olmstead v. United States*, 277 U.S. 438, 478 (1928) (Brandeis, J., dissenting).

478 U.S. at 199. The dissenters concluded that the ability of adults to engage in private voluntary sexual conduct that did not result in physical harm was an essential part of personal autonomy that could be appropriately protected under the Court's earlier privacy decisions.

4.   *Lawrence v. Texas*

Seventeen years after *Bowers*, the Court invalidated a Texas state law that prohibited persons from engaging in sodomy with a person of the same sex. In *Lawrence v. Texas*, 539 U.S. 558 (2003), the Court held that the state law violated the due process clause of the Fourteenth Amendment. Justice O'Connor concurred in the judgment of the Court, but instead argued that the Court should have invalidated the law based on the equal protection clause. This would have accomplished the same result by not overturning *Bowers*, but instead deciding a question left open in the earlier case—whether the state could punish sexual activity outside of marriage only by a group of persons defined by some trait that was disliked by the majority of persons in the political process. The dissenting Justices believed that the Court's ruling could not be justified in terms of the Supreme Court's prior cases, nor from the Court's role in the definition of fundamental rights based on the United States' history and traditions.

B. Privacy and Control of Information

Although numerous supporters of privacy rights have made strong arguments over the years that the Constitution should be interpreted to protect a right to control information, there has been little support for such a right from the Supreme Court. *Whalen v. Roe*, 429 U.S. 589 (1977), was the first case in which the Court squarely faced the question of whether the constitutional right to privacy encompasses the collection, storage, and dissemination of information in government databases. *Whalen* was also the first decision in which the Court acknowledged that the constitutional right of privacy consists of two branches: informational privacy and privacy-autonomy.

1.   Whalen v. Roe

Whalen addressed a New York law that required physicians to identify patients receiving prescription drugs that have a potential for abuse. Challengers noted that the resulting state-maintained database infringed on the right to privacy, arguing that individuals have a right to avoid disclosure of personal matters. 429 U.S. at 598–99. In balancing privacy interests against the police powers, the Court noted that the government had an important interest in monitoring the use of prescription drugs that might be abused, and a particular responsibility for the health of the community, which did not automatically amount to an impermissible invasion of privacy. The Court, however, did not reject the possibility that the right to privacy might be recognized in the future to include a right to control information:

> We are not unaware of the threat to privacy implicit in the accumulation of vast amounts of personal information in computerized data banks or other massive government files. The collection of taxes, the distribution of wealth and social security benefits, the supervision of public health, the direction of our Armed Forces, and the enforcement of the criminal laws all require the orderly preservation of great quantities of information, much of which is personal in character

and potentially embarrassing or harmful if disclosed. . . .

We therefore need not, and do not decide any question which might be presented by the unwarranted disclosure of accumulated private data-whether intentional or unintentional-or by a system that did not contain comparable security provisions. We simply hold that this record does not establish an invasion of any right or liberty protected by the Fourteenth Amendment.

429 U.S. at 605–06.

Whalen is a major example of judicial recognition that constitutional protection for limiting government access to personal, confidential, or intimate information about individuals is not confined to unreasonable searches and seizures in violation of the Fourth Amendment.

2. *Katz v. United States*

For many years, the major source of law on informational privacy arose under federal constitutional cases dealing with invasions of privacy in the form of personal searches or literal intrusions into physical places. The most litigated issue concerned judicial review of search and seizure actions by government entities, most often municipal police or federal law enforcement agents, engaged in collecting information for purposes of criminal prosecutions. Developments in this area of the law led to the landmark case of *Katz v. United States*, 389 U.S.

347 (1967), which still underlies most modern privacy jurisprudence in the context of constitutional
law.

In *Katz*, the Supreme Court considered electronic
eavesdropping on a telephone conservation in a
public telephone booth. The petitioner asked the
Court to approach the issue as presented in two
separate questions: first, whether a telephone booth
can be an area subject to protection against government searches under the Fourth Amendment; and
second, whether the fact that the eavesdropping
was accomplished by a non-physically invasive
method avoided turning the surveillance into a
"search" of the telephone booth. 389 U.S. at 349–
50. The Court rejected these formulations of the
issue on appeal, finding them overly narrow and
overbroad:

> [T]he Fourth Amendment cannot be translated
> into a general constitutional "right to privacy."
> That Amendment protects individual privacy
> against certain kinds of governmental intrusion,
> but its protections go further, and often have
> nothing to do with privacy at all. Other provisions
> of the Constitution protect personal privacy from
> other forms of governmental invasion. But the
> protection of a person's general right to privacy—
> his right to be let alone by other people—is, like
> the protection of his property and of his very life,
> left largely to the law of the individual States.

389 U.S. at 350 (footnotes omitted).

As the Court explained, both Katz and the Federal government placed far too much emphasis on the question of exactly which types of physical locations are the sort that should be protected against searches:

> [T]he Fourth Amendment protects people, not places. What a person knowingly exposes to the public, even in his own home or office, is not a subject of Fourth Amendment protection. But what he seeks to preserve as private, even in an area accessible to the public, may be constitutionally protected.

389 U.S. at 351 (citations omitted). The Court likewise rejected the argument over whether the use of electronic surveillance was a form of trespass within the scope of earlier Supreme Court decisions regarding searches. Recognizing that it had formerly found physical trespass was necessary, the Court acknowledged that it was discarding that approach and instead pursuing what could be identified as an anti-reductionist methodology:

> It is true that the absence of such penetration [into a physical space] was at one time thought to foreclose further Fourth Amendment inquiry.... But the premise that property interests control the right of the Government to search and seize has been discredited. * * * We conclude the underpinnings of [those earlier cases] have been so eroded by our subsequent decisions that the trespass doctrine there enunciated can no longer be regarded as controlling. The Government's activi-

ties in electronically listening to and recording the petitioner's words violated the privacy upon which he justifiably relied while using the telephone booth and thus constituted a search and seizure within the meaning of the Fourth Amendment. The fact that the electronic device employed to achieve that end did not happen to penetrate the wall of the booth can have no constitutional significance.

389 U.S. at 353–54 (parentheses, quotation marks, and citations omitted). Despite the broad reach of this holding, the majority opinion expressly declined to find that the ruling encompassed surveillance for purposes of national security.

The *Katz* decision produced two concurrences of particular significance. First, Justice Douglas, joined by Justice Brennan, warned that the deliberate limitation of the holding to regular criminal cases gave "a wholly unwarranted green light for the Executive Branch to resort to electronic eavesdropping without a warrant in cases which the Executive Branch itself labels 'national security' matters." 389 U.S. at 359. Douglas explained that there was nothing in the Fourth Amendment that could be read to distinguish "searches" made for purposes of national security from those made for purposes of ordinary criminal investigations. Second, Justice Harlan used his concurrence to explore under what circumstances an individual can expect to enjoy protection against unreasonable searches. It was here that the famous term "reasonable expectation of privacy" was coined. 389 U.S. at 360.

Justice Harlan articulated the rule as requiring a two part analysis, "first that a person have exhibited an actual (subjective) expectation of privacy and, second, that the expectation be one that society is prepared to recognize as 'reasonable.' " 389 U.S. at 361.

3.   *United States v. White*

In *United States v. White*, 401 U.S. 745 (1971), the Supreme Court considered whether certain conversations between the defendant White and a government informant, overheard by police by use of a radio transmitter, were constitutionally protected. The Court noted:

Inescapably, one contemplating illegal activities must realize and risk that his companions may be reporting to the police. If he sufficiently doubts their trustworthiness, the association will very probably end or never materialize. But if he has doubts, or allays them, or risks what doubt he has, the risk is his. In terms of what his course will be, what he will or will not do or say, we are unpersuaded that he would distinguish between probable informers on the one hand and probable informers with transmitters on the other. Given the possibility or probability that one of his colleagues is cooperating with the police, it is only speculation to assert that the defendant's utterances would be substantially different or his sense of security any less if he also thought it possible that the suspected colleague was wired for sound. At least there is no persuasive evidence that the difference in this respect between the electronically equipped and the unequipped agent is substantial enough to require discrete constitutional recognition, particularly under the Fourth Amendment which is ruled by fluid concepts of "reasonableness."

401 U.S. at 752–53. The principle emanating from *Unites States v. White* is that a person has no constitutionally protected expectation of privacy in information voluntarily disclosed to someone else, absent some recognized form of privilege. While the Court's analysis on its face appears uncontroversial under most of the definitions and philosophies of privacy discussed in Chapter 2, the breathtaking scope of this rule was revealed five years later in *United States v. Miller*.

4. *United States v. Miller*

In *United States v. Miller*, 425 U.S. 435 (1976), building on *United States v. White*, the Supreme Court held that a bank customer had no reasonable expectation of privacy in canceled checks and other transaction records held by his bank. The Court held that the otherwise personal information contained in transaction records was under control of his bank, and not the customer, notwithstanding that the records were in part held by the bank because a Federal statute compelled their retention. The specific ruling in *Miller* has been superseded in the Federal context by the Right to Financial Privacy Act,[2] as well as by numerous state statutes and state court decisions. The *Miller* decision has been interpreted by some scholars to give private entities that collect data in a proper and legal manner co-equal ownership of the right to use and disclose the data.

5. *Smith v. Maryland*

In *Smith v. Maryland*, 442 U.S. 735 (1979), the Supreme Court synthesized its rulings in *Katz* and *Miller*. In *Smith*, local police apprehended a man wanted for questioning in a robbery and series of stalking incidents by placing a "pen register" at the local telephone company's central office for purposes of monitoring which telephone numbers he was dialing. No warrant was obtained prior to installing the pen register. After the police confirmed the suspect was the individual calling the victim, they obtained a warrant for his house, where incriminating evidence was recovered and he was subsequently convicted.

On appeal, the defendant argued that the installation of the pen register without a warrant violated the rule set forth in *Katz* because he possessed a reasonable expectation of privacy. The Court rejected this argument on three major grounds. First, it observed that "a pen register differs significantly from the listening device employed in *Katz*, for pen registers do not acquire the *contents* of communica-

2. 12 U.S.C. § 340. The Right to Financial Privacy Act pertains to disclosures by banks to federal agencies. *See infra* Chapter 3, Part II(A)(5) for further discussion.

tions." 442 U.S. at 741 (emphasis in original). Second, the Court found that there was no reasonable expectation of privacy in the information as to which numbers were dialed because, "[a]ll telephone users realize that they must 'convey' phone numbers to the telephone company, since it is through telephone switching equipment that their calls are completed. All subscribers realize, moreover, that the phone company has facilities for making permanent records of the numbers they dial. . . ." 442 U.S. at 742. Finally, relying on *Miller*, the Court explained that "a person has no legitimate expectation of privacy in information he voluntarily turns over to third parties. . . . When he used his phone, petitioner voluntarily conveyed numerical information to the telephone company and 'exposed' that information to its equipment in the ordinary course of business." 442 U.S. at 744. Thus, the defendant could not avail himself of the protections of *Katz* and his conviction was affirmed.

The two *Smith* dissents highlighted important problems with the majority's analysis, which have become even more significant in the age of ubiquitous Internet usage. Justices Stewart and Brennan took issue with the majority's view that telephone numbers are effectively unconnected to the contents of the communication. Instead, Justice Stewart wrote, "that information is an integral part of the telephonic communication that under *Katz* is entitled to constitutional protection. . . ." 442 U.S. at 747–48. Meanwhile, Justice Marshall, with whom Justice Brennan also joined, emphasized that the majority ruling set up an inevitable conflict between privacy and technology, unlike the *Katz* ruling which had sought to make constitutionally protected privacy coextensive with technological change. Justice Marshall warned that once privacy rights became dictated by technology then "unless a person is prepared to forgo use of what for many has become a personal or professional necessity, he cannot help but accept the risk of surveillance." 442 U.S. at 750. Despite these trenchant criticisms, lower Federal courts have effectively interpreted *Smith* to mean that routing information on any sort of electronic communication is not "private" for Fourth Amendment purposes.[3]

II.   FEDERAL STATUTES

Due to the incomplete nature of constitutional privacy protection in the United States, numerous statutory schemes have been enacted to fill perceived gaps in those protections. As is the inherent nature of the legislative process, these statutes represent a compromise between the demands of diverse constituencies. The following section surveys the development of privacy protections in certain

3.   *See, e.g.,* United States v. Forrester, 512 F.3d 500, 504 (9th Cir. 2008) ("Alba challenges the validity of computer surveillance that enabled the government to learn the to/from addresses of his e-mail messages, the Internet protocol ('IP') addresses of the websites that he visited and the total volume of information transmitted to or from his account. We conclude that this surveillance was analogous to the use of a pen register that the Supreme Court held in *Smith v. Maryland*, 442 U.S. 735 (1979), did not constitute a search for Fourth Amendment purposes.").

subject areas and provides brief overviews of other significant pieces of legislation.

A. Financial Privacy

1. *Introduction*

Customers of financial institutions desire, and even presume, that their financial records are private. Law enforcement, on the other hand, presses a legitimate need for access to financial records. Prior to 1970, the law was largely implicit. Various courts held that customers had an implied right of financial privacy at common law, established by the contract between bank and customer. Starting with the Bank Secrecy Act and the Fair Credit Reporting Act, both passed in 1970, Congress began to define and limit the scope of financial privacy in the face of law enforcement pressure for ever greater access. In 1976, the U.S. Supreme Court handed down the landmark case *United States v. Miller*, establishing the constitutional boundary for financial records protection and disclosure.

Since 1976, three new laws have variously contracted and expanded the ability of third parties to share and/or subpoena financial records both with and without consent of the individual being targeted. The Right to Financial Privacy Act of 1978 established, in part, circumstances under which financial records may be disclosed to third parties without individual consent. Fearing the pendulum had swung too far in the direction of financial information sharing, the Gramm–Leach–Bliley Financial Modernization Act of 1999 established an individual's option to limit the sharing of financial information among affiliated institutions and with third parties. On the heels of the September 11, 2001 terrorist attacks, in an effort to enhance law enforcement's ability to "follow the money" as a means of thwarting future terrorist activity, Congress passed the USA PATRIOT Act of 2001.

2. Bank Secrecy Act

In 1970, with an eye toward preventing money laundering, Congress passed the Bank Secrecy Act ("BSA").[4] The BSA requires banks and other financial institutions to keep certain records and to report certain transactions as authorized by the Secretary of Treasury. The act formalized the definition of "financial institution."[5]

Upon becoming law, the United States Treasury Department promulgated regulations requiring financial institutions to report any deposit, withdrawal, currency exchange or other payment or transfer involving more than $10,000.[6] As became immediately apparent after passage, the BSA was easily thwarted by simply limiting the size of any single transaction to less than $10,000. As a result, Congress and the Treasury Department have ad-

4. Pub. L. No. 91–508, 84 Stat. 1114 (1970) (codified as amended in parts of 12 U.S.C., 15 U.S.C., 18 U.S.C., and 31 U.S.C.).

5. 31 U.S.C. § 5312(a)-(a)(2).

6. 31 C.F.R. § 103.11.

justed the regulations to require reporting of related transactions that, combined, exceed $10,000.[7]

3. *Fair Credit Reporting Act*

If the BSA was all about financial disclosure, the
Fair Credit Reporting Act ("FCRA"), simultaneously passed in 1970,[8] was all about not disclosing
financial information. Targeted at credit bureaus,
FCRA restricted the use of consumer credit reports
to specific purposes and required credit bureaus to
respond to consumer complaints.[9] The stated objective was to meet the commercial need for credit and
other financial information in a fair and equitable
way for the consumer, while assuring confidentiality, accuracy, and relevancy.[10]

Consumer credit reports contain truly sensitive
personal information. When an individual applies
for a charge account, personal loan, insurance, or
job, a file is created about that individual. The file
contains information on where the individual
works and lives, how bills are paid, and whether
the individual has ever been sued, arrested, or
filed for bankruptcy. Companies that gather and
sell this information are called Consumer Reporting Agencies (CRAs). The most common type of
CRA is the credit bureau. The activities of other

7. 31 U.S.C. § 5324.

8. Pub. L. No. 91–508, 84 Stat. 1114 (1970) (codified as
amended at 15 U.S.C. §§ 1681–1681t).

9. *See* 15 U.S.C. § 1681–1681t.

10. 15 U.S.C. § 1681b.

CRAs—including tenant or employment screening services, or agencies whose data is limited to an individual's check-writing history—that offer reports on consumers in specific situations are also governed by the FCRA. CRAs may sell information about individuals to creditors, employers, insurers, and other businesses in the form of a consumer report. In addition to credit reports on file with credit bureaus, the FCRA may govern other files of information collected and maintained on consumers, depending on their content and use. Medical information and information used to prevent and detect fraud are sometimes governed by the FCRA.

a. *FCRA remedies*

The FCRA provides some remedies for breaches of financial privacy. The FCRA regulates credit information and provides for the investigation and correction of disputed accounts in an effort to ensure the accuracy of consumers' creditworthiness. The FCRA imposes certain duties upon credit agencies, such as Experian, Equifax, and TransUnion, and places duties upon commercial entities as well as furnishers of information to those credit reporting agencies including banks and credit card companies. If a consumer alleges discrepancies exist in their credit report, then the credit reporting agency is required to investigate the complaint to ensure accuracy.[11] If the agency finds that the consumer information is in fact inaccurate, the agency must

11. *See* 15 U.S.C. § 1681i(a)(1).

delete or correct the inaccurate information and notify the consumer of the decision. Also, those who furnish credit information have a duty to investigate disputed consumer information, correct any inaccuracies, and then notify the reporting agency of any changes that resulted.[12]

If entities governed by the FCRA willfully or negligently disregard its terms, then a private cause of action against those violators may be brought.[13] Furthermore, entities that furnish credit information, or credit reporting agencies that fail to abide by the FCRA obligations are liable for actual damages, which can include mental damages, as well as attorney fees. Punitive and statutory damages may be levied against those who display a willful violation of the FCRA.

b. FCRA amendments of 2003

The prevalence of privacy breaches and identity theft issues were responsible for driving the amendments to the FCRA in 2003.[14] If consumers, in good faith, believe they have been, or are about to become, the victim of identity theft, the amendments require reporting agencies to place a "fraud alert" on the consumers' file. Once the fraud alert has been filed, the creditors are required to take addi-

12.   15 U.S.C. § 1681s–2(b).

13.   15 U.S.C. § 1681n to o.

14.   The amendment was formally titled the Fair and Accurate Credit Transactions Act of 2003, Pub. L. No. 108–159, 117 Stat. 1952 (2003).

tional steps to verify the identity of the applicant before taking any action regarding accounts for that consumer. In addition, identity theft victims are entitled to receive a free credit report.[15] If a credit reporting agency receives verification of consumer identity theft, it must also prevent the reporting of such information.

To ensure that incorrect information about identity theft victims is not redistributed, the furnishers of credit information must establish and follow reasonable procedures to ensure that, when they are notified by credit reporting agencies of a disputed account, they take the necessary steps to prevent inaccurate redistribution. If the furnisher of credit information learns that the information is in fact correct, then it can report negative credit information.[16]

c. *Individual claims under FCRA*

FCRA does not impose liability on a defendant for actually stealing the victim's identity or for a theft that resulted because of inadequate supervision or security. Instead, FCRA claims usually focus on the manner in which third parties, such as those who furnish credit information or credit agencies themselves, have investigated and reported the information and facts involving the incident of identity theft, which in turn negatively impacted the victim's credit report.

15.   15 U.S.C. § 1681c–1.

16.   15 U.S.C. § 1681s–2(a)(6)(A) and (B).

In some cases, however, the defendant may be liable for both FCRA violations and common law negligence. If a bank issued a credit card to an identity thief, for example, the bank could be liable for negligence or other common law theories. If the account subsequently went into default and the bank then incorrectly reported any negative information about the victim to a credit reporting agency, a claim under the FCRA may arise.

In a recent case involving an identity theft claim, the plaintiff was able to establish a violation of the FCRA under 15 U.S.C. § 1681c–1 when the credit reporting agencies ignored her complaints of identity theft as they published her credit report.[17] The claim was allowed even though the plaintiff did not identify which of the credit reports was inaccurate, could not specify which of the defendant credit reporting agencies had violated the FCRA, and did not identify which provision of the FCRA the defendants had violated. The plaintiff's complaint alleged that the defendants had her supposed signature but could not verify that it was actually hers, and that when the plaintiff told the defendants that the credit card bill did not come to her address, the plaintiff received no response from the defendants. She also notified the defendants that she had been a victim of identity theft, but they failed to notify the creditor of the identity theft. These actions by the plaintiff were found by the court to have sufficiently

17. Collins v. Experian Credit Reporting Serv., Case 04CV1905(MRK), 2005 WL 2042071 (D. Conn. Aug. 24, 2005).

informed the defendants of the plaintiff's claims under the FCRA identity theft provisions.

Those who furnish credit information and credit reporting agencies are obligated to investigate consumer disputes, and these actions are usually judged by a standard of reasonableness. In a case involving a plaintiff who was victimized by an identity theft resulting in a fraudulent student loan in the plaintiff's name, the defendant credit reporting agency did have procedures in place to deal with issues arising from identity theft, and upon following those procedures, did in fact remove the inaccurate information, but only temporarily.[18] An error in the defendant's computer system allowed the adverse information to reappear on the plaintiff's credit report, thus giving doubts about the reasonableness of the credit reporting agency's procedures. The company servicing the loan transferred the plaintiff's account to another servicer, but failed to ensure that the loan was appropriately categorized to reflect that it had been the result of identity theft. The loan servicer changed the account number and, despite being notified that the loan was fraudulently obtained via identity theft, continued reporting the loan as a "charge off," thus giving rise to noncompliance actions under the FCRA.

In another case, a court ruled that the plaintiff's lack of action, coupled with only her denial that a fraudulent account was hers, was not sufficient to

18.   Jordan v. Equifax Info. Servs., LLC, 410 F. Supp. 2d 1349 (N.D. Ga. 2006).

oblige the defendant to take further investigation under the FCRA.[19] The plaintiff's boyfriend allegedly used her Social Security number to obtain a credit account and then forged her signature on a personal guarantee letter to secure the account. The plaintiff did not file a police report regarding the matter, nor did she provide the defendant with any evidence that her supposed signature was forged, nor did she ever indicate that the account was the result of fraud, identity theft, or forgery. As such, the defendants owed her no duty to investigate her simple denial.

In a case involving a reasonableness standard, the defendant was entitled to summary judgment because its investigation of an identity theft allegation was determined to have been sufficiently reasonable.[20] The plaintiff discovered that a former friend had stolen his identity and had opened an account with the defendant credit bureau using the plaintiff's information. The plaintiff filed a statement with the credit reporting agency, TransUnion, regarding the fraud, along with information concerning the identity thief. Upon receipt of this information, TransUnion produced a Consumer Dispute Verification Form (CDV) and sent it to the defendant credit bureau for investigation. The CDV form, however, did not mention identity theft or fraud, and did not provide any information about the

19.   Robinson v. Equifax Info. Servs., LLC, Case No. Civ.A. CV 040229 RP, 2005 WL 1712479 (S.D. Ala. July 22, 2005).

20.   Westra v. Credit Control of Pinellas, 409 F.3d 825 (7th Cir. 2005).

identity thief that the plaintiff had provided. The lack of information did not enable the defendant to make a quick assessment as to whether the account was indeed fraudulent. In fact, it took several months for the defendant to determine the account was actually fraudulent. Before the defendant had concluded its investigation, the plaintiff refinanced his home, and alleged that he was denied the most advantageous interest rate because the defendant had failed to conduct a reasonable investigation as required by the FCRA. Considering the lack of information provided the defendant from TransUnion, the court reaffirmed that the defendant was entitled to summary judgment. If TransUnion had provided additional information, the defendant would have been obligated to conduct a more thorough investigation. Furthermore, the court held that the defendant, under these circumstances, was not required to contact the plaintiff directly as part of its investigation because requiring direct contact between every entity who furnishes credit information with every consumer who disputes an account would create inefficiencies and an undue burden upon the entity.

4.   *United States v. Miller*

The BSA and FCRA left financial privacy headed in two seemingly opposite directions. On one hand, any transaction or aggregate of related transactions over $10,000 was reported to the Treasury Department. On the other hand, credit report use was restricted to certain purposes only. The rationale for limiting use of one type of information, while opening the door on another related type, was somewhat ambiguous. In 1976, the U.S. Supreme Court sought to clarify the scope of financial privacy.

Although the holding of *United States v. Miller* has been briefly discussed before, a deeper exploration of the facts is necessary in understanding its specific impact on financial privacy. The case was rooted in the operation of an illegal still. On December 18, 1972, a deputy in Georgia, acting on a tip, stopped a van, occupied by two of three co-conspirators, containing distillery apparatus and raw material. On January 9, 1973, while fighting a fire in a warehouse rented to Mitch Miller, the third co-conspirator, firemen and sheriff department officials discovered a 7,500–gallon-capacity still and 175 gallons of non-tax-paid whiskey.

Two weeks later, agents from the Treasury Department's Bureau of Alcohol, Tobacco and Firearms presented blank grand jury subpoenas to the presidents of two banks where Miller maintained accounts. The subpoenas instructed the presidents to appear on a specified day with all records of any savings, checking, loan, or other accounts in Miller's name.

On February 12, 1973, Miller and the other co-conspirators were indicted, based in part on the information provided by the banks, which tied various incriminating purchases to Miller. Miller argued that the bank documents were illegally seized. Although convicted at trial, the Fifth Circuit Court of Appeals agreed with Miller, indicating that compulsory production of "private papers" for the purpose of establishing a criminal charge was prohibited.[21] Because it concluded that Miller's Fourth Amendment right against unreasonable search and seizure had been circumvented by requiring a third party to produce the records without sufficient legal process, the appellate court reversed the conviction.[22]

On appeal, the United States Supreme Court, with Justice Powell writing for the majority, dealt with the scope of the Fourth Amendment in relation to financial privacy, which the government argued did not extend to financial records. Powell began by noting that, when the government is involved in investigative activities, the Fourth Amendment is not implicated unless the investigation intrudes into the "zone of privacy." 425 U.S. at 440. The zone of privacy establishes the security relied upon when an individual is properly within a constitutionally protected area.

While "private papers" arguably fall within the "zone of privacy," the bank records provided to the investigating agents and the grand jury were not private papers because Miller could not assert either ownership or possession. Instead, the bank records, required to be kept under the Bank Secrecy Act ("BSA"), pertained to transactions to which the

21. *See* United States v. Miller, 500 F.2d 751, 757 (5th Cir. 1974) (citing Boyd v. United States, 116 U.S. 616, 622 (1886)).

22. *See id.* at 757–58.

bank was a party, making the records not "private papers," but business records.

Miller, however, argued that the combination of the BSA recordkeeping requirement and subpoena power enabled investigators to circumvent the Fourth Amendment by setting up a way to obtain private records without complying with the legal requirements of proceeding against Miller directly. The question, then, became whether or not the compulsion to keep and produce records contained in BSA created a Fourth Amendment right where one did not otherwise exist.

Miller contended that the bank records were not business records, but copies of personal records made available to the bank for a limited purpose and for which Miller had a reasonable expectation of privacy. Justice Powell responded, however, that the checks were not personal records, rather they were negotiable instruments used in commercial transactions. In fact, all of the documents obtained, including the financial statements and deposit slips, contain only information Miller voluntarily shared with the banks and bank employees in the ordinary course of business.

Further, Congress, in enacting BSA, which requires records be maintained because they are highly useful in criminal, tax, and regulatory investigations, creates a presumption that there is no legitimate privacy expectation in financial records. The bank customer then, in revealing his financial transactions to another, willingly and knowingly takes the risk that the information will be shared with the government. The BSA records retention and production requirements, therefore, are not aimed at circumventing Fourth Amendment protections, but are merely an attempt at ensuring these records are available when needed by law enforcement. As a result, Miller was left only with the general rule that a third party records subpoena does not violate a defendant's rights, even if the subpoena is in anticipation of a criminal prosecution.

The ruling in *United States v. Miller* established four principles relating to financial privacy that remain highly relevant today:

1. Records of an individual's bank accounts, maintained by a bank in compliance with the record keeping requirements of BSA, are not Fourth Amendment protected "private papers," but are the bank's business records.

2. Checks, deposit slips, and financial statements are not confidential communications, but either negotiable instruments used in commercial transactions or information voluntarily conveyed to the bank and bank employees in the ordinary course of business.

3. BSA requirements that a bank permanently retain account information are merely an attempt to ensure the records are available when needed by law enforcement.

4. There is no legitimate privacy expectation in bank records.

In short, following *United States v. Miller*, the needs of law enforcement largely take precedence over the individual right to financial privacy.

5. *Right to Financial Privacy Act*

Partly in response to *United States v. Miller*, Congress turned its attention to better defining and narrowing the circumstances under which financial records could be discovered, and establishing notice requirements to affected individuals. The result was the enactment of the Right to Financial Privacy Act of 1978 ("RFPA").[23]

RFPA focuses primarily on notice requirements where a government agency seeks financial records. In general, individual financial records may not be disclosed to a government authority without the individual's consent. Consent is not required, however, if the disclosure is sought subject to a judicial subpoena, search warrant, or administrative subpoena. Similarly, consent is not required where the information sought is not individually identifiable, when the financial institution itself is the subject of the investigation, or when disclosure is necessary to comply with Internal Revenue Code provisions or the provisions of other federal regulations or statutes. If consent is obtained, an individual may later choose to revoke that consent.

Whether consent is required or not, if the government agency seeks financial records, notice to the

23. Pub. L. No. 95–630, 92 Stat. 3697 (1978) (codified as amended at 12 U.S.C. §§ 3401 to 3422).

affected individual is required before release of the information to the requesting authority. In turn, the individual has the right to challenge the disclosure. RFPA does, however, contain important notice requirement exceptions. Pursuant to a court order, for example, notice may be delayed until after the financial information has been obtained if the government agency demonstrates that notice will result in a serious investigative compromise or lead to flight from prosecution, evidence destruction, or witness intimidation. RFPA is limited in application to individuals and small partnerships and, therefore, its protections do not extend to corporations or other organizations.

6. *"Know Your Customer"*

With the balance between the individual right to financial privacy and Government right to effective investigation set by the confluence of the BSA, FCRA and RFPA operating within the Fourth Amendment parameters established by *United States v. Miller* and related decisions, financial privacy regulations remained relatively unchanged until 1998.

In 1998, federal banking regulators put forth a series of proposed regulations under the heading "Know Your Customer."[24] The regulations sought to reduce the barriers to law enforcement seeking financial records. For example, Know Your Customer would require financial institutions: (1) to deter-

24. *See* Know Your Customer, 63 Fed. Reg. 67,536 (1998).

mine a customer's identity, (2) identify the source of a given customer's funds, and (3) establish an expected and normal level and type of transactions for monitoring accounts inconsistent with expectations to determine if the transactions were suspicious.

Know Your Customer essentially proposed a framework for circumventing the notice and consent requirements of the RFPA by expanding the recordkeeping and reporting requirements of BSA to include the kinds of activity actual individual records, if obtained, would disclose. Due to an overwhelming response opposing the rules, regulators withdrew the proposal in 1999. While the Know Your Customer proposal failed, the exercise ignited Congressional interest in strengthening the right to financial privacy by formally preventing the type of notice and consent "workaround" Know Your Customer attempted to establish. The result was a new piece of landmark legislation.

7. *Gramm-Leach–Bliley Financial Modernization Act*

The Gramm–Leach–Bliley Financial Modernization Act ("GLB"),[25] passed in 1999, repealed various provisions of the Glass–Steagall Act.[26] The Glass–Steagall Act was a New Deal regulation that restricted certain bank and securities firm affilia-

25. P.L. 106–102, 113 Stat. 1338 (1999) (codified in scattered sections of 12, 15, 16 & 18 U.S.C.).

26. Pub. L. No. 73–66, 48 Stat. 162 (1933) (formerly codified at scattered sections of 12 U.S.C.).

tions. Broadly, GLB lifted the restrictions, making bank, stock brokerage, and insurance company mergers and affiliations permissible. In turn, GLB raised the specter of previously unimagined volumes of financial information sharing among these entities, which are now permitted to affiliate with each other. As a result, Title V of GLB addresses the sharing of financial information, referred to as nonpublic personal information.[27] Title V is divided into two subtitles.

a.   GLB Subtitle A

In general, Subtitle A establishes specific obligations for financial institutions relative to disclosing nonpublic personal information to unaffiliated third parties. Financial institutions are required to establish and implement procedures that ensure the confidentiality of nonpublic personal information, and to protect nonpublic personal information from unauthorized access. As part of the protection process, financial institutions are required to provide customers with an annual notice explaining the policies and procedures for protecting nonpublic personal information. The annual notice must further describe the financial institution's policies for disclosing nonpublic personal information with both affiliated and non-affiliated entities. In turn, financial information may not be disclosed without first giving customers the opportunity to "opt-out" of the disclosure. The "opt-out" is not absolute. Non-

27. See 15 U.S.C. §§ 6801 to 6809.

public personal information, for example, may be disclosed to credit reporting agencies and particular regulatory agencies.

b. GLB Subtitle B

Subtitle B establishes federal criminal penalties for either fraudulently obtaining or fraudulently using nonpublic personal information.[28] The target is information brokers that obtain nonpublic personal information, which they use to defraud either individuals or financial institutions.

c. GLB scope

Recalling that BSA established a formal definition of "financial institution," GLB refines the definition to include any institution that section 4(k) of the Bank Holding Company Act[29] describes as engaging in financial activities. The Bank Company Holding Act describes financial activities as any activity that the Federal Reserve Board determines—by order or regulation—which closely relates to banking, managing or controlling a bank, or incident to banking.[30]

A number of institutions have sought clarification as to whether or not they are closely enough related to banks or banking to make them subject to the

28.   *See* 15 U.S.C. §§ 6821 to 6827.

29.   Pub. L. No. 84–511, 70 Stat. 133–146 (codified as amended at 12 U.S.C. sections 1841 to 1850).

30.   15 U.S.C. § 6809.

requirements of GLB. As a result, the courts have been asked to particularly address the scope of GLB in at least three instances concerning organizations not traditionally thought to be "financial institutions." Specifically, credit-reporting agencies and credit counseling services are covered by GLB; however, law firms are not covered.[31]

Beyond issues defining "financial institution" and what entities fall within GLB's scope, GLB has resulted in challenges regarding whether or not GLB preempts state law, and how GLB impacts litigation discovery, which helps to further illuminate the scope of GLB.

d.   GLB and state law preemption

The U.S. Congress and Supreme Court are not the only players on the privacy stage. Individual states have also exhibited a keen interest in striking the right balance between keeping financial information private and providing access where needed for law enforcement or regulatory oversight. As a result, state and federal law inevitably come into contact. GLB in particular has been a source of contention in determining if, and when, state law is preempted. States have sought to regulate the sharing of nonpublic personal information among affiliated entities, and whether individualized customer

31.   *See* Trans Union LLC v. FTC, 295 F.3d 42, 48 (D.C. Cir. 2002); FTC v. AmeriDebt, Inc., 343 F. Supp. 2d 451, 461–62 (D. Md. 2004); American Bar Ass'n v. FTC, 430 F.3d 457, 468 (D.C. Cir. 2005).

consent is required for sharing with unaffiliated entities.

GLB specifically provides that state statutes are not preempted as long as the state law is consistent with GLB. In addition, GLB provides that state statutes are not preempted unless the state law is less protective than GLB. The challenge is determining when a state statute is consistent with and/or more protective than GLB. California enacted the California Financial Privacy Act ("California Act") in 2004.[32] Like GLB, the California Act restricted the use of nonpublic personal information by targeting information sharing among affiliated and unaffiliated entities. The California Act was explicitly intended to provide greater protection than GLB.

Recalling that under GLB nonpublic personal information may be shared with both affiliated and unaffiliated entities unless the individual customer "opts-out" of the sharing, the California Act required, instead, that nonpublic personal information may not be shared with unaffiliated entities unless the individual customer "opts-in" to the sharing. On the other hand, affiliated entities may share nonpublic personal information subject to the individual customer "opting-out."

In *American Bankers Ass'n v. Lockyer*, 412 F.3d 1081 (9th Cir. 2005), three financial services industry trade associations sued arguing that the California Act was preempted by GLB, and that the

32.   CAL. FIN. CODE §§ 4050 to 4060.

California Act was incorporated in the FCRA information sharing restrictions. The United States District Court for the Eastern District of California found that GLB, in expressly allowing states to pass laws consistent with GLB, and to pass more restrictive information sharing laws, made the California Act not only permissible but anticipated by GLB. The decision was appealed to the United States Court of Appeals for the Ninth Circuit.

The Ninth Circuit analyzed the California Act primarily in light of the FCRA, framing the issue simply as whether or not the FCRA preempted the California Act. The Ninth Circuit began by noting that FCRA regulates the use of "consumer reports" by "consumer reporting agencies." A "consumer report" is any communication of any information that reflects on a consumer's credit worthiness, credit standing, credit capacity, character, general reputation, personal characteristics, or mode of living.

Communication among entities, whether related by common ownership or corporate control, of information that only shows transactions or experiences between a customer and the person making the report is not considered part of a "consumer report." A "consumer report" also does not include any other information sharing among entities related either by common ownership or corporate control if the customer receives clear and conspicuous disclosure that such information may be shared along with an opportunity to "opt-out" of such sharing before sharing occurs. In other words, the

FCRA sets out exceptions for "experience" information and "non-experience" information, which, then, would not fall within FCRA protections. A "consumer reporting agency" is an entity regularly engaged in assembling or evaluating consumer credit information or other information on consumers for the purpose of providing the information to third parties.

The FCRA contains a specific preemption clause, which provides that no State law may impose restrictions respecting the exchange of information among entities affiliated by either common control or common ownership. The preemption clause precludes any state "requirements" and "prohibitions" on the communication of information among affiliated entities. "Information" has a specific meaning in the statute, including only that information described in the "consumer report" definition of FCRA.

Taken together, Congress, through FCRA, specifically precludes states from regulating the sharing of "information" as defined by FCRA. As a result, the Ninth Circuit concluded that the California Act was preempted to the extent FCRA—defined information is regulated, *i.e.*, information relating to credit worthiness, credit standing, credit capacity, character, general reputation, personal characteristics, or mode of living. The Ninth Circuit remanded the case for determination if, in fact, the California Act did regulate sharing of information that FCRA preempts. On remand, the California Act was found to be preempted by FCRA.[33]

While the Ninth Circuit is the highest court to address the scope of federal preemption of state law protecting nonpublic personal information, courts in Massachusetts and Vermont have dealt with the scope of GLB state law preemption from different angles. The Massachusetts Consumer Protection Act Relative to the Sale of Insurance by Banks[34] prohibited bank referrals to insurance agents without the customer having first inquired about insurance. The Act further prohibited the payment of referral fees to the referring banker, and required that any insurance solicitation be conducted in a physically separate area of the bank. The Massachusetts Bankers Association challenged the Act on the grounds that the law was preempted by GLB.[35] The issue was whether GLB preempted laws aimed at interfering with the ability of banks to cross-market. GLB was found to preempt the referral, referral fee, and separation requirements of the Massachusetts law, because the requirements "significantly curtailed" banks' ability to cross-market.

On the other hand, a Vermont Department of Banking, Insurance, Securities, and Healthcare Administration regulation creating "opt-in" provisions for the sharing of nonpublic personal information,

33. *See* American Bankers Ass'n v. Lockyer, Case No. Civ. S 04–0778MCE KJM, 2005 WL 2452798 (E.D. Cal. Oct. 5, 2005).

34. Mass. Gen. Laws ch. 167F, § 2A.

35. *See* Massachusetts Bankers Ass'n v. Bowler, 392 F. Supp. 2d 24 (D. Mass. 2005).

similar to those in the California Act, was not preempted by GLB.[36] GLB set a floor with the "opt-out" provision, and the "opt-in" provision of the Vermont regulation provided greater protection than GLB, which is permitted by GLB, and thus the Vermont regulation is not preempted.

Given the various interpretations of GLB found in the California, Massachusetts and Vermont examples, the extent and scope of preemption is unclear and likely ripe for a unifying interpretation by the U.S. Supreme Court.

e. *GLB and litigation discovery*

Is GLB violated when a financial institution discloses nonpublic personal information during discovery in a court proceeding? As with the state law preemption issue, the courts are split, but a majority view has emerged. The U.S. District Court for the Southern District of West Virginia reasoned that, even though GLB does not contain an explicit exception for discovery, the general prohibition against financial information disclosure does not create a right to circumvent the discovery process.[37] When a party responds to a discovery request, the response is to the "judicial process," which requires the disclosure of non-public personal information. A

36. *See* American Council of Life Insurers v. Vermont Dept. of Banking, Docket No. 50–1–02 Wncv, 2004 WL 578737 (Vt. Super. Ct. Feb. 12, 2004).

37. Marks v. Global Mtg. Group, Inc., 218 F.R.D. 492, 496 (S.D. W. Va. 2003).

majority of those courts reviewing the issue have adopted the "judicial process" exception.[38]

f. *GLB summary*

In repealing the New Deal prohibition of bank, insurance, and securities firm affiliations, GLB opened nonpublic personal information to the possibility of disclosure across a broad spectrum of consumer financial service organizations. Recognizing the potential to decimate real financial privacy, GLB contains specific rules about such sharing financial information:

1. Financial institutions are required to establish and implement procedures keeping nonpublic personal information confidential and protecting the information from unauthorized use;

2. Customers must receive an annual notice detailing how nonpublic personal information is protected and on what basis information is shared;

3. Customers must be given the right, though not absolute, to opt-out of information sharing;

4. Fraudulently obtaining or using nonpublic personal information is a federal crime;

38. *See*, *e.g.*, Ex parte Mutual Savings Life Ins. Co., 899 So.2d 986 (Ala. 2004); Martino v. Barnett, 595 S.E.2d 65 (W. Va. 2004); McGuire v. Rawlings Co., Case No. CV000375212S, 2005 WL 895870 (Conn. Super. Ct. Mar. 14, 2005).

5. While the courts are split, states may not regulate the sharing of information included in the definition of "consumer report" contained in the FCRA;

6. A financial institution, despite GLB restrictions, is expected to respond to information requests made as part of the judicial process.

8. *USA PATRIOT Act*

As codified by BSA, anti-money laundering law traditionally aimed at tracing criminal proceeds. In the period following the terrorist attacks of September 11, 2001, the Federal government sought to expand the use of financial information from merely tracking the result of crime to intercepting criminal financing in order to prevent crime. In October 2001, the Uniting and Strengthening America by Providing Appropriate Tools Required to Intercept and Obstruct Terrorism Act (emphasis added), or USA PATRIOT Act ("Patriot Act") was signed into law.[39] Among hundreds of pages of provisions, the Patriot Act significantly altered the rules regulating financial privacy in three main areas.

a. *"Financial institution" redefined*

The Patriot Act reached back to the BSA and expanded the definition of "financial institution" to include entities ranging from traditional ones as commercial banks or trust companies and credit

39. Pub. L. No. 107–56, 115 Stat. 272 (2001) (codified as amended at scattered sections of 12, 15, 18, and 31 U.S.C.).

unions, to logical newcomers including issuers of travelers' checks and money transfer agencies, to organizations whose possible connections to international terrorism are obscure, such as persons involved in real estate closings and settlements. Furthermore, the Secretary of the Treasury may expand the definition to include any other business or agency "whose cash transactions have a high degree of usefulness in criminal, tax, or regulatory matters."[40] In other words, the definition of "financial institution" is now so broad that criminals may not simply avoid the old BSA restrictions by using non-traditional financial channels. In turn, law enforcement may now cast a stunningly wide and diverse net in gathering financial information.

b.   *The return of "Know Your Customer"*

Reviving the "Know Your Customer" rules attempt of 1998, the Patriot Act directed the Secretary of Treasury to establish regulations setting standards for financial institutions regarding customer identity. The resulting regulations require a financial institution to establish and implement procedures for verifying the identity of any person seeking to open an account. In addition, financial institutions must maintain records of the information used to verify identity, including name and address and any other identifying information. Government agencies are in turn to provide financial institutions with lists of known or suspected terror-

40.   31 U.S.C. § 5312(a)(2).

ists and terrorist organizations, which financial institutions are to compare to each customer identity for a match.

In contrast, prior to the Patriot Act, the then-narrower list of entities considered "financial institutions" were only required to identify customers when the BSA reporting requirements were triggered by transactions exceeding $10,000, singly or in a related series. In addition, BSA required reporting transactions if "suspicious" and more than $3,000 or any transaction when selling cashier's checks and money orders or when wire transferring money. Although not formally repealed, these provisions of BSA have been largely mooted by the Patriot Act's more stringent requirements.

A transaction or related series of transactions greater than $10,000 triggers the requirement that the financial institution file a Currency Transaction Report ("CTR"). A suspicious transaction results in filing a Suspicious Activity Report ("SAR"). A CTR or SAR is filed with the Financial Crimes Reporting Network ("FinCEN").

c. Information sharing

The pivot point for the sharing of financial information in the Patriot Act is FinCEN. Law enforcement agencies may gather information about the financial arrangements of any person under investigation for either terrorist activity or money laundering. FinCEN responds to the request by disclosing information provided by financial institutions or by requiring financial institutions to search their records to see if a given institution has conducted transactions or maintained an account for an identified individual. Of note, then, records may be requested that do not follow from the usual CTR or SAR transactions. Law enforcement may request any financial record for any individual under investigation.

Procedurally, the Patriot Act only requires that the requesting agency provide FinCEN information identifying the individual under investigation and a certification that the target of the investigation is engaged in , or reasonably suspected of, engagement in terrorist activity or money laundering. Put another way, the Patriot Act does not require that law enforcement, in requesting financial information, have a search warrant, grand jury subpoena, or even an administrative subpoena, provided that the request is capable of being couched in those categories.

The financial institution, upon receipt of a Fin-CEN information request, is required to "expeditiously" search for any records related to the named individual. If a record is found, the financial institution is to report to FinCEN the name, Social Security number, date of birth, account number, and any other identifying information provided when the account was opened or a transaction was performed. A financial institution is prohibited from disclosing to anyone that a request was received from Fin-CEN, or that information was provided to FinCEN, unless disclosure of the information request is necessary to provide the information.

The Patriot Act includes an incentive for financial institutions to comply with FinCEN requests. When a financial institution seeks regulatory approval for a merger or acquisition, banking regulators are required to consider the institution's record of combating crime by responding to FinCEN. The implication is that the regulators will look favorably on those financial institutions that are more forthcoming with requested information.

If, after a financial institution has reported the identifying information indicating a match for an individual under investigation, and the investigating agency wants the actual documents, then the agency must comply with regular procedural safeguards for securing the documents. The investigating agency may, for example, request a search warrant, which issues only upon a showing of probable cause to a judge. In the alternative, a grand jury subpoena may be requested through a prosecutor's office. Here, the showing required is not probable cause but virtually any information the prosecutor deems adequate. Unlike with a search warrant, however, the receiver of the subpoena may challenge the request, before the documents are provided, on the basis that compliance is unreasonable, oppressive, or requests privileged information. In turn, a court may modify or quash the subpoena.

An investigative agency may, however, elect to forgo the search warrant or grand jury subpoena, with the accompanying required showing and right to challenge, in favor of an administrative subpoena issued by a federal or state agency. An administrative subpoena does not require a showing of probable cause or court order, but a showing only of relevance. In 1989 the Office of Thrift Supervision ("OTS") was created to regulate the safe and sound operation of savings and loan associations. The OTS is authorized to subpoena information relevant to the affairs or ownership of any bank, financial institution, or affiliate.[41]

During a routine examination in 1990, the OTS discovered that the subject Bank was nearly insolvent.[42] Upon further investigation, OTS discovered that two of the Bank's directors owned a mortgage company and law firm. Large overdrafts in the law firm deposit accounts were covered by overnight transfers from the mortgage company escrow accounts, suggesting violation of fiduciary duties of the Bank and Mortgage Company Act, as well as a violation of OTS regulations regarding loans to affiliated parties and overdraft restrictions on director maintained accounts.

As a result, OTS issued a subpoena to each director seeking personal financial documents belonging to them, spouses and any entity owned, controlled by or through which either director or their spouse did business. Included in the subpoena was a request for financial statements, tax returns, and

41. 12 U.S.C. § 1820(c).

42. The factual background is found at *In re* Sealed Case, 42 F.3d 1412, 1414–15 (D.C. Cir. 1994).

bank account statements. The directors refused to comply.

Arguing in district court, OTS claimed three reasons for the subpoena. First, OTS wanted to determine if either director benefited from the use of the escrow funds to cover the law firm overdrafts. Second, it was seeking to determine the extent to which the directors could pay civil money penalties. Third, the agency wanted to determine if there was any other as yet unknown wrongdoing. The district court found that the information sought was reasonably relevant, not too burdensome, and within OTS's authority to request. The directors appealed on the basis that the Fourth Amendment limited the ability of OTS to obtain personal financial documents.

The test for deciding whether a subpoena should be enforced is three pronged: (1) is the request within the authority of the agency; (2) is the request not too indefinite; and (3) is the information sought reasonably relevant.[43] The directors argued that the first and third prongs were not met.

The D.C. Circuit found the first and second prongs were met because the requested information would facilitate OTS's statutory duty to assess civil penalties, issue orders of removal and determine liability.[44] Because the subpoenas satisfied the first and second prong, the directors were left with their argument that the information requested was not

43. *Id*. at 1415.

44. *Id*. at 1416.

relevant. The test for relevance is simply that the requested information is "reasonably relevant" to the general purpose of the agency investigation, thus there was no question the requested information, including personal financial and banking records, was relevant to the OTS's investigation to determine if the directors benefited personally and were able to pay a civil penalty.[45]

The subject of an administrative subpoena, therefore, must comply unless they can overcome the relatively low agency burden of showing relevance to the investigation. The only practical protection afforded the recipient of an agency subpoena is to refuse to comply. An agency may not enforce the subpoena, but must seek enforcement through the courts, as demonstrated by *In re Sealed Case*. The subpoena power only comes into play, however, when an agency wants actual documents. After all, through FinCEN and the authority granted in the Patriot Act, a vast amount of information may be collected without notice.

d.   The Patriot Act at work

In practice, the Patriot Act authority has not been limited to terrorist or money laundering investigation, but has been used in relatively routine criminal investigations. The financial transactions of particular individuals targeted by law enforcement agencies in an investigation called "Operation G–Sting," who suspected of bribing public officials

45.   *Id.* at 1419.

in exchange for votes changing the regulations for a Las Vegas strip club, were tracked under authority of the Patriot Act.

A Honduran lobsterman was also convicted of illegally importing lobster into the United States in violation of Honduran size regulations.[46] The Lacey Act prohibits the importation of fish caught in violation of United States or any foreign law.[47] The investigation was enabled in part due to the use of the Patriot Act to gather financial information on the basis that money from the proceeds of the lobster sales was deposited in banks.

e. *The Patriot Act and the future*

The Patriot Act liberalizes the ability of law enforcement to gather financial information and relaxes the safeguards imposed by prior law such as BSA and GLB. There is a constant stream of proposed amendments to the Patriot Act, some of which would create greater privacy protections. Much has been written about safeguards that should be considered. Congress or the courts could be given an oversight role in monitoring FinCEN activity. In turn, FinCEN could be required to make periodic reports to a designated judge or adjunct of Congress in order to ensure that designated procedural safeguards are, in fact, followed. A particular problem which may need to be addressed is that, financial

46.   *See* United States v. McNab, 324 F.3d 1266 (11th Cir. 2003).

47.   *See* 16 U.S.C. § 3372.

institutions can be penalized by banking regulators for being uncooperative with FinCEN. Financial institutions are increasingly dropping customers on the merest suspicion of illegal activity out of fear of FinCEN requests for records.

In the meantime, various agencies continue to explore the scope and test the limitations of the Patriot Act. Many actions are the first of their kind and, as a result, are new to all involved parties. The Securities and Exchange Commission ("SEC"), for example, did not bring its first case against a brokerage firm for failure to report suspicious transactions until 2007. In that case, the SEC accused Park Financial and its principal of executing numerous trades in Spear & Jackson securities, despite obvious red flags, and of failing to file SARs. Spear & Jackson's former CEO allegedly used brokerage accounts, opened in the name of a series of British Virgin Island-based companies he controlled, to illegally trade Spear & Jackson stock. The brokerage accounts were opened at Park Financial, which, given the nature of the transactions and foreign base of the accounts, the SEC argued, represented the type of conduct Park Financial knew fell under SAR.

The SEC action highlights the rigor with which any financial institution is expected to use in alerting FinCEN. In turn, the action highlights the extent to which financial transactions are monitored, and the related information shared. The Patriot Act is left, then, as both the current and most questioned financial privacy related law. Congress is wrestling, as has been the case since the BSA of 1970, with the proper balance between the right to financial privacy and the real need for disclosure of nonpublic personal information for the benefit of law enforcement.

B. Medical Privacy

1. *Introduction*

Many people characterize their medical records as being among the information they most want kept out of the public eye. Medical records, however, have historically not been subject to systematic privacy regulations. Instead, the health care industry relied mainly on principles of medical ethics and tort law to protect the privacy of such records. Increasing concern over the use and distribution of individuals' medical records though, has led to an increasingly formalized regulatory regime.

2. *Health Insurance Portability and Accountability Act*

At the Federal level the privacy of medical records is primarily governed by the Health Insurance Portability and Accountability Act of 1996 (HIPAA).[48] The Federal Privacy Rule, which officially implements HIPAA, became effective in April 2003.[49] HIPAA was enacted to prevent fraud and unauthorized access, use, and disclosure of "individ-

48. Health Insurance Portability and Accountability Act (HIPAA) of 1996, Pub. L. No. 104–191,110 Stat. 1936 (1996).

49. 45 C.F.R. § 164.534.

ually identifiable health information." It also is intended to reduce the costs of administrative operations in the healthcare industry by simplifying the exchange of electronically stored medical information and preventing fraud or unauthorized access, use, and disclosure of health information.

a. Protected health information

HIPAA regulates protected health information as it is used and disclosed by covered entities.[50] The health information protected under HIPAA includes any information relating to treatment or payment of healthcare. Health information is defined as any information that "relates to the past, present, or future physical or mental health or condition of an individual, the provision of health care to an individual, or the past, present, or future payment for the provision of health care to an individual."[51]

In addition, HIPAA seeks to protect elements of health information that could identify the patient. The statute defines "individually identifiable health information" as any information collected from an individual that relates to the past, present, or future physical or mental health or condition of an individual. It also includes in the definition the provision of health care to an individual, or the past, present, or future payment for the provision of health care to an individual, which identifies the individual, or which creates a reasonable basis to

50.   45 C.F.R. § 164.502(a).

51.   42 U.S.C. § 1320d(4)(B) (2000).

believe that the information can be used to identify the individual.[52]

The United States Department of Health and Human Services (HHS) lists some of the identifiers, which include name, social security number, address, zip code, phone number, photograph, employer, treatment date, and names of spouse and children.[53] If there is other healthcare information that has the potential to identify the patient, this information is also protected.

b.   Covered entities

HIPAA applies to "covered entities," which consist of three particular categories of persons. Those three categories are: (1) a health plan; (2) a health care clearinghouse; and (3) a health care provider who transmits any health information in electronic form.[54] A "health plan" is defined quite broadly, and includes individual and group plans providing or paying the cost of medical care, as well as most employer health benefit plans established pursuant to the Employee Retirement Income Security Act of 1974 ("ERISA"), Medicaid, Medicare, HMOs, other state and federal healthcare programs, and insurance companies that issue healthcare policies. The statute exempts small plans, meaning those with fewer than 50 participants and purely employer managed plans.

52.   42 U.S.C. § 1320d(5)(M).

53.   45 C.F.R. § 164.514(b).

54.   42 U.S.C. § 1320d(2), (3), (5).

A "health care clearing house" is an "entity that processes or facilitates the processing of nonstandard data elements of health information into standard data elements."[55] A health plan or provider may contract with a healthcare clearinghouse to handle the transmitting or receiving of any of the HIPAA standard electronic transactions, which converts both the provider and the clearinghouse into a covered entity subject to HIPAA.[56]

A "health care provider" is defined as "a provider of medical or health services ... and any other person or organization who furnishes, bills, or is paid for health care."[57] Once again, coverage under this definition is rather wide as it includes all types of medical doctors and other licensed professionals who provide treatment and/or diagnostic testing to patients. It also includes any healthcare professional who provides medical drugs or devices to patients.

Providers excluded under HIPAA are those who do not conduct any of the HIPAA-regulated electronic transactions. HIPAA only applies to those health care providers that transmit "health information in electronic form in connection with a transaction."[58] There are nine electronic transactions regulated by HIPAA, which include: claims, claim status, benefit eligibility inquiries, enrollment and disenrollment, healthcare payments, premium

55.   42 U.S.C. § 1320d(2).

56.   42 U.S.C. § 1320d–4(a)(2)(B).

57.   45 C.F.R. § 160.103.

58.   42 U.S.C. § 1320d–1(a)(3).

payments, referral authorization requests, coordination of benefits, and claims attachments. If a health care provider does not conduct any of the foregoing transactions electronically with any covered entity, the provider is not regulated by HIPAA.

Determining whether an entity is indeed a "covered entity" under HIPAA is not an easy task due to the complex language of the statute. An online resource made available by the Centers for Medicare and Medicaid Services, divisions of HHS, gives guidance and provides a helpful chart for navigating through the complexities.[59]

"Health Plans" include ERISA group health plans that have 50 or more participants, or that are administered by a third party other than the plan sponsor.[60] If an organization does have a group health plan with 50 or more participants or has a plan administered or insured by someone other than the plan sponsor, then a plan is required to comply with the HIPAA privacy and security rules. Conversely, if no group health plan exists, or if the plan is self-administered, self-insured and contains fewer than 50 participants, the HIPAA rules do not apply. HIPAA still applies to the employer even if it would otherwise appear to be exempt, albeit indirectly. If the employer is performing functions for the group health plan, including processing claims, conducting audits, obtaining payment for denied

59. The resource is entitled "Covered Entity Charts" and is *available at* http://www.cms.hhs.gov/HIPAAGenInfo/06_AreYoua CoveredEntity.asp.

60. 45 C.F.R. § 160.103.

claims, or administering flex account spending, HIPAA applies.

Compliance with the HIPAA provisions is required for all covered entities whenever protected health information is used or disclosed. Disclosure is mandated in only two circumstances. First, when the patient requests access to his or her healthcare information and, second, when the Secretary of HHS requests access to the information as part of an investigation or enforcement action concerning a covered entity's compliance with HIPAA.[61] In addition to these two mandatory disclosures, there exist six categories under HIPAA that permit or otherwise excuse limited use and disclosure of healthcare information: (1) To the individual, who is the subject of the information; (2) Treatment, Payment, or Healthcare Operations; (3) Inadvertent Disclosures; (4) When Authorized in Writing; (5) Agreed to Disclosures; and (6) Public Interest Disclosures.

c.   *Individual rights*

Since HIPAA is designed to protect an individual's healthcare privacy, there are eight fundamental rights afforded to individuals:

1. The right to access, inspect, and obtain a copy of protected health information about him or herself;

2. The right to have the covered entity correct the individual's protected health information;

61.   45 C.F.R. § 164.502(a)(2)(ii).

3. The right to receive an accounting of disclo-
    sures made by a covered entity;

4. The right to request that a covered entity
    restrict the uses or disclosures of the individ-
    ual's protected health information related to
    treatment, payment, or health care opera-
    tions, although the covered entity is not re-
    quired to agree to such a restriction;

5. The right to request confidential communica-
    tions from providers of protected health infor-
    mation;

6. The right to object or agree before covered
    entities make certain disclosures, such as list-
    ing the individual's name in a facility directo-
    ry;

7. The right to authorize disclosures to third
    parties pursuant to an authorization;

8. The right to receive adequate notice of the
    uses and disclosures that may be made by the
    covered entity.

d. *Administrative Simplification*

The "Administrative Simplification" provisions
were designed to give the HHS power to create
and publish rules to improve the electronic exchange of health information. Since patient privacy
is vital, and electronic storage and transmission of
records can pose serious threats of such privacy
being compromised on a vast scale, Congress
granted the HHS authority to adopt rules to pro-

tect the confidentiality of individually identifiable health information. The most significant rule promulgated pursuant to the Administrative Simplification provisions is the Privacy Rule discussed above.

Civil and criminal penalties may be imposed for failure to adhere to the rules adopted by HHS. The HHS Secretary may issue a penalty of not more than $100 per violation, up to a maximum of $25,000 per type of violation per year.[62] HHS determines civil monetary penalties for violations of the Administrative Simplification provisions. The Privacy Rule is enforced through the Office for Civil Rights (OCR), which is a division of HHS. The OCR estimates that it receives over one hundred privacy-related complaints per week, but, as of July 2007, it has never assessed a civil penalty for a violation of the Act. This is at least in part because civil penalties cannot be imposed if any of three criteria are met. First, criminal enforcement overrides civil enforcement, thus, where there is an overlap of jurisdiction between the OCR and the U.S. Department of Justice, which prosecutes criminal violations of HIPAA, OCR must accede to DOJ's control of the investigation. Second, the HHS Secretary may waive penalties if it is established that the person or entity responsible for the violation "did not know, and by exercising reasonable diligence would not have known," that a violation had been committed. Third, the Secretary can also excuse the violation if it is determined that "the failure to comply was due

62.   42 U.S.C. § 1320d–5.

to reasonable cause and not to willful neglect; and the failure to comply is corrected." Finally, even if none of the criteria are met, the Secretary has the discretion to waive the penalty to the extent that "payment of such penalty would be excessive relative to the compliance failure involved."

Criminal violations can bring a fine of up to $50,000 and/or imprisonment for not more than one year. If the crime was perpetrated using false pretenses, then the fine can increase to $100,000 and/or not more than fives years in prison. Furthermore, if the offender commits the crime for personal gain, or to inflict malicious harm, the penalty can be up to $250,000 and/or imprisonment for up to ten years.[63]

e. *HIPAA Enforcement Rule*

On March 16, 2006, the Enforcement Rule took effect in an effort to create a unified and comprehensive approach to enforcing all the HIPAA Administrative Simplification rules, which includes, in addition to the Privacy Rule, the Security Rule, the Electronic Transaction and Code Set Rule, and the Identifier Standards.[64] The new Enforcement Rule follows some of the same principles of previous individualized rules, including the Privacy rule, by encouraging voluntary compliance. The Secretary of HHS may also provide technical assistance to cov-

63. 42 U.S.C. § 1320d–6.

64. HIPAA Administrative Simplification: Enforcement, 71 Fed. Reg. at 8391.

ered entities to enhance voluntary compliance.[65]

The Enforcement Rule stresses the use of self-regulatory means to ensure compliance. Self-regulatory includes "demonstrated compliance, or a completed corrective action plan or other agreement."[66] The Secretary has broad discretion to settle any matter of noncompliance and to encourage covered entities to comply voluntarily. If a covered entity does not comply via informal means, then HHS must give notice to the entity and provide an opportunity "to submit written evidence of any mitigating factors or affirmative defenses for consideration...."

The Secretary of HHS is to consider six factors in determining civil monetary penalties. Fist, the nature of the violation, in light of the purpose of the rule violated. Second, the circumstances and consequences of the violation, including but not limited to: (a) the time period during which the violation occurred, (b) whether physical harm was caused by the violation, (c) whether the violation facilitated or hindered an individual's ability to obtain health care, and (d) whether financial harm resulted from the violation. Third, the degree of culpability of the covered entity, which includes but is not limited to: (a) whether the violation was intentional, and (b) whether the violation was beyond the direct control of the covered entity. Fourth, whether the company

65. HIPAA Administrative Simplification: Enforcement, 71 Fed. Reg. at 8425, 8394.

66. HIPAA Administrative Simplification: Enforcement, 71 Fed. Reg. at 8425.

had a history of prior compliance with the administrative simplification provision. Fifth, the financial condition of the covered entity. And finally, whether there are any other matters as justice may require.[67]

As was noted above, there have been no formal civil penalties yet assessed under HIPAA. There have been, however, a handful of criminal cases brought. The first of these was *United States v. Gibson*, Case No. CR04–0374RSM, 2004 WL 2188280 (W.D. Wash. 2004). Gibson was a phlebotomist who used a cancer patient's name, date of birth, and Social Security number to obtain four credit cards in the patient's name. This information, which is protected health information under HIPAA, was collected by Gibson's employer for payment of health care services. After obtaining the credit cards, Gibson charged more than $9,000 on the cards for various items. When Gibson's employer discovered what he had done, he was terminated. The Department of Justice filed criminal charges against Gibson and, under a plea agreement, he was sentenced to sixteen months in prison and ordered to pay $15,000 in restitution.

Interestingly, Gibson was prosecuted despite not meeting the definition of a "covered entity." HIPAA states that it only applies to "covered entities," as defined above, and HHS has repeatedly stated that the imposition of privacy standards do not extend beyond these entities. The DOJ's deci-

67. HIPAA Administrative Simplification: Enforcement, 71 Fed. Reg. at 8427.

sion to prosecute Gibson under HIPAA was specifically influenced by the fact that Gibson unlawfully obtained the health information while carrying out his employment duties as a health care technician.

Within a year after the *Gibson* case, the DOJ issued a memorandum that spoke to the issues present in the action, namely that he was not a covered entity within the scope of HIPAA. The opinion stated that only "covered entities" and "those persons rendered accountable by general principles of corporate criminal liability" may be prosecuted for violations under 42 U.S.C. § 1302d–6.[68] Despite this reserved language, the DOJ's determination that HIPAA could be extended to directors, officers, and employees of covered entities radically increased the reach of privacy protection under the statute.

f. Emergency exception

In response to Hurricane Katrina in 2005, the OCR issued two separate Special Bulletins to give guidance to covered entities in emergencies. The first bulletin stated that the HIPAA Privacy Rule allows the sharing of health information to assist disaster relief efforts. The second bulletin expanded on the first. It allowed that "business associates that are managing such information on behalf of covered entities may make these disclosures to the

68. Office of General Counsel, U.S. Dept. of Justice, Scope of Criminal Enforcement Under 42 U.S.C. § 1320d–6 (2005), *available at* http://www.usdoj.gov/olc/hipaafinal.htm.

extent permitted by their business associate agreement with the covered entities, as provided in the Privacy Rule."[69] It also emphasized that HIPAA permits HHS to take into consideration the circumstances surrounding violations of the Privacy Rule, proper allowance would be made for the complications created by the hurricane in any investigation. The bulletin cautioned that, even in emergency situations, proper safeguards still need to be in place for exchange of the information.

g.   *HIPAA requirements*

As has been previously discussed, health information of an individual, which also includes information about the payment for the individual's health care, is protected under HIPAA. HIPAA does allow, however, health plans to disclose some protected health information as necessary to carry out internal operations and to provide payment for a participant's treatment.[70]

HIPAA requires a "firewall" between the plan and the employer to prevent the plan from disclosing health information to the employer for purposes of employment-related actions. Otherwise, a plan participant must give written authorization for any

69.   Bulletin from Office of Civil Rights, U.S. Dept. of Health & Human. Services, Hurricane Katrina Bulletin #2: HIPAA Privacy Rule Compliance Guidance and Enforcement Statement for Activities in Response to Hurricane Katrina (Sept. 9, 2005), *available at* http://www.hhs.gov/ocr/hipaa/EnforcementState ment.pdf.

70.   45 C.F.R § 164.506.

other disclosures, barring certain exceptions. Furthermore, HIPAA requires the plan to enter "business associate contracts." The contracts are with third-party administrators who handle protected health information on behalf of the plan and require the business associate to follow the basic HIPAA confidentiality and security rules. Examples of third-party administrators include lawyers, accountants, IT personnel, and benefits consultants.

h. Rights of plan participants

Participants are allowed to access and amend their health information from group health plans. The participants must also be allowed to obtain an accounting of when their health information for certain disclosures was made.[71]

i. HIPAA preemption rules

Although many states may have their own laws which create a privilege for medical records and contain rules about the disclosure of such information, HIPAA's general preemption rule is that any conflicting state law is superseded by HIPAA.[72] Any preemption by HIPAA will not be triggered unless the state law is contrary to the HIPAA provisions.[73] To give guidance, HIPAA defines "contrary" in two ways. First, the statutory schemes are considered

71. 45 C.F.R §§ 164.524–164.528.

72. 45 C.F.R. § 160.203 (2005).

73. 45 C.F.R. § 160.203.

contrary where a covered entity would find it impossible to comply with both the state and federal requirements. If a covered entity were required by state law to take some type of action that would violate HIPAA, then HIPAA prevails. The second definition of "contrary" recites that a state law is contrary to HIPAA when it "stands as an obstacle to the accomplishment and execution of the full purposes and objectives" of HIPAA.[74]

The Secretary of HHS can determine that a contrary state law will not be preempted if the law is necessary for regulating the state's healthcare and insurance.[75] For example, the Secretary may determine that a state law is designed to prevent healthcare fraud and abuse or that it concerns efforts to regulate the manufacture or distribution of controlled substances. Furthermore, HIPAA's preemption provision serves as a "floor," rather than a "ceiling," in that it expressly does not preempt contrary state laws to the extent such laws provide more stringent protection for individually identifiable health information than HIPAA.

j. Genetic information

The HIPAA Privacy Rule includes "genetic information" as a possible form of "protected health information."[76] The term "genetic information" en-

74.   45 C.F.R. § 160.202(2).

75.   45 C.F.R. § 160.203(a).

76.   Office for Civil Rights, U.S. Dept. of Health & Human Services, Your Frequently Asked Questions on Privacy, *available at* http://hhs.gov/ocr/hipaa/.

compasses "information about genes, gene products, and inherited characteristics that may derive from the individual or a family member," whether collected through direct testing or through the assembly of family medical histories. Genetic information gains protection under HIPAA as long as it relates to medical records and other personal health information maintained by covered entities. Any genetic information that is individually identifiable, in the sense of being associated with a personal identifier, cannot be disclosed or used by any covered entities, except as permitted by the Privacy Rule. The key limitation here is that these restrictions on disclosures apply only to covered entities (and potentially their directors, officers, and employees under the DOJ's interpretation of the statute in *Gibson*), thus many educational institutions and private genetics labs are not subject to the Rule.

Pursuant to the HIPAA's allowance for more stringent health information privacy laws at the state level, many jurisdictions have enacted their own legislation governing genetic privacy. Before disclosing previously provided genetic information, informed consent is required in twenty-six states. Furthermore, criminal and/or civil penalties exist in eighteen states for violations of their respective genetic privacy laws. The remaining states do not create a specific penalty for similar violations, which could give rise to inequities for the same violation in different states. Partly as a result of this inconsistent coverage, efforts are underway to enact comprehensive genetic privacy legislation at the Federal level.

3. *Genetic Privacy Bill (H.R. 493)*

The Genetic Information Nondiscrimination Act of 2007 (GINA) was introduced to prohibit discrimination on the basis of genetic information with respect to health insurance and employment. GINA would bar group health plans and health insurers from denying coverage or charging higher premiums to individuals based solely on a genetic predisposition to a specific disease. GINA amends the ERISA as well as the Public Health Service Act.

GINA prohibits two main practices. First, it prohibits enrollment and premium discrimination based on information about a request for or receipt of genetic services. Second, it prohibits requiring genetic testing. In addition, the Act sets forth penalties for violations. It also amends the Medicare section of the Social Security Act to prohibit issuers of Medicare supplemental policies from discriminating on the basis of genetic information. Furthermore, the Act extends medical privacy and confidentiality rules to the disclosure of genetic information. The Act makes it an unlawful for employers to discriminate against an individual or to deprive an individual of employment opportunities because of genetic information. The collection and disclosure of genetic information is also prohibited, unless certain exceptions apply. The proposed Act also establishes a Genetic Nondiscrimination Study Commission. This commission would review the developing science of genetics and advise Congress on providing for a disparate impact cause of action under GINA.

C.   Other Privacy Legislation

The following are some of the more notable Federal statutes that address the many privacy concerns that exist today.

1.   *Privacy Act of 1974*

Congress passed the Privacy Act of 1974[77] to protect federal records containing personally identifiable information by prohibiting agencies from disclosing such information without consent, and to address the dangers posed by the widespread use of Social Security numbers as personal identifiers. Under the Privacy Act, a governmental agency cannot deny a right, benefit, or privilege simply because the individual refused to disclose his or her Social Security number. The Act also gives individuals access to consumer records collected by federal agencies, including the right to correct or delete the records. When an agency requests an individual's Social Security number, it must inform the individual whether the disclosure is voluntary or mandatory, to what purposes the number will be used, and by what statutory authority the number is solicited. Social Security numbers may be collected under the

77.   Pub. L. No. 93–579, 88 Stat. 1896 (1974) (codified at 5 U.S.C. § 552).

Privacy Act if it is in conformity with other federal laws, including collection of tax and immigration information.

The Privacy Act does not protect the privacy of non-governmental records, such as bank statements, credit reports, and medical records (although these may be protected by state laws or other federal laws), and thus does not apply in disputes arising between private institutions, including credit card issuers and banks, and identity theft victims.

2. *Driver's Privacy Protection Act*

The Drivers Privacy Protection Act of 1994 (DPPA)[78] allows criminal and civil liability to be imposed upon any person who knowingly obtains, discloses, or otherwise uses personal information from motor vehicle records. The DPPA allows for a private cause of action to remedy violations. The plaintiff can recover actual damages, reasonable attorney fees, other litigation costs reasonably incurred, and other preliminary and equitable relief the court deems to be appropriate. The plaintiff can recover punitive damages upon showing proof of reckless or willful disregard of the law. A plaintiff can recover liquidated damages under DPPA without having to prove actual damages, leaving the finding of an appropriate award to the court's discretion given the circumstances. Although Con-

78.   Pub. L. No. 103–322, 108 Stat. 2099 (codified at 18 U.S.C. § 2721 *et seq.*).

gress' express legislative intent was not to combat identity theft in passing the DPPA, some courts have allowed identity theft claims to proceed under that law.

A potential plaintiff under DPPA is any individual whose personal information has been improperly obtained from a motor vehicle record. In *Margan v. Niles*, 250 F. Supp. 2d 63 (N.D.N.Y. 2003), a workers' compensation claimant learned he was being followed by private investigators. The subject obtained the license plate numbers of the investigators' cars. Then he asked a police officer, who happened to be his friend, to use a police database to gather information about the investigators, including their identities, addresses, and other identifying information. Upon receiving such information, the claimant began to harass the investigators and their families. The investigators and their family members were allowed to bring claims under DPPA since their information had been obtained through the use of a police database.

3. *Electronic Communications Privacy Act*

The Electronic Communications Privacy Act of 1986 ("ECPA")[79] was enacted to regulate how the government and individuals obtain access to electronic communications and how these communications are kept and maintained by "electronic communications services" or by "remote computing

79. Pub. L. No. 95–351, 82 Stat. 212 (1986) (codified at 18 U.S.C. § 2701 *et seq.*).

services." The definition of "electronic communications service" under the ECPA includes any service that provides users "the ability to send and receive wire or electronic communications."[80] The entities regulated by the ECPA include internet service providers, banks, and telephone companies. The ECPA protects information stored by communication services by requiring the service provider to restrict access to only authorized individuals. If the information is in electronic storage, it is illegal for any person to read or alter the information unless one of the limited exemptions provided for under the statute applies.

There are three categories of information covered by the ECPA as stored electronic communication services: (1) subscriber information, (2) transaction records, and (3) actual content of communications. "Subscriber information" includes the subscriber's name, physical address, IP address, type of service, and method of payment. Subscriber information can be obtained via a subpoena without having to notify the account holder. The transaction records can be obtained through a court order. These records contain information pertaining to particular communications, but such records do not include the actual communications content. In order for the government to access transaction records, it must show reasonable grounds that the information sought is relevant to an ongoing criminal investigation.

The actual content of the communication may also be obtained, but stricter requirements must be

80.   18 U.S.C. § 2510(15).

met before access is granted. If the information has been in electronic storage for less than 180 days and is unopened, then the government must have a search warrant to access the information. The issuance of a search warrant requires the government to show probable cause that a crime has been committed and that evidence of the crime is contained in the contents of the information. The subscriber must be notified that the information is sought after, but a prosecutor can delay notification if permission is granted from the court. If the government seeks to delay the notification to the subscriber, it must show that the notification would endanger an individual's life, bring about the tampering or destruction of evidence, seriously jeopardize an investigation, or lead to the intimidation of witnesses. In a situation where the communication is older than 180 days and unopened, the government may access the information via a subpoena or court order, or by search warrant as well.

The ECPA's protections of privacy in the workplace are narrow. The ECPA has categorized communications in two ways: (1) stored communications, and (2) live communications. Electronic storage is defined as "any temporary or intermediate storage of wire or electronic communication incidental to the electronic transmission thereof."[81] While electronic communication is defined as "any transfer of signs, signals, writing, images, sounds, data, or intelligence of any nature, transported in whole or in part by wire, radio, electro-

81.   18 U.S.C. § 2520(17).

magnetic, photoelectric, or photo-optical system.''[82] An employer is not restricted from accessing stored communications. A number of courts have held that, even though an employer may not intercept an e-mail during its transmission, an employer may nevertheless access stored copies as it pleases.[83] This necessarily creates an exception that swallows the rule in numerous instances, as electronic communications are often automatically stored on a computer hard drive or server as part of the sending/receiving process.

An exception to the ECPA for monitoring of live communications exists if employees give consent to interception, and even if an employer does not seek their permission, such monitoring may still fall under an exception if the violation occurs during the ordinary course of business. Although an employee does retain a reasonable expectation of privacy in the workplace, the employer's interests in preventing illegal, disruptive, or inappropriate communications is typically considered to outweigh the employee's workplace privacy interests.

4. *Children's Online Privacy Protection Act*

The Children's Online Privacy Protection Act of 1998 ("COPPA") was designed to protect children from unfair and deceptive acts in connection with

82.   18 U.S.C. § 2510(12).

83.   *See, e.g.,* Wesley College v. Pitts, 974 F. Supp. 375, 377 (D. Del. 1997); United States v. Reyes, 922 F. Supp. 818, 836 (S.D.N.Y. 1996); Bohach v. Reno, 932 F. Supp. 1232, 1236–37 (D. Nev. 1996).

the collection and use of personal information from and about children on the Internet by prohibiting the unauthorized online collection of personal information from children under age 13.[84] The FTC's final regulations implementing COPPA became effective on April 21, 2000.[85] COPPA's primary goals are to give parents control over what information is collected from their children online and how the information may be used.

COPPA applies to operators of: (1) commercial websites and online services directed at children under 13 that collect personal information from them; (2) general audience sites that knowingly collect personal information from children under 13 and; (3) general audience sites that have a separate children's area and which collect personal information from children under 13.[86] In determining if a site is "directed at children" the FTC looks at the site based on subject matter, visual or audio content, age of models on the site, language, and if the site uses animated characters or other child-oriented features.

If a site qualifies as "directed at children" the act places numerous requirements on the site operator. First, it must post a privacy policy on the front page of the website and link to the privacy policy on every page where personal information is collected. The policy must describe the information collected.

84. Pub. L. No. 105–277, 112 Stat. 2681 (1998) (codified at 15 U.S.C. § 6501 *et seq.*).

85. 16 C.F.R. § 312 *et seq.*

86. 16 C.F.R. § 312.4(b).

Second, the operator must provide notice about the site's information collection practices to parents and obtain verifiable parental consent before collecting personal information from children. Third, parents must be given a choice as to whether their child's personal information will be disclosed to third parties. Fourth, parents are to be given access to their child's personal information and the opportunity to delete that information and opt-out of future collection or use of the information. Fifth, the operator cannot condition a child's participation in a game, contest or other activity on the child's disclosure of more personal information than is reasonably necessary to participate in the activity. Finally, the operator must maintain the confidentiality, security, and integrity of personal information collected from children.[87] This can be a significant burden on operators because if they give a child's personal information to a third party, they must have a procedure for recovering and deleting all such information, notwithstanding that it is no longer in their possession.

In order to encourage active industry self-regulation, COPPA also includes a safe harbor provision, which allows industry groups and others to request FTC approval of self-regulatory guidelines to govern the participating websites' compliance with the COPPA rules. If an operator can demonstrate full compliance with approved guidelines, that operator will be deemed to be in compliance with the regula-

87.   16 C.F.R. § 312.3.

tions. Self-regulatory guidelines are those issued by representatives of the marketing or online industries or by others, who after notice and comment, are approved by the FTC. The regulations also detail the step-by-step procedure and criteria for approval of the guidelines.

5. *Family Education Rights and Privacy Act*

As the name suggests, the Family Education Rights and Privacy Act of 1974 ("FERPA")[88] protects the privacy of student educational records. It applies to all schools that receive funds under applicable programs of the U.S. Department of Education, and these schools must comply to enjoy continued eligibility for funding. The rights the Act affords extend to parents until the student reaches the age of 18, whereupon the rights transfer to the student. FERPA also governs how state agencies must transmit testing data to federal agencies.

FERPA allows parents to inspect their minor children's educational records. A student or parent may request that a school correct records they believe to be inaccurate or misleading. If the school refuses, the school must provide a formal hearing. If after the hearing, the student or parent is not satisfied, they have the right to put a dissenting statement into the student's record.

88. Pub. L. No. 93–380, 88 Stat. 484 (1974) (codified as amended at 20 U.S.C. § 1232g).

Under the Act, schools must get written permission in order to release any information from a student's education record unless it is for:

1. School officials with a legitimate education interest;

2. Other schools to which a student is transferring;

3. Appropriate parties in connection with financial aid to a student;

4. Organizations conducting studies for or on behalf of the school;

5. Accrediting organizations;

6. By order of law;

7. Appropriate officials in cases of health and safety emergencies.

Schools can also give out "directory" information (name, address phone number, date of birth and dates of attendance). Schools must give notice, and afford the student or parent an opportunity to deny the release of such information. In addition, the Act allows student records to be released to qualified persons, including school officials who have a reason to know the information, research organizations, federal and state education officials, and individuals with a lawful subpoena.[89]

6. *E–Government Act*

To ensure agency compliance with privacy laws and regulations, the E–Government Act was passed

89. 20 U.S.C. § 1232g(b)(1).

in 2002 requiring agencies to publish Privacy Impact Assessments ("PIA").[90] Agencies are required to submit PIAs any time personal information is collected on ten or more people. Assessments must include what information is collected and why, how the information is used and secured, and with whom the information is shared.

D.   Significant Legislation With Incidental Privacy Impacts

In addition to statutory schemes expressly enacted, in whole or in part, for purposes of protecting personal privacy, numerous other Federal statutes impact individuals' privacy interests. The legislation discussed below is by no means a comprehensive list as the complexity of different statutory and regulatory schemes can have interactions with other statutes and regulations that were not contemplated even by the legislators voting on the bills.

1.   *Freedom of Information Act*

The Freedom of Information Act of 1966 ("FOIA")[91] was passed to give the public access to information collected by federal government agencies. Under FOIA, an individual may request public information from an executive branch government

90.   Pub. L. No.107–347, 116 Stat. 2899 (2002) (codified as amended in scattered sections of 5, 10, 13, 15, 18, 28, 31, 40, 41, and 44 U.S.C.).

91.   Pub. L. No. 89–554, 80 Stat. 383 (1966) (codified as amended at 5 U.S.C. § 552).

agency and that agency is required to make a full disclosure, baring any applicable exemptions.

FOIA has nine exemptions, one of which protects privacy interests of individuals regarding their own sensitive personal information.[92] Information contained in medical, personal, or similar types of files is covered, for example. To determine if the personal identifying information exemption applies, the standard is whether the requested information includes information applicable to a particular individual. This is preliminarily determined by the agency that has been served the request. A court thereafter must determine if the release of the information would constitute a clearly unwarranted invasion of privacy, which turns on a balancing test weighing the individual's right to privacy against the basic policy of disclosing information under public request and scrutiny.

2. *Economic Espionage Act*

The Economic Espionage Act of 1996 ("EEA"),[93] makes the theft or misappropriation of a trade secret a federal crime. It was passed to fill the void between existing federal and state laws, and as a general American economic protection initiative. The Department of Justice is responsible for regulating and enforcing the EEA. Although "trade secrets" are usually thought of as chemical formulas

92. 5 U.S.C. § 552(b)(6).

93. Pub. L. No. 194–294, 110 Stat. 3488 (1996) (codified at 18 U.S.C. § 1831 *et seq.*).

or other scientific data, customer lists and personal information concerning customers are potentially protectable as a trade secret under the Act, although the power to enforce protection of that information is actually vested in the commercial entity that originally collected the information, rather in the individual customers themselves.

The EEA has two provisions that criminalize two types of activities. First, 18 U.S.C. § 1831 criminalizes the theft of trade secrets to benefit foreign powers. Second, 18 U.S.C. § 1832 criminalizes the theft of trade secrets for commercial or economic purposes. The two provisions differ in their target, and in the severity of the punishment. Section 1831 applies to someone who intends, or knows, that a violation will benefit any foreign government or agent. Under Section 1831 an individual can be fined up to $500,000, and imprisoned for up to 15 years, while businesses can be fined up to 10 million dollars. Section 1832 targets theft more generally, without specifying a foreign beneficiary. Under Section 1832, individuals can be fined up to $500,000, and imprisoned up to 10 years, while businesses can be fined $5 million.

The EEA has a very broad definition of a trade secret. Encompassed are thoughts and ideas in someone's head and purely oral communications; there is no requirement that the information be stored electronically or have been stolen in hardcopy form. This broad definition has serious implications for businesses that hire workers from competitors. The act punishes anyone who knowingly:

(1) steals, or without authorization appropriates takes, carries away, or conceals, or by fraud, artifice, or deception obtains a trade secret;

(2) without authorization copies, duplicates, sketches, draws, photographs, downloads, uploads, alters, destroys, photocopies, replicates, transmits, delivers, sends, mails, communicates, or conveys a trade secret, or

(3) receives, buys, or possesses a trade secret, knowing the same to have been stolen or appropriated, obtained, or converted without authorization.[94]

3. *USA PATRIOT Act*

Although the USA PATRIOT Act[95] was discussed above in regard to its impact on financial privacy, the Act contains numerous other provisions that also affect individual privacy. A complete examination of the Act's provisions is beyond this book's scope, however certain key sections with privacy implications include:

Section 105: Creates a "national network of electronic crimes task forces" to be set up by the Secret Service throughout the country to prevent, detect, and investigate various electronic crimes "including potential terrorist attacks against critical infrastructures and financial payment sys-

94. 18 U.S.C. § 1831

95. Pub. L. No. 107–56, 115 Stat. 272 (2001) (codified as amended at scattered sections of 12, 15, 18, and 31 U.S.C.).

tems"—which encompasses a wide variety of computer crimes.

Section 203: Requires information sharing, including previously secret grand jury testimony, between any number of federal agencies, so long as the information involves "foreign intelligence." The broad definition of that term found in the Foreign Intelligence Surveillance Act ("FISA") includes the following: "information, whether or not concerning a United States person, with respect to a foreign power or foreign territory that relates to the national defense or the security of the United States or the conduct of the foreign affairs of the United States." This information, which is in the possession of any federal investigative or law enforcement officer or attorney can be shared, without any court review or involvement, with any other federal "law enforcement, intelligence, protective, immigration, national defense, or national security official."

Section 212: Provides for voluntary and required disclosures to federal investigators by firms such as Internet service providers.

Section 218: Changes the scope of warrants under FISA from foreign intelligence being "a significant purpose" to "a purpose" of the investigation and so lowers the standard for obtaining a FISA warrant. Note that an investigation under FISA even though it usually involves foreign nationals or aliens does not have to be so restricted, and under the broad definition of "foreign intelligence" can include United States citizens.

Section 403: Mandates a dramatic new information system to allow State Department access to certain criminal files kept by the FBI, such as National Crime Information Center files. NCIC is a computerized index of criminal justice information. It provides authorized agencies with information such as criminal record histories, fugitives, stolen properties, and missing persons.

Section 507 and 508: Allow government investigators access to educational records, without a court order.

4. Federal Information Security Management Act

The Federal Information Security Management Act of 2002 ("FISMA") was designed to protect the information systems of the federal government.[96] Government agencies and contractors must establish a security program to improve and protect the information systems. These security programs must include the creation of security procedures and policies, annual reporting to Congress, security safeguard implementation, and continuous evaluations. While not specifically directed at the protection of individuals' privacy, the fact that government agencies maintain databases replete with personal information and which are frequently the target of identity thieves or other criminals, means that the benefits of increased security for these

96. Pub. L. No. 107–347, 116 Stat. 2899 (2002) (codified as amended in scattered sections of 15, 40, and 44 U.S.C.).

databases will accrue at least in part to the individuals whose personal information is stored therein.

E.   Federal Agencies

Numerous federal agencies are tasked with policing the statutory schemes discussed above, both externally and internally. A complete review of these agencies and their respective privacy law enforcement duties is beyond the scope of this Nutshell. Instead, in this section we will examine two agencies, which in many ways represent the outer limits of external and internal privacy regulation: the Federal Trade Commission ("FTC"), which is the primary enforcer of many federal privacy laws, and the Department of Homeland Security ("DHS"), which must work to balance its mission of collecting information essential for national security with traditional American concerns regarding concentration of surveillance powers.

1.   *The Federal Trade Commission*

Privacy is a key element of the FTC's consumer protection mission. Advances in computer technology have made it possible for detailed information about individuals to be compiled and shared more easily than ever. These advances have resulted in many benefits for both society as a whole, and individual consumers. Yet, as personal information is more frequently transmitted and becomes more accessible, steps to prevent and protect against the misuse of this information become more important at every stage of a transaction.

Congress established the FTC as the primary agency responsible for protecting consumers and preserving competition between businesses, while curbing the worst abuses of the free market.[97] To these ends, the FTC investigates reports of unfair competition and deceptive trade practices. The main tool provided to the FTC for this purpose is Section 5 of the Federal Trade Commission Act ("FTCA," codified as 15 U.S.C. § 45), but the FTC also has the power to promulgate quasi-legislative regulations and quasi-judicial orders addressing more specific issues within the scope of its Section 5 authority. Additionally, due to its status as the Federal government's primary defender of consumers' interests, Congress has also vested it with authority to enforce many specific pieces of privacy legislation enacted in recent years.

a. *Section 5 of the FTCA*

Section 5 of the FTCA was intended to permit a flexible approach to regulating business practices.[98] As a result, Section 5 avoids the approach of some consumer protection legislative schemes which attempt to exhaustively list what constitutes a "deceptive" or "unfair" trade practice in favor of the

97. Federal Trade Commission Act, Pub. L. No. 63–203, 38 Stat. 717 (1914) (codified as amended at 15 U.S.C. §§ 41 to 58).

98. *See* FTC v. Sperry & Hutchinson Co., 405 U.S. 233, 239–40 (1972).

simple statement, "Unfair methods of competition in or affecting commerce, and unfair or deceptive acts or practices in or affecting commerce, are hereby declared unlawful."[99] The FTC is therefore "empowered and directed to prevent persons, partnerships, or corporations ... from using unfair methods of competition in or affecting commerce and unfair or deceptive acts or practices in or affecting commerce," except for certain types of businesses which are separately regulated by other Federal agencies, such as financial institutions.[100] Section 5 does not, however, extend to export trade with foreign nations unless the unfair methods of competition employed against foreign competitors or consumers also injure U.S. consumers or businesses or "involve material conduct occurring within the United States."[101]

The FTC was also authorized to provide a wide range of remedies for Section 5 violations. The most typical remedy is a cease-and-desist order, which enjoins the illegal conduct and prohibits future violations. Other remedies include "fencing-in," which involves the FTC not only entering a cease-and-desist order regarding a specific practice or product, but also covering related practices or products so as to prevent the sanctioned party from circumventing the FTC's action. Corrective advertising to rectify misleading impressions created by earlier false advertising, redress to injured consumers, and civil penalties may also be assessed.

99.   15 U.S.C. § 45(a)(1).

100.   15 U.S.C. § 15 U.S.C. § 45(a)(2).

101.   15 U.S.C. § 45(a)(3), (4).

In extreme circumstances, the FTC may order a "sweep" of an entire industry based on pervasive unfair trade practices. The FTC's "Operation Bidder Beware," for example, was aimed at online auction fraud by sellers and payment escrow services. That sweep resulted in over fifty separate legal actions filed in twenty-nine different states.[102]

b. *The evolution of the Unfairness Doctrine*

Congress left it to the FTC and courts to determine how to define "unfair" in the context of Section 5. This has led to a gradual expansion of the definition of what constitutes unfair competition. Originally, Section 5 only specifically proscribed "unfair methods of competition," and thus it was understood that the FTC's main concern was protecting competitors and preventing the formation or abuse of monopoly power. Yet it did not take long before the FTC began to interpret the language of the FTCA to permit an emphasis on consumer protection. As early as 1916, in the *Circle Cilk Co.* decision, 1 F.T.C. 13 (1916), the FTC entered a cease-and-desist order based on practices found to have "deceived some of the consuming public." *Id.* at 15. Originally, the FTC indicated that a finding of actual deception was necessary,[103] but by 1919,

102. Federal Trade Commission, *Internet Auction Fraud Targeted by Law Enforcers* (Apr. 30, 2003), *available at* http://www.ftc.gov/opa/2003/04/bidderbeware.htm.

103. Circle Cilk Co., 1 F.T.C. 13, 19 (1916); *see also* Geographical Publ'g Co., 1 F.T.C. 235, 239 (1918) (finding intentional deception).

the FTC expanded the scope of unfair competition to include a mere "tendency" to deceive.[104]

The courts, however, acted to limit the FTC's efforts to expand the range of conduct it could punish. In *FTC v. Gratz*, 253 U.S. 421 (1920), the first U.S. Supreme Court decision to address the scope of the FTC's authority under Section 5, the Court found that the term "unfair methods of competition" did not reach "practices never heretofore regarded as opposed to good morals because characterized by deception, bad faith, fraud or oppression, or as against public policy because of their dangerous tendency unduly to hinder competition or create monopoly." *Id*. at 427. Eleven years later, in *FTC v. Raladam Co.*, the Supreme Court held that for conduct to be punishable under Section 5 the conduct must have injured, or have the tendency to injure, an actual or potential competitor or competition generally and that consumer injury alone was insufficient.[105] The Court noted that public interest is only one part of the analysis the FTC must consider before issuing a cease-and-desist order.

Congress responded to the *Raladam* decision by passing the Wheeler–Lea Act amending Section 5(a)(1) to apply to both unfair competition and deceptive acts or practices.[106] This clarified that the FTC's jurisdiction extended to the protection of consumers without needing to consider whether the

104. Gordon Van Tine Co., 1 F.T.C. 316 (1919).

105. FTC v. Raladam Co., 283 U.S. 643, 652–54 (1931).

106. Wheeler-Lea Act of 1938, Pub L. No. 75–447, 52 Stat. 111 (1938) (codified as amended at 15 U.S.C. §§ 45 to 57).

conduct could also be considered anticompetitive. The FTC broadly defined the term "deceptive" as any act or practice that has the tendency to mislead a substantial amount of the consuming public in a material way. As the Second Circuit Court of Appeals explained in affirming an FTC order against a skin cream manufacturer, the "fact that a false statement may be obviously false to those who are trained and experienced does not change its character, nor take away its power to deceive others less experienced. The important criterion is the net impression which the advertisement is likely to make upon the general populace."[107] The FTC also found favor with the courts on the question of whether representations with the capacity or tendency to deceive are sufficient to find a Section 5 violation.[108] As one court explained, "since the purpose of the statute is not to punish the wrongdoer but to protect the public, the cardinal factor is the probable effect which the advertiser's handiwork will have upon the eye and mind of the reader."[109] This was drawn from the conclusion that the main purpose of the Wheeler–Lea Act's amendment to Section 5 of the FTCA was to give "to the consumer the right to rely upon representations of facts as the truth."[110]

107.   Charles of the Ritz Distribs. Corp. v. FTC, 143 F.2d 676, 679–80 (2d Cir. 1944) (internal quotation marks and citations omitted).

108.   *See* FTC v. Sterling Drug, Inc., 317 F.2d 669 (2d Cir. 1963).

109.   Id. at 674.

110.   *See In re* Pfizer, Inc., 81 F.T.C. 23 (1972).

During the 1960s, the FTC continued its jurisdictional expansion. In 1964, it issued the "Cigarette Rule," which became the first of several policy statements to provide a better understanding of what constituted an unfair act or practice.[111] The FTC gave three criteria to consider when investigating possible unfair acts or practices: (1) whether the practice offends established public policy concepts of unfairness; (2) whether it is immoral, unethical, oppressive, or unscrupulous; and (3) whether it causes substantial injury to consumers or competitors. All three elements did not have to be satisfied and a practice could be determined to be unfair based on a sufficiently severe infraction of one of the elements. The U.S. Supreme Court affirmed this approach in *FTC v. Sperry & Hutchinson Co.*, 405 U.S. 233, 244 (1972), holding that Section 5 empowered the FTC to proscribe practices as unfair or deceptive regardless of their effect on competition because Section 5 "considers public values beyond simply those enshrined in the letter or encompassed in the spirit of the antitrust laws."

c. The 1980s: The halt of FTCA Section 5 jurisdictional expansion

By the late 1970s and early 1980s, public policy

111. Statement of Basis and Purpose of Trade Regulation Rule 408, *Unfair or Deceptive Advertising and Labeling of Cigarettes in Relation to the Health Hazards of Smoking,* 29 Fed. Reg. 8325, 8355 (July 2, 1964). The regulation was preempted by the Federal Cigarette Labeling and Advertising Act, Pub. L. No. 89–92, 79 Stat. 283 (1965) (codified as amended at 15 U.S.C. §§ 1331–1340).

began placing increased emphasis on free markets as efficient and self-correcting means of regulating business behavior, while mergers were viewed as expanding business and creating growth benefiting the overall economy. Courts, following influential scholarship from a variety of sources that hybridized traditional legal and economic principles, also increasingly agreed that antitrust and other forms of market regulation imposed substantial costs on the American economy. Meanwhile, Congress was expressing growing apprehension over the FTC's aggressive pursuit of alleged Section 5 violators, and began to take steps to pass legislation which would have sharply reduced the FTC's discretion in defining "unfair" and "deceptive" practices. To respond to these pressures and head off Congressional action, the FTC introduced two key policy statements in the early 1980s that were designed as a form of self-restraint and which led to a significant decrease in FTC Section 5 actions.

(i) The Unfairness Policy Statement, 1980

In the 1980 "Unfairness" Policy Statement ("Unfairness Statement"), the FTC changed its approach to the unfairness doctrine from the moral and ethical concepts emphasized by the "Cigarette Rule" and the *Sperry & Hutchinson* decision to one based on a cost-benefit analysis. The Unfairness Statement set forth that a practice is unfair if: 1) it causes substantial consumer injury as monetary harm; 2) the injury is not outweighed by benefits to the consumer or to competition; and 3) the injury caused by practice could not be reasonably avoided by the consumer. The Statement narrowed the effective scope of Section 5 by adding the need for "substantial" consumer injury; adopting a cost-benefit analysis which included weighing the harm against competitive benefits; and by limiting public policy to only "clear and well-established" statements.[112]

(ii) The Deception Policy Statement, 1983

In 1983, the FTC issued another policy statement (the "Deception Statement"), this time limiting what constitutes "deceptive" conduct by defining it as a material representation, omission, or practice that is likely to mislead a reasonable consumer to that consumer's detriment.[113] The FTC defined an act or practice as material if it is "likely to affect a consumer's conduct or decision with regard to a product or service." A "reasonable consumer" is defined by the circumstances of each case, but in any event, it does not automatically equate to a majority of consumers, because a practice may still

112. *FTC Policy Statement on Unfairness*, Letter from Michael Pertschuk, FTC Chairman, to Sens. Wendell H. Ford & John C. Danforth (Dec. 17, 1980), *available at* http://www.ftc.gov/bcp/policystmt/ad-unfair.htm. Congress codified the Unfairness Statement in 1994. *See* Pub. L. No. 103–312, § 9, 108 Stat 1691, 1695 (1994) (codified as 15 U.S.C. § 45(n)).

113. *FTC Policy Statement on Deception*, Letter from James C. Miller, III, FTC Chairman, to Rep. John D. Dingell (Oct. 14, 1983), *available at* http://www.ftc.gov/bcp/policystmt/ad-decept.htm.

be deceptive if it "misleads a significant minority of reasonable consumers." The deception must be material, although there is no requirement that the manufacturer intended any deception or that anyone was actually deceived or injured.

d. Unfair competition in the Internet Age: protecting privacy

Although the FTC still operates under the constraints of the Unfair and Deception Statements, it began to find new vigor during the Internet boom of the late 1990s. The growth of online commerce, which often involves consumers engaging in transactions with parties that they have little or no prior business relationship with, stimulated both a quantitative and qualitative change in the types of unfair and deceptive practices unscrupulous individuals could engage in. As consumer deception online typically features victims and perpetrators located in different states or even different nations, the FTC naturally found itself obliged to play a greater role in such investigations. The Commission has shown major concern over a few areas of the internet including misrepresentations of how information is collected and used including violations of company privacy policies, consumer fraud including deceptive advertising and marketing, inadequate security measures to avoid security breaches, and COPPA violations.

The FTC generally supported industry self-regulation as the primary means of addressing online

privacy concerns. As the FTC itself explained in a
report to Congress, "Self-regulation is the least
intrusive way and most efficient to ensure fair
information practices, given the rapidly evolving
nature of the Internet and computer technology."[114]
Self-regulation avoids the heavy burdens of cost and
inflexibility of government regulations, and the
FTC has expressed concern that overly formalizing
privacy standards through the bureaucratic process
could stunt technological growth and market development. To this end, the FTC mostly relied on
industry organizations to adopt their own codes of
conduct or best practices for the first several years
of the Internet's growth. With the growth of e-
commerce and corresponding fears about the security of consumers' personal data, however, in recent
years the FTC has begun to more actively use its
authority to protect consumers under Section 5.

Early enforcement actions concerning privacy or
personal data on the internet stemmed principally
from consumer deception. The first major case the
FTC brought concerning Internet privacy was in
1998 against the operators of the GeoCities online
community.[115] Although GeoCities had a posted privacy policy which stated that it distributed users'
personal information to third parties on only an
"opt-in" basis, evidence suggested that GeoCities

114. *See* FTC, *Self-Regulation and Privacy Online: A Report
to Congress*, 6 (July 1, 1999), *available at http://www.ftc.gov/os/
1999/07/privacy99.pdf.*

115. *See* FTC, *Analysis of Proposed Consent Order to Aid
Public Comment*, Aug. 1998, *available at* http://www.ftc.gov/os/
1998/08/9823015.ana.htm.

was in fact selling or otherwise disseminating its users' personal information without their knowledge. Furthermore, to be able to access certain parts of the website, users were required to provide personal information through forms that suggested GeoCities was handling the information, when in fact the users' information was being directly collected by third parties, which had partnered with GeoCities. The following year, GeoCities settled with the FTC, and agreed to the entry of a consent order prohibiting GeoCities from making further misrepresentations and required the company to post notice of their informational practices. GeoCities was further ordered to revise its privacy policy to accurately reflect how it uses data collected through the website and also ordered it to contact all individuals it had collected personal information from to give them the option to have their collected data deleted.[116]

In response to the concerns raised by the *GeoCities* case, the FTC began to demonstrate increased skepticism toward self-regulation. Whereas only two years earlier the FTC had praised self-regulation, in 2000 the Commission stated that due to the fact that "self-regulatory initiatives to date fall far short of broad-based implementation of effective self-regulatory programs, the Commission has concluded that such efforts alone cannot ensure that the online marketplace as a whole will emulate the stan-

116. *See In re Geocities*, 127 F.T.C. 94, No. 9823015, Feb. 1999, *available at http://www.ftc.gov/os/1998/08/geo-ord.htm.*

dards adopted by industry leaders."[117] The FTC reasoned that a company's privacy policy should be easily accessible and understandable so that the consumer is aware of what information is being collected and how the information is used. The FTC also stressed that companies take appropriate steps to ensure the security and integrity of the collected information. The FTC concluded that most consumers do not realize that companies were collecting and using their personal information. To rectify this situation while awaiting specific legislation from Congress, the FTC began to place greater emphasis on what it termed the "Fair Information Practice Principles" to provide guidance to companies that were collecting personal information.[118] The "Fair Information Practice Principles" were first articulated by the FTC in 1998 and were modeled on the OECD's privacy guidelines. The Principles are defined by the FTC as:

1. Notice: those collecting data must disclose their information practices before collecting it from consumers;

2. Choice: consumers must be given options if and how their personal info may be used for other purposes;

117.   FTC, *Privacy Online: Fair Information Practices in Electronic Marketplace*, ii-iii (2000), *available at* http://www.ftc.gov/reports/privacy2000/privacy2000.pdf.

118.   Id.

3. Access: consumers should be able to access and correct data collected about them; and

4. Security: data collectors must take reasonable steps to assure info collected from consumers is secure from public use.

In 2001, the FTC further committed itself to greater use of its Section 5 powers to attack practices that compromise consumers' privacy online by using both its deception and unfairness standards. Under this more aggressive standard, a company's violation of its own privacy policy is considered by the FTC to be an unfair and deceptive practice. Likewise, the FTC has increasingly pursued Section 5 violations pertaining to privacy when a company makes affirmative misrepresentations in collecting information, and particularly when such information is collected from children. As part of this effort, the FTC uses the Fair Information Practice Principles as its guide.

The FTC's pursuit of an action against Gateway Learning Corp.[119] is an example of this stepped up enforcement. Gateway was a seller of popular educational materials and products for children. Its privacy policy represented that it did not sell, rent, loan, or otherwise disclose personal information that it collected from its customers. Notwithstanding this policy, Gateway leased information to third parties without disclosing to its customers that it was doing so. Gateway then altered its privacy

119. *In re Gateway Learning Corp.*, No. C–4120, 2004 WL 2618647 (Sept. 10, 2004), *available at* http://www.ftc.gov/os/caselist/0423047/0423047.shtm.

policy on a retroactive basis to state that it was entitled to disclose personal information to third parties, but again failed to notify its existing customers of the change despite the fact that its posted privacy policy stated that Gateway would provide notice of any material changes in the terms of the policy.[120]

The FTC commenced an enforcement action on the grounds that this behavior constituted both deceptive and unfair trade practices. As set forth in the FTC's complaint, the dissemination of personal information to third parties in violation of the published privacy policy constituted a form of deceptive trade practice, while the retroactive amendment of the policy was an unfair practice.[121] The FTC and Gateway ultimately settled the action with Gateway being required to disgorge the profits it had earned from improperly sharing its customers' information and to agree not to disclose previously collected customer information, or to alter its privacy policy retroactively, without express affirmative consent from the customers.

(i) Misrepresentations in collecting personal information

Although this discussion has mainly focused on the FTC's activities concerning privacy issues on-

120. FTC, Analysis of Proposed Consent Order to Aid Public Comment, Jul. 7, 2004, *available at* http://www.ftc.gov/os/caselist/0423047/040707anl0423047.pdf.

121. Complaint, *In re Gateway Learning Co.*, ¶¶ 11–16, *available at* http://www.ftc.gov/os/caselist/0423047/040707cmp0423047.pdf.

line, it bears mention that even before the Internet, the FTC found that a company had acted both deceptively and unfairly in collecting consumers' personal privacy. In the case of *In re Metromedia, Inc.*, 78 F.T.C. 331 (1971), a company sent consumers a form letter with a questionnaire that could be returned in exchange for the opportunity to be eligible for prizes. The company claimed the letter was sent to find out people's habits and characteristics and assured them that no salesperson would call and that there was nothing to buy. The FTC found that the company violated Section 5 by failing to disclose that the real purpose for collecting the information was to compile and sell mailing lists to third parties.[122] The FTC stressed the importance of the consumers' interest in privacy, noting that most consumers prefer that their names not be placed on mailing lists because they feel it is an invasion of personal privacy being subject to advertisers.

(ii) Protecting children

As discussed above in Chapter 3, Part II.C.4, Congress enacted the Children's Online Privacy Protection Act (COPPA) in 2000 to protect the personal information of children under the age of 13.[123] Under COPPA, both the state attorneys general and the FTC can bring enforcement actions.[124]

122.   *In re Metromedia, Inc.*, 78 F.T.C. 331, 337 (1971).

123.   15 U.S.C. § 6501 to 6506.

124.   15 U.S.C. §§ 6502(c) and 6504(a)(1).

The FTC has the right to intervene in any action brought under the statute by a state attorney general.[125] To implement its enforcement regime for COPPA, the FTC promulgated the Children's Online Privacy Protection Rule ("COPPR"), also discussed above.[126]

Although some critics have suggested that COPPA has not been effective because of surveys that suggest most businesses which would be subject to the statute are not in compliance, there is little doubt that the FTC has sought sizeable penalties in those instances where it has brought enforcement actions under the statute. In 2006, the FTC settled a COPPA enforcement action against the social networking website Xanga.com for $1 million dollars.[127] The FTC had alleged that Xanga.com knowingly allowed minors to sign up for services on the site without parental consent. Although Xanga.com had a stated policy that children under the age of 13 were not allowed to join the site, all children had to do to join was to check a box confirming they were over 13 even if they had entered a birth date showing otherwise.

(iii) Spyware

So-called "spyware," and its associated privacy implications, have been an increasing concern for

125. 15 U.S.C. § 6504(b)(1).

126. 16 C.F.R. § 312.

127. Consent Decree and Order for Civil Penalties, Injunction, and Other Relief, ¶ 11, United States v. Xanga.com, Inc., Civ. Act. No. 06–CIV–6853, *available at* http://www.ftc.gov/os/caselist/0623073/xangaconsentdecree.pdf.

the FTC. The FTC defines spyware as "software that aids in gathering information about a person or organization without their knowledge and which may send such information to another entity without the consumer's consent, or that asserts control over a computer without the consumer's knowledge."[128]

The FTC has successfully pursued a number of Section 5 enforcement actions related to spyware in recent years. In 2006, for example, the FTC settled two spyware cases,[129] for a combined judgment of $3.61 million.[130] In both cases, the FTC had alleged that companies covertly placed software on webusers' computers by exploiting security defects in their Internet browsers. The primary manifestation of the spyware in both instances were "pop-ups," advertisements that appear in new browser windows over the user's original screen, and redirection of users to commercial websites. The software also collected personal information from the users' machines, including websurfing habits and passwords entered online.

128. FTC, Press Release, *Spyware Poses Risks to Consumers*, Apr. 29, 2004, *available at* http://www.ftc.gov/opa/2004/04/spywaretest.shtm.

129. FTC v. Seismic Entertainment Prods., 04–CV–00377–JD (D.N.H. 2006); FTC v. Odysseus Mktg., Inc., Case No. 05–cv–00330–SM (D.N.H. 2006).

130. FTC, Press Release, *FTC Permanently Halts Unlawful Spyware Operations,* Nov. 21, 2006, *available at* http://www.ftc.gov/opa/2006/11/seismicodysseus.shtm.

(iv) Inadequate security: expanding FTC jurisdiction

The FTC has used deception standards to bring enforcement actions against companies for failing to provide information security consistent with the companies' public representations regarding security, or for not following their own privacy policies. But after several major breaches of computer databases in 2005, the FTC began bringing enforcement actions pursuant to its ability to prosecute unfair trade practices against companies that were failing to provide reasonable and adequate security, even without having made false representations to their customers or other parties.[131]

In early 2006, the FTC settled with ChoicePoint, a data mining company, for a $10 million penalty and $5 million for compensation to injured customers after the company sold personal information on over 150,000 individuals to people with ties to identity theft rings.[132] The FTC concluded that Choice-Point did not have reasonable procedures for ascertaining what purpose its customers intended to use the personal information for. The FTC was able to

131.   Thomas J. Smedinghoff, *The Challenge of Electronic Data: Corporate Legal Obligations to Provide Information Security*, Wallstreetlawyer.com, Mar. 2006, *available at* 10 No. 3 GLWSLAW 1 (Westlaw).

132.   Jason Krause, *Stolen Lives*, 92 Mar A.B.A.J. 36, 38 (2006); Evan Perez & Rich Brooks, *File Sharing: For Big Vendor of Personal Data, A Theft Lays Bare the Downside*, WALL ST. J., May 3, 2005, at A1; *see also* Bob Sullivan, *Database Giant Gives Access to Fake Firms*, MSNBC.com, Feb. 14, 2005, *available at* http://msnbc.msn.com/id/6969799.

identify over 1400 consumers who had experienced an out-of-pocket loss due to ChoicePoint's inadequate security measures.[133] The settlement bars ChoicePoint from selling personal information without taking reasonable precautions to ensure that the information is only provided to customers with lawful purposes in mind.

Several other companies experienced security breaches around this same time, causing heightened concern for consumer privacy and leading to yet further FTC scrutiny.[134] CardSystems Solutions, Inc. settled with the FTC in 2006 on charges for failure to use appropriate security measures to protect sensitive information of millions of consumers.[135] The FTC found the breach of CardSystems' database resulted in millions of dollars of fraudulent charges. FTC determined that the company did not adequately manage its security practices and failed to prevent unauthorized access to its database. CardSystems was required to implement a formal security program that met certain minimum guarantees and agree to third-party audits of its privacy practices every other year for 20 years.

133. Stipulated Final Judgment and Order for Civil Penalties, Permanent Injunction, and Other Equitable Relief, United States v. ChoicePoint, Inc., FTC No. 052 3069 (N.D. Ga. Jan. 26, 2006), *available at* http://www.ftc.gov/os/caselist/choicepoint/choicepoint.htm

134. See Privacy Rights Clearinghouse, *A Chronology of Data Breaches Reported Since the ChoicePoint Incident*, Nov. 11, 2007, *available at* http://www.privacyrights.org/ar/ChronDataBreaches.htm.

135. Agreement Containing Consent Order, *In re CardSystems Solution, Inc.*, FTC File No. 052 3148 (Feb. 23, 2006), *available at* http://www.ftc.gov/opa/2006/02/cardsystems_r.htm.

Also in 2006, the FTC ordered Qchex, an online checking company, to stop its business practice of e-mailing personal checks without first verifying the identity of the maker of each check.[136] The FTC commenced the investigation after receiving over 600 consumer complaints claiming Qchex had fraudulently withdrawn money from their accounts, as well as at least twenty fraudulent checks processed by Qchex that were drawn on the FTC and Federal Communications Commission's own accounts.[137] The FTC argued that by not requiring identity authentication before sending the checks, the company committed an unfair trade practice in violation of Section 5 of the FTCA.[138] The checks did not have to be signed and were instead stamped "signature not required" which allowed users to write fraudulent checks.

Guidance Software, Inc. also settled with the FTC in late 2006 for failing to use reasonable security measures to protect consumer data and for not following its own privacy policy.[139] Guidance's inad-

136. Press Release, FTC, *Court Halts Illegal Operations of Online Check Processing Firm*, Oct. 2, 2006, *available at* http://www.ftc.gov/opa/2006/10/qchex.shtm.

137. Bob Sullivan, *Targeted in Online Check Scam, FTC Sues*, Sept. 25, 2006, *available* at http://www.msnbc.msn.com/id/14995196/.

138. Complaint, FTC v. Neovi, Inc., Case No. 06–cv–1952–WQH-JMA, *available at* http://www.ftc.gov/os/caselist/0523155/060919neovicmplt.pdf.

139. Press Release, FTC, *Guidance Software Inc Settles FTC Charges*, Nov. 16, 2006, *available at* http://www.ftc.gov/opa/2006/11/guidance.htm.

equate security measures allowed hackers to obtain credit card information from thousands of customers. The settlement requires Guidance to implement a security program and to be subject to biannual third-party audits. This was FTC's fourteenth challenge against companies for unreasonable data security measures in handling sensitive consumer data. Despite the success of these enforcement efforts, however, identity theft will remain a major challenge for the FTC into the foreseeable future. In 2006, 36% of almost 700,000 complaints to the FTC concerned identity theft, the seventh year in a row where identity theft topped the list of complaints.[140]

e. Recent regulations: the Disposal Rule

The Disposal Rule became effective June 1, 2005 giving the FTC authority to require businesses to take appropriate measures in disposing of sensitive information from consumers' files.[141] The Disposal Rule applies to "consumer reports" or information derived from consumer reports. Consumer reports include information such as establishing an individual's credit, employment or insurance history, background checks, past checks, residential history and medical history.[142] Any company that uses consum-

140. FTC, *Consumer Fraud and Identity Theft Complaint Data* (Feb. 2007), *available at* http://www.consumer.gov/sentinel/pubs/Top10Fraud2006.pdf.

141. Press Release, FTC, *FACTA Disposal Rule Goes into Effect June 1*, (June 2005), *available at* www.ftc.gov/os/2004/11/041118disposalfrn.pdf.

142. Id.

er reports must comply with the disposal rule including lenders, insurers, employers, landlords, government agencies, auto dealers, debt collectors, and credit reports. Proper disposal is reasonable and appropriate if measures are taken to prevent unauthorized access or use of information derived from consumer reports. The company must use due diligence by hiring a document destruction company or otherwise following proper in-house document destruction procedures for both hardcopy and electronic data. The rule emphasizes self-regulation, leaving it up to the regulated businesses and organizations to determine what measures are reasonable for disposal depending on the sensitivity of the information, the costs and benefits of disposal methods, as well as changes in technology.[143]

2. *The Department of Homeland Security*

The Department of Homeland Security (DHS) was established in 2002 by the Homeland Security Act.[144] DHS is a cabinet-level executive department tasked with preventing terrorist attacks within the United States, reducing vulnerability to terrorist attacks, and otherwise minimizing the damage of these attacks if they occur.[145] The Homeland Security Act brought over a dozen Federal agencies that had either been independent or under the supervi-

143.   Release, *FACTA Disposal Rule Goes into Effect June 1*, (June 2005), *available at* www.ftc.gov/os/2004/11/041118disposal frn.pdf.

144.   6 U.S.C. § 111(a).

145.   6 U.S.C. § 111(a), (b).

sion of different executive departments, including the Immigration and Naturalization Service, the Federal Emergency Management Agency, and Secret Service, under the umbrella of the DHS. The concentration of so many different agencies, many of which have reason to collect individuals' personal information under a variety of circumstances, under one supervising authority raised unparalleled concerns about the threat this newly created entity would pose to individual privacy.

To address these concerns, the DHS has an intricate system to ensure adequate measures are taken to ensure privacy protection inside and outside of the agency. The DHS is the first federal agency to have a statutorily required chief privacy officer ("CPO"),[146] something that had become increasingly common in the business world over the preceding years. (Private sector CPOs are discussed in Chapter 3, Part V(E)). The CPO reports directly to the Secretary of Homeland Security and oversees the DHS Privacy Office.[147]

The mission of the DHS Privacy Office is to protect individuals' privacy rights, with particular emphasis on maintaining the security of their "personally identifiable information." The DHS Privacy Office defines "personally identifiable information" as information in a system or online collection that "directly or indirectly identifies a specific individu-

---

146. 6 U.S.C. § 142.

147. DHS, *The Privacy Office of the U.S. Dept. of Homeland Security*, *available at* http://www.dhs.gov/xabout/structure/editor ial_0338.shtm.

al."[148] This can include information such as names, Social Security numbers, date and place of birth, and biometric records, among others. The Privacy Office establishes contracts and relationships with vendors and ensures that they have adequate protections to safeguard consumer privacy. Pursuant to the E–Government Act of 2002, discussed above, the Privacy Office also issues PIAs concerning any new information technology or programs implemented by DHS's subsidiary agencies, such as the "Secure Flight" program, a proposed passenger screening system developed by the Transportation Security Administration ("TSA"). These assessments address how long collected personal information is retained, with whom it is shared, and rights of individuals to access and correct the information.[149] To determine whether individuals reasonably believed that their personal information would be kept private, DHS will look at the circumstances of how the data was collected, whether the consumer had notice, and the risk of harm to the consumer by using the data, such as medical or financial information.

The DHS also established the Data Privacy and Integrity Advisory Committee in 2004 to advise the

148. DHS, Office of Inspector General, *Better Administration of Automated Targeting System Controls Can Further Protect Personally Identifiable Information*, 2 (Oct. 2007), *available at* http://www.dhs.gov/xoig/assets/mgmtrpts/OIG_08–06_Oct07.pdf.

149. DHS, Privacy Office, *Privacy Impact Assessment for the United States Visitor and Immigrant Status Indicator Technology (US–VISIT) Program*, 3–4 (2005), *available at* http://www.dhs.gov/interweb/assetlibrary/privacy_pia_usvisit_update_12–22–2005.pdf.

CPO and Secretary on issues affecting individual privacy. The goal of the committee is to limit information disclosure to ensure that it is only used for authorized purposes, maximize security and confidentiality in the handling of information, protect the constitutional and statutory rights of individuals whose personal information has been collected, and improve both the integrity of data and increase personal privacy through timely destruction of information that has been collected. The committee advises DHS on length of data retention, limits, and methods of enhancing security. The committee must have at least 12 members appointed by the Secretary for a period of four years in staggered terms.[150] Since its creation, DHS has published almost 30 new or revised public notices describing operations concerning collection and use of personally identifiable information.[151]

Given its broad powers, the DHS has been under scrutiny by a number of organizations concerned with privacy issues. In July 2004, for example, the Electronic Privacy Information Center (EPIC), a non-profit group, challenged the release of data from the U.S. Census Bureau to the DHS, which had included municipal and zip code-level breakdowns on Arab American populations, including

150. *See* DHS Data Privacy and Integrity Advisory Committee Charter (Apr. 26, 2004) *available at* http://www.dhs.gov/xlibrary/assets/privacy/privacy_advcom_ctr_rev.pdf.

151. Daniel Pulliam, *DHS Privacy Office Steps up Scrutiny of Tech Projects*, Dec. 14, 2006, *available at* http://govexec.com/story_page.cfm?articleid=35700 & prtinerfriendlyvers=1 & .

their countries of origin.[152] DHS explained that information was needed to determine which airports needed Arabic language signage.[153] In any event, setting aside truth or falsity of DHS's explanation, the release of information from the Census Bureau would not have triggered Privacy Office oversight because the data was "anonymized," *i.e.*, no specific individuals could be identified from it, thus it did not constitute "personally identifiable information."

III.   STATE CONSTITUTIONS

Privacy interests are a matter of great concern at the level of state government, particularly as a number of state constitutional provisions provide better articulated and broader protection for individual privacy than the U.S. Constitution.

In 1905, the Georgia Supreme Court recognized privacy as an independent and distinct right under the Georgia Constitution. In *Pavesich v. New England Life Ins. Co.*, 50 S.E. 68 (Ga. 1905), the Georgia Supreme Court found the state's residents to have a "liberty of privacy" guaranteed by the Georgia constitutional provision: "no person shall be deprived of liberty except by due process of law." The court grounded the right to privacy in the doctrine of natural law:

152.   Douglas J. Sylvester & Sharon Lohr, *Counting on Confidentiality: Legal and Statistical Approaches to Federal Privacy Law after the USA Patriot Act*, 2005 WIS. L. REV. 1033, 1043.

153.   *See* Lynette Clemetson, *HS Given Data on Arab Americans*, NY TIMES, July 30, 2004 at A14.

The right of privacy has its foundations in the instincts of nature. It is recognized intuitively, consciousness being witness that can be called to establish its existence. Any person whose intellect is in a normal condition recognizes at once that as to each individual member of society there are matters private and there are matters public so far as the individual is concerned. Each individual as instinctively resents any encroachment by the public upon his rights which are of a private nature as he does the withdrawal of those rights which are of a public nature. A right of privacy in matters purely private is therefore derived from natural law.

Pavesich, 50 S.E. at 69. The Georgia court's decision in *Pavesich* represented the first time any court of last resort recognized an independent constitutional right to privacy. Over the next fifty years, the majority of states adopted the principle of an individual right to privacy, whether by express constitutional provisions or by interpretation of existing constitutional language.

A. Explicit Right-to-Privacy Clauses

At least ten state constitutions contain explicit right-to-privacy clauses.

State	Clause
Alaska	The right of the people to privacy is recognized and shall not be infringed.[154]

154. ALASKA CONST., art. I, § 22.

State	Clause
Arizona	No person shall be disturbed in his private affairs, or his home invaded, without authority of law.**155**
California	All people ... have inalienable rights. Among these are enjoying and defending life and liberty, acquiring, possessing, and protecting property, and pursuing and obtaining safety, happiness, and privacy.**156**
Florida	Every natural person has the right to be let alone and free from governmental intrusion into his private life except as otherwise provided herein.**157**
Hawaii	The right of the people to privacy is recognized and shall not be infringed without the showing of a compelling state interest.... The right of the people to be secure in their persons, houses, papers, and effects against unreasonable searches, seizures and invasions of privacy shall not be violated....**158**
Illinois	The people shall have the right to be secure in their persons, houses, papers, and other possessions against unreasonable searches, seizures, invasions of privacy or interceptions of communications by eavesdropping devices or other means ... No warrant shall issue without probable cause, supported by affidavit particularly describing the place to be secured and the persons or things to be seized.**159**
Louisiana	Every person shall be secure in his person, property, communications, houses, papers and effects

155.   ARIZ. CONST., art. II, § 8.

156.   CAL. CONST., art. I, § 1.

157.   FLA. CONST., art. I, § 23.

158.   HAW. CONST., art. I, §§ 6–7.

159.   ILL. CONST., art. I, § 6.

State	Clause
	against ... invasions of privacy.[160]
Montana	The right of individual privacy is essential to the well-being of a free society and shall not be infringed without the showing of a compelling state interest.[161]
South Carolina	The right of the people to be secure in their persons, houses, papers, and effects against unreasonable searches and seizures and unreasonable invasions of privacy shall not be violated, and no warrants shall issue but upon probable cause, supported by oath or affirmation, and particularly describing the place to be searched, the person or thing to be seized, and the information to be obtained.[162]
Washington	No person shall be distributed in his private affairs, or his home invaded, without authority of law.[163]

B. Extending the Right to Privacy

Most other states have recognized some form of a right to privacy through courts' interpretations of their state constitutions. Colorado and New Jersey are two representative examples.

1. *Colorado*

The Colorado state constitution provides in relevant part:

160. LA. CONST., art. I, § 5.

161. MONT. CONST., art. II, § 10.

162. S.C. CONST., art. I, § 10.

163. WASH. CONST., art. I, § 7.

The people shall be secure in their persons, papers, homes and effects, from unreasonable
searches and seizures; and no warrant to search
any place or seize any person or things shall issue
without describing the place to be searched, or
the person or thing to be seized, as near as may
be, nor without probable cause, supported by oath
or affirmation reduced to writing.

Colo. Const., art. II, sec. 7. This language is substantially similar to the Fourth Amendment of the
U.S. Constitution, but the Colorado Supreme Court
has concluded that the scope of privacy protection it
affords can be construed more broadly. The Court
has declined to articulate a precise standard for
determining, "[w]here, as a result of a government
surveillance practice, the amount of privacy and
freedom remaining to citizens would be diminished
to a compass inconsistent with the aims of a free
and open society, a court may require regulation of
the government practice by means of a warrant."
People v. Oates, 698 P.2d 811, 816 (Colo. 1985). The
Colorado Court of Appeals recently explained that,
"in every case in which our supreme court has
recognized a greater protection under the state constitution than that afforded by the federal constitution, it has identified a privacy interest deserving of
greater protection than that available under the
Fourth Amendment." *People v. Rossman*, 140 P.3d
172, 176 (Colo. Ct. App. 2006).

This has resulted in a case-by-case approach to
constitutional privacy by the Colorado courts, usual-

ly involving the courts reacting to earlier U.S. Supreme Court decisions, which the Colorado courts perceive as lowering the threshold of federal privacy protections. Examples of this include determinations that an individual possesses a reasonable expectation of privacy in:

1. Commercially purchased goods, so that the installation of a tracking device in goods without a warrant is unconstitutional. *People v. Oates*, 698 P.2d 811 (Colo. 1985) *contra United States v. Karo*, 468 U.S. 705 (1984) (finding warrantless installation of tracking device in goods constitutional under Fourth Amendment);

2. Telephone numbers dialed, so that warrants are required for pen registers. *People v. Sporleder*, 666 P.2d 135 (Colo. 1983) *contra Smith v. Maryland*, 442 U.S. 735 (1979) (permitting warrantless pen registers under Fourth Amendment);

3. Bank records, so that properly issued subpoenas or warrants are required unless the bank otherwise voluntarily discloses the information. *Charnes v. DiGiacomo*, 612 P.2d 1117 (Colo. 1980) *contra United States v. Miller*, 425 U.S. 435 (1976) (no reasonable expectation of privacy in bank records under Fourth Amendment).

2. *New Jersey*

The New Jersey state constitution provides in relevant part:

All persons are by nature free and independent, and have certain natural and unalienable rights, among which are those of enjoying and defending life and liberty, of acquiring, possessing, and protecting property, and of pursuing and obtaining safety and happiness.

N.J. Const., art. 1, para. 1. The New Jersey Supreme Court has found that this language is "an analogue" to "the right of privacy guaranteed under the Fourteenth Amendment" to the U.S. Constitution. *State v. Saunders*, 381 A.2d 333, 341 (N.J. 1977). This right "is not necessarily broader in all respects" than the protections of the U.S. Constitution, but the New Jersey courts may demand "stronger and more persuasive showings of a public interest" than would be demanded under federal standards. *Id.* Notwithstanding this characterization, the New Jersey Supreme Court has subsequently interpreted the state constitution in a manner that lower courts have characterized as expanding the right to privacy "to areas not afforded such protection by the Fourth Amendment." *State v. Reid*, 914 A.2d 310, 313 (N.J. Super. Ct. 2007). Most significantly, the New Jersey courts have found that the state constitution protects "informational privacy," *i.e.*, the ability to control the acquisition, disclosure, or use of personally identifiable information. *Id*. at 314. Applying these standards, the New Jersey courts have found unconstitutional:

1. Statutes prohibiting consensual sexual intercourse between unmarried adults. *State v. Saunders*, 381 A.2d 333 (N.J. 1977);[164]

2. Acquisition of records of telephone numbers called without a warrant or other judicial proceeding. *State v. Hunt*, 450 A.2d 952 (N.J. 1982) *contra Smith v. Maryland*, 442 U.S. 735 (1979) (permitting warrantless pen registers under Fourth Amendment);

3. Searches of garbage left outside for pick-up without a warrant. *State v. Hempele*, 576 A.2d 793 (N.J. 1990) *contra California v. Greenwood*, 486 U.S. 35 (1988) (permitting warrantless searches of garbage placed in location accessible to public under Fourth Amendment);

4. Acquisition of account information from an Internet service provider without a warrant or valid subpoena. *State v. Reid*, 914 A.2d 310 (N.J. Super. Ct. 2007).[165]

164.   The U.S. Supreme Court's later decision in Lawrence v. Texas, 539 U.S. 558 (2003) has now arguably raised federal constitutional privacy protections for consensual adult sexual activities above the level set by *Saunders* (which specifically noted it was not addressing sodomy statutes).

165.   Although not directly in opposition to existing U.S. Supreme Court precedent, the New Jersey court noted that lower

IV. STATE STATUTES

From January 1, 2005 through November 1, 2007, over 500 reported security breaches involving personal information occurred in the United States alone, resulting in the theft of records containing information on millions of individuals.[166] Consequently, it is unsurprising that the enactment of privacy laws and regulations has become an increasing priority for state governments, particularly given the perception that the federal government has failed to address the issue in a timely or systemic manner.

Three common obligations emerge from the patchwork of state laws, regulations, and government enforcement actions. First, businesses have a duty to provide reasonable security for personal information in their possession. Second, businesses have a duty to disclose security breaches concerning such personal information in their possession. Third, publicly traded companies increasingly are required to regularly advise shareholders of the adequacy of their security measures even in the absence of an actual breach.

Federal courts have consistently interpreted the holding *Smith v. Maryland*, 442 U.S. 735 (1979) to reach a contrary result to what the New Jersey constitution compels.

166. Privacy Rights Clearinghouse, *A Chronology of Data Breaches*, www.privacyrights.org/ar/ChronDataBreaches.htm (last updated November 2, 2007).

A. Mandatory Privacy Policies

A number of states have introduced legislation that either requires businesses to maintain formal privacy policies for their customers and/or employees' personal data or, at a minimum, establishes criteria for privacy policies to be considered legally valid. The California Online Privacy Act of 2003,[167] requires operators of commercial websites or online services that collect "personally identifiable information through the Internet" to "conspicuously post" a privacy policy on their websites or otherwise make the privacy policy available in compliance with the statute. The statute also specifies what information must be contained in the privacy policy and sets forth certain formatting rules that the party posting the policy must follow.[168]

Pennsylvania has approached this area in its Unfair Acts and Practices Act. In 2004, Pennsylvania added the following language to its unfair acts and practices statute, to include as an unfair act, any person who "knowingly makes a false or misleading statement in a privacy policy, published on the Internet or otherwise distributed or published, regarding the use of personal information submitted by members of the public."[169]

Some states impose the requirement of the creation of a privacy policy in selected cases. Michigan,

167. CAL. BUS. & PROF. CODE §§ 22575 *et seq.* (2005).

168. *Id.* §§ 22575(b), 22577(b) (2005).

169. 18 PA. CONS. STAT. ANN. § 4107(a)(10) (2004).

for example, mandates the creation of a privacy policy containing specified items for any person who obtains one or more Social Security numbers in the ordinary course of business.[170]

B. Opt-in Privacy Standards

One important issue in opt-in laws has been whether to provide for a right to "opt-out" of particular uses, or whether to require that the individual "opt-in" by expressly permitting the use of personal information before it can be made. "Opt-out" laws typically leave the data or information holder with broad discretion in handling the information, especially because few data subjects exercise their rights to "opt-out." The states of California, Vermont, North Dakota, Alaska, Connecticut, Illinois, and Maryland have "opt-in" privacy standards.

C. Mandatory Security for Personal Information

States that have enacted open record statutes or similar "sunshine laws" permitting public access to state records have uniformly adopted companion statutes designed to protect the privacy of at least some types of personal information of individuals who submit information to the government. Those statutes are discussed in more detail in Chapter 3, Part IV(G) below.

170.   MICH. COMP. LAWS ANN. § 445.84.

Five states, Arkansas, California, Nevada, Rhode Island, and Utah, require security for personal information held by private entities. California, the first state to require these measures, mandates that businesses that own or license personal information about a California resident "shall implement and maintain reasonable security procedures and practices appropriate to the nature of the information, to protect personal information from unauthorized access, destruction, use, modification, or disclosure."[171] Arkansas requires that a person or business that acquires, owns, or licenses personal information about an Arkansas resident shall implement and maintain reasonable security measures.[172] Nevada requires reasonable security measures from "data collectors" who maintain records that contain personal information.[173] Rhode Island and Utah have similar requirements.[174] Rhode Island's statute is prefaced with comments discussing the intent of the statute, which demonstrate the legislature's primary concern about identity theft, and a secondary focus on privacy. "There is a growing concern regarding the possible theft of an individual's identity and a resulting need for measures to protect the privacy of personal information. It is the intent of the general assembly to ensure that personal information about Rhode Island residents is protected."[175]

171. CAL. CIV. CODE § 1798.81.5 (2006).

172. ARK. CODE ANN. § 4–110–104 (2006).

173. NEV. REV. STAT. ANN. § 603A.210 (2006).

174. *See* R.I. GEN. LAWS § 11–49.2–2 (2006); UTAH CODE ANN. § 13–44–201 (2007).

D. Data Destruction Laws

An increasingly recognized component of data security is assuring that personal information and other data is destroyed in a timely manner once it is no longer needed. Eight states have data destruction laws.[176] Arkansas requires that the person or business:

> shall take all reasonable steps to destroy or arrange for the destruction of a customer's records within its custody or control containing personal information that is no longer to be retained by the person or business by shredding, erasing, or otherwise modifying the personal information in the records to make it unreadable or undecipherable through any means.[177]

Nevada requires that businesses "shall take reasonable measures to ensure the destruction" of personal information records.[178] "Reasonable measures" require a method that modifies the records in such a way as to render the personal information unreadable or undecipherable, including shredding or erasing.[179]

175.   R.I. Gen. Laws § 11–49–2.2 (1) (2006).

176.   These states are Arkansas, California, Kentucky, New Jersey, Nevada, North Carolina, Texas and Utah.

177.   Ark. Code Ann. § 4–110–104 (a) (2006).

178.   Nev. Rev. Stat. Ann. § 603A.200(1) (2006).

179.   Nev. Rev. Stat. Ann. § 603A.200(1)-(2).

E. Consumer Notification of Security Breaches

Thirty-eight states have "data breach notification" laws.[180] The development and proliferation of notification laws is considered to be a particularly important advancement in protecting individuals' privacy interests. In the absence of these disclosure requirements, individuals are often unable to determine where their personal information was compromised.

Nevada requires disclosure of any breach of the security of the system data following discovery or notification of the breach where unencrypted personal information was, or is reasonably believed to have been, acquired by an unauthorized person.[181] Nevada provides three different methods of notification: (1) written notification; (2) electronic notification; or (3) substitute notification.[182]

Substitute notification is permitted if the data collector demonstrates that the cost of notification exceeds $250,000, the affected class of subject persons to be notified exceeds 500,000, or the data

180. States with data breach notification laws include: Arizona, Arkansas, California, Colorado, Connecticut, Delaware, Florida, Georgia, Hawaii, Idaho, Illinois, Indiana, Kansas, Louisiana, Maine, Maryland, Massachusetts, Michigan, Minnesota, Missouri, Montana, Nebraska, Nevada, New Hampshire, New Jersey, New York, North Carolina, North Dakota, Ohio, Pennsylvania, Rhode Island, Tennessee, Texas, Utah, Vermont, Wisconsin, Washington, Wyoming.

181. NEV. REV. STAT. ANN. § 603A.220(1) (2006).

182. NEV. REV. STAT. ANN. § 603A.220(4)(a)-(c).

collector does not have sufficient contact information.[183] Substitute notification must consist of: (1) notification by electronic mail when the data collector has electronic mail addresses for the subject persons; (2) conspicuous posting of the notification on the Internet website of the data collector, if the data collector maintains an Internet website; and (3) notification to major statewide media.[184]

Nevada also provides that data collectors who are subject to, and comply with, the privacy and security provisions of the Gramm–Leach–Bliley Act[185] shall be deemed to be in compliance with Nevada laws.[186]

F.   Spyware Control

Utah, California and 12 other states have "spyware" control laws. As described in more detail in Chapter 3, Part II(E)(1)(d)(iii) above, spyware is software that is covertly installed on a computer to monitor users' activities, particularly websurfing, and transmit information concerning those activities to another party. Spyware is often identified as one of the biggest ongoing threats to personal privacy. Concerns have emerged, however, over the risk of a proliferation of conflicting state laws; software and practices affected by the various statutes vary

183.   NEV. REV. STAT. ANN. § 603A.220(c).

184.   NEV. REV. STAT. ANN. § 603A.220(c).

185.   15 U.S.C. § 6801 *et seq*. *See* Chapter 3, Part II(A)(7) for further discussion of the Gramm–Leach–Bliley Act.

186.   NEV. REV. STAT. ANN. § 603A.220(5)(b) (2006).

widely as well as the specific restrictions and the methods of enforcement. As a result, bills have been introduced on the federal level several times to address these concerns,[187] but all have either expired in committee or otherwise not passed.

G. Open Records & Freedom of Information Laws

All fifty states have enacted statutes that, to varying degrees, open government records to public inspection.[188] These statutes are known by many different names, but are often called "open records acts," "sunshine laws," or "freedom of information statutes." Open records acts are focused on requiring government agencies to provide access to information they hold. Similar to the federal Freedom of Information Act, these state statutes have some form of exemption that allows an agency to redact or withhold information if disclosure would expose certain types of personally identifiable information, particularly Social Security numbers.[189]

187. *See, e.g.*, Securely Protect Yourself Against Cyber Trespass Act, H.R. 2929, 109th Cong. (2007); Internet Spyware Prevention Act, H.R. 744, 108th Cong. (2005); Software Principles Yielding Better Levels of Consumer Knowledge, S. 687, 108th Cong. (2005).

188. *See, e.g.*, **Colorado:** COLO. REV. STAT. § 24–72–203 (2006); **Connecticut:** CONN. GEN. STAT. § 1–212 (2006); **Florida:** FLA. STAT. ANN. §§ 119.01 to 119.15 (2006); **Vermont:** VT. STAT. ANN., tit. 1, §§ 315–320 (2005).

189. *See, e.g.*, **Delaware:** 29 DEL. CODE ANN. § 10002(g) (2007); **Georgia:** GA. CODE ANN. § 50–18–72(a)(11.3)(A); **Kansas:** Kan. Stat. Ann. § 75–3520(a)(1) (2007).

V. PRIVATE LAW

Beyond the realm of statutes and regulations that expressly protect privacy rights, there is a considerable range of private law techniques that can be used. All of these operate primarily on contract law principles, although many, including trade secret protections, also have a statutory and/or tort law component as well. Private law approaches to protecting privacy rights highlight the complex question of what a "right to privacy" truly means.

A. Privacy Policies

The most explicit form of privacy right created by private law is the category of contracts and representations collectively referred to as "privacy policies." These statements range from highly detailed descriptions of what a party's obligations are with regard to particular types of information and what security measures will be in place to assure the appropriate level of protection, to single sentence promises not to "share" an individual's "information" without further definition of those terms. While these policies have become ubiquitous over the past decade, their enforceability is heavily dependent on how they are drafted and what rights they purport to protect.

Privacy policies may exist in the form of traditional contracts or, especially on the Internet, as statements superficially subject to promissory estoppel principles. Unless clearly stated as not being contractual in nature, the breach of a privacy policy theoretically could give rise to contractual damages. Most efforts at enforcing privacy policies through litigation, however, have failed for one or two reasons. First, in many instances the "privacy policy" merely recites that a customer or user's information will be protected without sufficiently setting forth what the "protection" will consist of, or what obligations the recipient of the information has with regard to handling the information. The policy thus fails to rise to the level of an enforceable contract because its terms are too vague or otherwise fail to establish the necessary exchange of consideration.[190] Second, even where a privacy policy is determined to be an enforceable contract, courts have found that breach of the policy without specific evidence of quantifiable harm flowing from the breach will not support a breach of contract claim.[191] The ongoing difficulty of enforcing privacy policies through private litigation has been a major factor in driving the activities of the FTC and state governments concerning privacy policies discussed above in Chapter 3, Parts II(E)(1) and IV.

B. Trade Secrets

The intersection between the law of trade secrets and privacy rights demonstrates the paradox of economic interests simultaneously promoting and

190. *See, e.g., In re N.W. Airlines Privacy Litig.*, No. Civ. 04–126(PAM/JSM), 2004 WL 1278459 (D. Minn. June 6, 2004).

191. *In re JetBlue Airways Corp. Privacy Litig.*, 379 F. Supp. 2d 299 (E.D.N.Y. 2005).

compromising personal privacy. Personal information may be protected as a trade secret, but rarely by the individual whose personal information is at issue.

The law of trade secrets evolved from the recognition by American courts in the mid-to-late Nineteenth Century that information generated or received by a business could become the property of the business itself and have concrete economic value, rather than simply being something "known" by the individual employees. Early trade secret cases primarily concerned recipes or manufacturing techniques, but by the turn of the Twentieth Century, it became recognized that a list of names and addresses of customers, *i.e.*, personal information, could be a protectable trade secret in and of itself. One of the earliest cases addressing this issue was *Hackett v. A.L. & J.J. Reynolds Co.*, 62 N.Y.S. 1076 (N.Y. Sup. Ct. 1900), which found that a former employee of a grocery delivery business could be barred from contacting its customers:

> The value of the defendant's business consisted not merely of the property invested and the goods sold by it, but, as well, in the knowledge of the location of its routes, and the names of the customers to whom it was accustomed to make sales. This knowledge was in the nature of a trade secret, and was imparted to the plaintiff at the time he was employed by the defendant, solely to enable him to profitably and intelligently attend to the business of the defendant.

Id. at 1078. The employee had signed a contract agreeing not to compete with the employee's former employer, and the customer lists were trade secrets provided only for his use while employed. Therefore, it was a breach of the contract to use the information in a manner that was economically disadvantageous to the employer.

Today, most American jurisdictions[192] have adopted some form of the Uniform Trade Secrets Act. The Act defines a "trade secret" as:

information, including a formula, pattern, compilation, program, device, method, technique, or process, that: (i) derives independent economic value, actual or potential, from not being generally known to, and not being readily ascertainable by proper means by, other persons who can obtain economic value from its disclosure or use, and (ii) is the subject of efforts that are reasonable under the circumstances to maintain its secrecy.[193]

Theft or misappropriation of a secret occurs when an individual or entity, either directly or indirectly, knowingly learns of or discloses a trade secret

192. Including Alabama, Alaska, Arizona, Arkansas, California, Colorado, Connecticut, Delaware, District of Colombia, Florida, Georgia, Hawaii, Idaho, Illinois, Indiana, Iowa, Kansas, Kentucky, Louisiana, Maine, Maryland, Michigan, Minnesota, Mississippi, Missouri, Montana, Nebraska, Nevada, New Hampshire, New Mexico, North Dakota, Ohio, Oklahoma, Oregon, Pennsylvania, Rhode Island, South Carolina, South Dakota, Tennessee, Utah, Vermont, Virgin Islands, Virginia, Washington, West Virginia, Wisconsin, Wyoming.

193. Uniform Trade Secrets Act § 1(4) (2007).

through improper means or in violation of a duty to the owner of the trade secret.[194] Customer lists are typically protectable under the Act even if they consist exclusively of publicly available information, so long as the creator of the list expended significant effort to gather or organize the information and has taken sufficient steps to preserve its confidentiality.[195]

Trade secret law thus expresses in a microcosm the difficulties of protecting personal privacy through traditional legal means. A specific individual's personal information will rarely derive "independent economic value" from being known only to him or herself. Indeed, based on the fact that many businesses are willing to compensate consumers (through "loyalty" card programs, sweepstakes entries, etc.) for providing their personal information, it would appear that for the vast majority of individuals, their personal information is most valuable when shared. Yet the party that receives the information can, if it has devoted sufficient time and energy to collecting, filtering, and otherwise organizing the information, protect it as a trade secret.

194. Uniform Trade Secrets Act § 1(2) (2007).

195. See, e.g., Fireworks Spectacular, Inc. v. Premier Pyrotechnics, Inc., 86 F. Supp. 2d 1102, (D. Kan. 2000) ("Customer lists containing merely public information that could be easily compiled by third parties will not be protected as trade secrets; however, where 'the party compiling the customer lists, while using public information as a source, . . . expends a great deal of time, effort and expense in developing the lists and treats the lists as confidential in its business, the lists may be entitled to trade secret protection.") (quoting Robert B. Vance & Assocs., Inc. v. Baronet Corp., 487 F.Supp. 790, 799 (N.D. Ga. 1979)).

C. Shrink–Wrap and Click–Wrap Agreements

A common type of contract encountered by software users and websurfers is known as "shrink-wrap"[196] or "click-wrap"[197] agreements. These agreements can contain privacy policies, but in most instances they actually function as "anti-privacy policies," containing terms expressly allowing the party serving the agreement to collect, use, and distribute the personal information of the user. This may be done candidly through an electronic registration form or surreptitiously through forms of spyware.

Numerous cases challenging the validity of electronically delivered contract terms were brought when businesses began incorporating them into software in the 1990s. The state of the law today is in favor of these agreements so long as they sufficiently comply with traditional contract principles, particularly knowing acceptance of the terms by the user.[198]

196. A "shrink-wrap" agreement is any sort of contract packaged in a container or box that advises the purchaser of the terms of use of the product and is typically only discoverable after having purchased the product. The term is most often applied to "end user license agreements" included with software.

197. Also known as click-through agreement, point-and-click agreement, user agreement, web-wrap agreement, and browse-wrap agreement. Click-wrap agreements are simply electronic versions of a shrink-wrap agreements. In a typical click-wrap agreement, a user is asked to assent to the terms of an agreement displayed upon reaching a website or running a piece of software by clicking a button, box, or other graphic on the computer screen with the mouse cursor.

D. Confidential Settlement Agreements

The term "confidential settlement agreements" refers to a range of practices that result in agreements to resolve a legal dispute between parties with terms not subject to public disclosure. Confidential settlements agreements are a form of contract between the parties and in most instances are not filed with the court. Information that remains private as a result of these agreements can include the allegations, evidence, settlement terms, or even the fact that there was ever a dispute between the parties.

There has been sharp criticism of confidential settlement agreements in recent years, particularly when these agreements are used to resolve litigation that initially attracted significant public attention. The main argument is that confidential settlements conceal misconduct that had an impact on the broader public beyond the specific parties to the litigation, and thus others are either left uninformed of the true facts or must file their own litigation. Supporters of confidential settlement agreements contend that this type of contract promotes settlements in many cases where parties might otherwise feel compelled to go to trial simply to "clear their names," with the resulting expense and burden on the judicial system. Most courts

198. *See* ProCD, Inc. v. Zeidenberg, 86 F.3d 1447, 1449 (7th Cir. 1996); Specht v. Netscape Commc'n Corp., 306 F.3d 17, 22 n.4 (2d Cir. 2002).

eagerly embrace these types of confidential settlements, stating, "secrecy of settlement terms ... is a well-established American litigation practice."[199] The "well-established" acceptance of confidential settlement agreements has lost ground in recent years, however. Some jurisdictions preclude confidential settlements without court approval.[200] In addition, a number of states regulate confidential settlements out of concern that these agreements may be used to conceal harmful conduct.[201]

E. Chief Privacy Officers and Related Concepts

To the extent privacy issues within businesses were specifically addressed at all, they were traditionally handled by several different departments, including legal, human resources, and information technology. Yet as contractual privacy rights have proliferated and compliance with local, state, federal, and international privacy laws has become a critical issue in business operations, companies have

199. Goodyear Tire & Rubber Co. v. Chiles Power Supply, Inc., 332 F.3d 976, 980–81 (6th Cir. 2003) (quoting Palmieri v. New York, 779 F.2d 861, 865 (2d Cir. 1985)).

200. *See, e.g.*, Local Rule 5.03(E) of the U.S. District Court for the District of South Carolina.

201. *See, e.g.*, Florida Sunshine in Litigation Act, Fla. Stat. Ann. § 69.081(4) (2005) ("Any portion of an agreement or contract which has the purpose or effect of concealing a public hazard, any information concerning a public hazard, or any information which may be useful to members of the public in protecting themselves from injury which may result from the public hazard, is void, contrary to public policy, and may not be enforced.").

increasingly recognized the importance of tasking particular individuals with the responsibility of coordinating privacy protection across different departments.[202] Although these positions are known by many names, the most common descriptor is "Chief Privacy Officer" or "CPO" for short.

A CPO's responsibilities will encompass the activities of many different areas of the business, and the CPO should have experience with not just privacy laws but must also understand how and why the company collects personal information, as well as how this information is stored and transmitted. A CPO must work closely with management to balance the benefits of collecting personal information with the legal risks that come with the practice.

For companies that either cannot afford a permanent CPO, or otherwise do not wish to create a position, there are other solutions intended to accomplish a similar result. Some companies set up a "privacy committee" with members from different departments to discuss privacy and security concerns. Yet other companies hire outside consultants, including law, accounting, or IT firms, to audit compliance with privacy laws and make recommendations on changes to operations or security measures. Entities specializing in privacy compliance, include the Privacy and American Business and the Better Business Bureau, have developed as consul-

202. In 1992, Equifax became the first U.S. company to formally designate a CPO. Patrick Friel, *Protecting Customer Information: Can You Afford Not to Have a Chief Privacy Officer?*, *available at* 4 http://www.heidrick.com/NR/rdonlyres/8A657 CD1–7532–4215–ACD5–A8FD00B4BF4A/0/HS_CPO.pdf.

tants to companies to ensure security through the best possible practices.

The International Association of Privacy Professionals ("IAPP") was established in 2001 to define, promote, and improve the privacy profession.[203] Growing very rapidly, the IAPP is the world's largest association of privacy professionals, with over 4,000 members from 32 countries. The IAPP provides a forum to allow members to share best practices, issues, and trends with other privacy professionals and also offers training and certification programs on privacy law.

VI. PROFESSIONAL PRIVACY ETHICS

In stark contrast to the numerous discrete statutory provisions outlining privacy law in the United States, are the ethical considerations governing the practices of law and medicine. The legal profession's requirement of client privacy and confidentiality is imposed in a largely self-governing manner,[204] while the medical profession adheres to a similar code of ethical conduct designed to protect and benefit the patient.[205]

203. *International Association of Privacy Professionals Mission*, (2001) https://www.privacyassociation.org/index.php?option=com_content & task=view & id=2 & Itemid=148 (last visited Nov. 8, 2007).

204. MODEL RULES OF PROF'L CONDUCT, *Preamble* (2005).

205. American Medical Association, Principles of Medical Ethics: Preamble, http://www.ama-assn.org/ama/pub/category/2512.html.

A. Legal Ethics

At the intersection of legal ethics and client privacy is the concept of the attorney-client privilege.
"Privilege," generally, refers to the right to withhold information from a legal proceeding. The attorney-client privilege acts to protect a client's private
information at the expense of the court's truth-
seeking process; the privilege is a balance between
the rights of, and to, the clients, and the courts. The
attorney-client privilege has been characterized as
"the most widely respected and applied common-
law privilege. . . ."[206] It applies to confidential client
communications made to an attorney for the purpose of seeking legal services. As the U.S. Supreme
Court has stated, the "privilege is intended to encourage 'full and frank communication between attorneys and their clients and thereby promote
broader public interests in the observance of law
and the administration of justice.' " *Swidler & Ber-
lin v. United States*, 524 U.S. 399, 403 (1998).

The extent of the attorney-client privilege can be
shaped by statute, but it has been carved from the
common law. While the heart of the attorney-privi-
lege lies within innumerable state and federal court
decisions and state rules of professional conduct, its
basics tenets of respecting a client's right to privacy
are enumerated in both the Model Rules of Professional Conduct, and the *Restatement (Third) of the
Law Governing Lawyers*. These works set forth the

206.   FED. R. EVID. 501 cmt (2007).

ethical standards that lawyers are bound to abide by concerning the protection of client communications. While these rules do not create an independent basis for criminal or civil liability (although in some jurisdictions it may be considered as evidence), violation of the ethical rules of conduct will subject an attorney to professional discipline from the governing bar.

1. Model Rules of Professional Conduct

The ABA Model Rules of Professional Conduct ("Model Rules") are the main "influence on the rules of professional conduct governing lawyers in the United States."[207] The Model Rules do not bind lawyers to maintain a specific level of conduct, rather, the Model Rules must be adopted by a jurisdiction to become enforceable, although many courts and disciplinary bodies have found them to be persuasive authority even when not formally adopted. While no jurisdiction has adopted the Model Rules in their entirety, close analogues to the Model Rules regarding attorney-client confidentiality and privacy are in effect in all U.S. jurisdictions. The Model Rules set standards for attorney conduct concerning current,[208] former,[209] and prospective clients.[210]

207.   MODEL RULES OF PROF'L CONDUCT, *Preamble, Editor's Introduction* (2005).

208.   MODEL RULES OF PROF'L CONDUCT R. 1.6.

209.   MODEL RULES OF PROF'L CONDUCT R. 1.9.

210.   MODEL RULES OF PROF'L CONDUCT R. 1.18.

Lawyers have a duty to not reveal private or confidential information relating to the representation of a current client unless the client provides "informed consent."[211] Absent informed consent, an attorney may reveal confidential information in only limited situations, namely:

(1) to prevent reasonably certain death or substantial bodily harm;

(2) to secure legal advice about the lawyer's compliance with these [Model] Rules;

(3) to establish a claim or defense on behalf of the lawyer in a controversy between the lawyer and client, to establish a defense to a criminal charge or civil claim against the lawyer based upon conduct in which the client was involved, or to respond to allegations in any proceedings concerning the lawyer's representation of the client; or

(4) to comply with other law or court order.[212]

Trust is fundamental to the attorney-client relationship. For assistance of counsel to be effective, an attorney needs the client to fully and frankly disclose private information necessary to the representation. To facilitate this discourse, attorneys are bound by the rules of ethics to not disclose such private information in a manner adverse to clients'

211. "Informed consent" is agreement by a client to allow certain conduct after the attorney has fully explained and communicated the nature of the proposal, and explained the risks and alternatives. MODEL RULES OF PROF'L CONDUCT R. 1.0(e).

212. MODEL RULES OF PROF'L CONDUCT R. 1.6(b)(1)-(4).

interests. Attorneys must act with competence to safeguard clients' information against "inadvertent or unauthorized disclosure," and must take reasonable precautions when transmitting the clients' private information.[213]

The duty to protect confidential client information extends even after completion of the attorney-client relationship. This continuing duty prevents an attorney from using a former clients' private information to the client's disadvantage, or to the benefit of a new client whose interests are adverse to the former client. Essentially, absent informed consent by the former client, the lawyer is forever barred from utilizing private information of a former client to the former client's detriment or for the benefit of another.

In addition to current and former clients, the attorney also has a duty to protect some, but not all, of communications with prospective clients. Any discussions with an attorney regarding the possibility of forming an attorney-client relationship are considered communications with a prospective client.[214] Regardless of whether an attorney-client relationship is formed after the initial discussion, the attorney has a duty not to reveal private information learned through these consultations.

213. MODEL RULES OF PROF'L CONDUCT R. 1.6 cmt. 15 and 16.

214. MODEL RULES OF PROF'L CONDUCT R. 1.18(a).

2. *Restatement (Third) of the Law Governing Lawyers*

The *Restatement (Third) of the Law Governing Lawyers* ("*Restatement*") is the American Law Institute's attempt to define the prevailing ethical rules and standards applied to lawyers.[215] As with the Model Rules, the *Restatement* defines the lawyers' duty to keep client information private and confidential for current, former, and prospective clients. With the exception of duties to prospective clients, the professional duty of confidentiality usually does not adhere to lawyers in the absence of an attorney-client relationship. Under the *Restatement*, an attorney-client relationship arises when the client intends for the lawyer to provide legal services, and the lawyer either consents to provide such service, or fails to consent to service when he knows that the client is relying on him for legal service. While the attorney-client relationship is normally "a consensual one," the "consent requirement ... is not symmetrical."[216] It is the client's manifestation of intent to form an attorney-client relationship that controls. Intent does not need to be reduced to writing, and may be inferred from the surrounding circumstances, conduct, or communication from the client or its agent. In this respect, the legal profession displays a unique trait: duties of privacy and confidentiality that bind attorneys may be created without explicit acts of acceptance and consent on the part of the attorney.

215. *See generally* RESTATEMENT (THIRD) OF THE LAW GOVERNING LAWYERS § 1 (2000).

216. Id. § 14 cmt. b.

The attorney-client privilege set forth in the *Restatement* applies to confidential communications between "privileged persons" made with the intent of extending or receiving legal services. A "communication" includes "any expression ... undertake[n] to convey information to another privileged person and any document or other record revealing such an expression."[217] Parties to the privilege include current, prospective, and former clients, the attorneys, and agents of those parties. The privilege remains in effect, unless waived through agreement or disclosure, both during and after the representation of a client.

Once a duty of confidentiality arises, it becomes necessary to consider what exactly qualifies as confidential client information. The *Restatement* defines confidential client information as being "information relating to the representation of a client, other than information that is generally known."[218] Information can be in any form, whether written, oral, electronic recording, or others. The information must also be protected regardless of the ultimate source of the information, including whether or not the source itself is protected by the attorney-client privilege.

A lawyer's duty to maintain the confidential status of a client's information arises from the lawyer's status as a fiduciary of the client, which requires a commitment of loyalty to the client. The lawyer

217.   RESTATEMENT (THIRD) OF THE LAW GOVERNING LAWYERS § 69.

218.   Id. §59 (2000).

ordinarily must not use or disclose a client's confidential information and is required to "take reasonable measures to safeguard" the information.[219] A lawyer may disclose confidential client information in certain limited situations. A lawyer is allowed to disclose confidential client information:

1. if the lawyer reasonably believes that disclosure is necessary to protect or advance the client's interests;

2. if ordered to by a court or pursuant to a subpoena or similar legal document, so long as the lawyer first "takes reasonably appropriate steps to assert that the information is privileged or otherwise protected against disclosure;"[220]

3. if the lawyer reasonably determines that the disclosure is necessary to defend against a claim that the lawyer committed malpractice or otherwise engaged in bad conduct in the course of the representation, but only to the extent necessary to rebut the claim;

4. if the lawyer reasonably determines that the disclosure is necessary to resolve a billing dispute with the client;

5. if the lawyer reasonably believes the disclosure is "necessary to prevent reasonably certain death or serious bodily harm to a per-

219.   RESTATEMENT (THIRD) OF THE LAW GOVERNING LAWYERS § 16 cmt. e.

220.   Id. § 63.

son;"[221] or to prevent the future commission of a crime or fraud by the client or its agent which "threatens substantial financial loss," and which would result from the client's use of the lawyer's services.[222]

Alternatively, the lawyer may almost always disclose a client's confidential information if the client has agreed after having been provided a sufficiently detailed explanation of the planned disclosure, to permit a reasoned determination as to whether to permit the lawyer to proceed, *i.e.*, "informed consent."

When the attorney-client relationship terminates, the attorney must take reasonable steps to protect the client's interests. As with present clients, in most instances an attorney cannot use a former client's confidential information without first seeking the former client's informed consent. These requirements are applied regardless of the reason for the termination, and regardless of which party initiates the termination.

The duties to prospective clients arise as soon as the lawyer begins discussing the *possibility* of forming an attorney-client relationship. Even if following the discussion, no actual attorney-client relationship forms, the duties still attach to the attorney. Most relevant to privacy concerns is the lawyer's duty not to disclose confidential information that was learned in the course of the initial

221. RESTATEMENT (THIRD) OF THE LAW GOVERNING LAWYERS § 66.
222. Id. § 67(1).

consultation and other preparatory communications. Under the *Restatement*, the duty of confidentiality to prospective clients exists no matter how brief the initial consultation or screening.

3. *Unauthorized Disclosure*

While instances of civil liability for breach of the attorney's duty of confidentiality are rare, the doctrinal basis supporting a claim is sound and can result in awards for monetary and/or injunctive relief. In *Prudential Insurance Co. of America v. Massaro*,[223] for example, equitable relief in the form of a permanent injunction barring further disclosure was granted following the unauthorized disclosures of an attorney acting in an in-house capacity. As the court explained, essential to the attorney-client privilege is the requirement that "lawyers must not themselves voluntarily divulge information covered by their client's ... privilege."[224] In *Perez v. Kirk & Carrigan*, 822 S.W.2d 261 (Tex. Ct. App. 1991), disclosure of confidential client information was held to allow for tort based recovery upon proof of damages. Perez was employed by Coca–Cola as a truck driver and was involved in a tragic automobile accident resulting in the death of 21 children.[225] Coca–Cola attorneys represented to Perez that they would represent him in the ensuing legal action, and with this understanding, Perez

223. Civ. Act. No. 97–2022, 2000 WL 1176541 (D.N.J. Aug. 11, 2000).

224. *Prudential Ins.*, 2000 WL 1176541 at *7.

225. *Perez*, 822 S.W.2d at 263.

provided a sworn statement regarding the accident. Without the consent of Perez, the Coca–Cola attorneys disclosed this statement to the District Attorney resulting in a grand jury indictment for involuntary manslaughter. The statement was found to be a protected attorney-client communication revealed without client consent, and thus, the mental anguish and emotional distress that Perez suffered as a result of his conviction created a valid claim for damages.

4. *The Brobeck Closed Archive*

The "Brobeck Closed Archive" represents a unique challenge to traditional principles of client confidentiality, but it bears discussion due to of the possibility that similar situations will arise in the future. Brobeck, Phleger & Harrison ("Brobeck") was a large, national law firm founded in San Francisco in 1926. In the 1990s, the growth of Brobeck's business was driven by the wave of dot-com companies through its representation of numerous technology startups. Following the burst of the dot-com bubble, mismanagement and the loss of key personnel forced the firm to announce its intention to liquidate in February 2003, and ultimately filed for liquidation through a Chapter 7 bankruptcy proceeding.

What exactly is the Brobeck Closed Archive? Pursuant to the terms of its bankruptcy plan, "[t]he Brobeck Closed Archive is a secure digital repository authorized by Order of Judge Dennis Montali,

United States Bankruptcy Court, Northern District of California, San Francisco Division on August 9, 2006."[226] Judge Montali's Order effectively places confidential client records, previously private and clearly protected by the attorney-client privilege in most instances, into a digital repository sponsored by the Library of Congress and its National Digital Information Infrastructure Preservation Program ("NDIIPP"). Former clients have been given the opportunity to opt-out of the program, but absent affirmative communication from the former clients, their private information will automatically become available to researchers.

Strangely, through the course of bankruptcy proceedings, previously confidential client information has been transformed into historical "artifacts" containing, in the words of the Archive's managers, "a wealth of historical information" which must be preserved at the expense of any existing privilege.[227] Justification for this sweeping abrogation of settled principles of client confidentiality include: "if no action is taken to preserve these records, they will be lost to history forever;" "these digital records document one of the most extraordinary episodes in the history of capitalism, the explosion of internet technology companies in the 1990s;" and, lastly, Congress has charged the "Library of Congress to

226. Brobeck Closed Archive, *Frequent Questions*, http://brobeckclosedarchive.org/faq.html (last visited Nov. 8, 2007).

227. Brobeck Closed Archive, http://brobeckclosedarchive.org (last visited Nov. 8, 2007).

develop a national strategy for digital preservation" of "non-public digital objects."[228]

The Archive purports to keep access to the client files limited to "a small number of archivists or scholars who have signed strict non-disclosure agreements," with physical access taking "place in an on-site institutional setting, and only for specific ... purposes [approved] ... by the Court."[229] Given today's digital economy and appetite for sensationalized news, there is a high risk that this archived information will be leaked to the public. More importantly, the events surrounding the formation of the Archive suggest critical questions for both law firms and their clients concerning what steps should be taken to preserve the confidentiality of client information beyond the life of a particular law firm. While the Brobeck Closed Archive perhaps represents a truly extreme and unique situation, it still serves to unsettle the very foundation of the legal tradition: communication between attorney and client will be private, confidential, and privileged forever.

B. Medical Ethics

The medical profession has long been governed by ethical rules directed to the benefit of the patient. Physicians adhere to ethical rules in the form of an accepted standard of conduct; these rules are not

228. Brobeck Closed Archive, *Frequent Questions*, http://brobeckclosedarchive.org/faq.html (last visited Nov. 8, 2007).

229. *Id.*

legally binding and typically exceed any legal duty imposed.[230]

1. *Ethical rules*

The medical profession arguably has the longest tradition of protecting privacy rights of any group or organization. The importance of promising patients confidentiality in order to provide effective medical care was recognized as early as the classical Greek Oath of Hippocrates from the Fourth Century B.C.E.:

> Whatsoever things I see or hear concerning the life of men, in my attendance on the sick or even apart therefrom, which ought not be noised abroad, I will keep silence thereon, counting such things to be as sacred secrets.[231]

This principle continues to be reflected in the modern Hippocratic Oath:

> I will respect the privacy of my patients, for their problems are not disclosed to me that the world may know.[232]

In 2001, the American Medical Association House of Delegates adopted the Revised Principles of Medical

230. American Medical Association, Canon E–1.02: The Relation of Law and Ethics, http://www.ama-assn.org/ama/pub/category/8312.html (last visited Nov. 9, 2007).

231. Oath of Hippocrates, 4th Century, B.C.E., *available at* http://www.chcpf.state.co.us/HCPF/HIPAA/Info_Sheet1.doc (last visited Nov. 9, 2007).

232. MedicineNet.com, *Definition of Hippocratic Oath*, *at* http://www.medterms.com/script/main/art.asp?articlekey=20909 (last visted Nov. 9, 2007).

Ethics.[233] The Revised Principles continue to emphasize that the privacy of patient information remains a paramount concern:

A physician shall respect the rights of patients, colleagues, and other health professionals, and shall safeguard patient confidences and privacy within the constraints of the law.[234]

In addition to the American Medical Association's Principles of Medical Ethics, the Judicial Council of the Association has issued opinions related to the privacy of patient information.[235] AMA Canon E–5.05 states in part:

The information disclosed to a physician by a patient should be held in confidence. The patient should feel free to make a full disclosure of information to the physician in order that the physician may most effectively provide needed services. The patient should be able to make this disclosure with the knowledge that the physician will respect the confidential nature of the communication. The physician should not reveal confidential information without the express consent of the patient, subject to certain exceptions which are

233. American Medical Association, *Principles of Medical Ethics* (June 17, 2001), *available at* http://www.ama-assn.org/ama/upload/mm/369/2001_principles.pdf.

234. American Medical Association, Principles of Medical Ethics: Section IV, http://www.ama-assn.org/ama/pub/category/2512.html (last visited Nov. 9, 2007).

235. *See generally* American Medical Association, Canon E–5.00: Opinions on Confidentiality, Advertising and Communications Media Relations, http://www.ama-assn.org/ama/pub/category/8299.html (last visited Nov. 9, 2007).

ethically justified because of overriding consider-ations.[236]

2. *Doctor-patient privilege*

Patient confidentiality and privacy is a funda-mental principle of the medical profession. The doc-tor-patient privilege allows candid discussion, en-suring the patient's medical needs are met. The privilege is not absolute, however, the doctor-pa-tient privilege may fall where concerns over public health are raised (*e.g.*, to warn partners of sexually transmitted diseases), or where a legal duty re-quires disclosure of information.[237]

Doctors must maintain procedural safeguards on private patient information, and public discussion of patients' medical problems without their consent represents a grave breach of professional ethics. Only with a patient's explicit consent may their personal information be disclosed outside of an aca-demic medical setting. Doctors are also encouraged to be advocates for improving measures and proce-dures for protecting the confidentiality of patients' information.

236. American Medical Association, Canon E–5.05: Confiden-tiality, http://www.ama-assn.org/ama/pub/category/8353.html (last visited Nov. 9, 2007).

237. AMERICAN COLLEGE OF PHYSICIANS, ETHICS MANUAL 576 (4th ed. 1998), *available at* http://www.annals.org/cgi/content/full/128/7/576.

3. *Unauthorized disclosure*

Recovery for unauthorized disclosure of medical information is based, in part, on the implied contract between doctor and patient.

Any time a doctor undertakes the treatment of a patient, and the consensual relationship of physician and patient is established, two jural obligations ... are simultaneously assumed by the doctor. Doctor and patient enter into a simple contract, the patient hoping that he will be cured and the doctor optimistically assuming that he will be compensated. As an implied condition of that contract, ... the doctor warrants that any confidential information gained through the relationship will not be released without the patient's permission. Almost every member of the public is aware of the promise of discretion contained in the Hippocratic Oath, and every patient has a right to rely upon this warranty of silence.... Consequently, when a doctor breaches his duty of secrecy, he is in violation of part of his obligations under the contract.[238]

In order to be entitled to the doctor-patient confidentiality, the patient must specifically be seeking medical care or treatment from the doctor.[239] Discussion of a non-present, third-party's medical concerns between doctor and patient and not covered by the doctor-patient privilege. On the other hand,

238. Hammonds v. Aetna Cas. & Sur. Co., 243 F.Supp. 793, 801 (N.D. Ohio 1965).

239. Howes v. United States, 887 F.2d 729, 732 (6th Cir. 1989).

disclosing confidential patient information during litigation without having at least notified the patient of the planned disclosure, even if it would appear to fall within an exception to the privilege, can be considered a breach of doctor-patient privilege.[240] These disclosures may create tort liability.[241] The privilege, however, can be compromised even without notice in extreme situations. Where a patient is considered a danger to himself and others, a physician's disclosure of confidential information does not amount to breach of the duty of confidentiality nor commission of a tort; "[t]he protective privilege ends where the public peril begins."[242] Thus the court in *McDonald v. Clinger*, ruled that "disclosure of confidential information by a psychiatrist to a spouse will be justified whenever there is a danger to the patient, the spouse or another person."[243]

240. Sorensen v. Barbuto, 143 P.3d 295, 300 (Utah Ct. App. 2006).

241. *See* Id. at 301–2.

242. Tarasoff v. Regents of Univ. of Cal., 551 P.2d 334, 347 (Cal. 1976).

243. 446 N.Y.S.2d 801, 805 (N.Y. App. Div. 1982).

CHAPTER FOUR

INTERNATIONAL PRIVACY

As the "right to privacy" has evolved from a "right to be let alone" to the right to control other's use and dissemination of one's personal data, so too has the economic and technological background of the world changed. Now that global data networks are ubiquitous, personally identifiable data is no longer tied to the locality of its owner or even to the owner's nation of residence. Exchanges of personal data regularly cross national borders, often between countries where the "right to privacy" means two different things. This chapter considers how international and non-U.S. privacy protection regimes operate, both on their own and where they intersect with U.S. privacy law.

I. INTERNATIONAL AGREEMENTS

A true binding international agreement protecting privacy does not exist. The differences in national legal systems are a clear obstacle to any agreement, but the many types and forms of data that might be considered "personal" further exacerbate these legal differences. Over the past several decades, however, there has been increasing progress toward identifying and agreeing on at least certain foundational issues.

The single most influential document of this subject has been the OECD Guidelines on the Protection of Privacy and Transborder Flows of Personal Data ("Guidelines").[1] The realization that market forces would create both challenges and opportunities for privacy rights happened during the 1970s, when the OECD began to see arguments over national privacy laws in the context of trade negotiations. After several years of negotiations, the OECD produced the Guidelines to try to bring commonality to the *mechanisms* of privacy protections within different countries without attempting to craft a complete regulatory framework. The Guidelines are only a "soft law" agreement and are not legally binding on the signatories. They also represented a pragmatic consensus that inconsistent privacy laws can be a block to economic development. The preamble to the Guidelines states:

> although national laws and policies may differ, Member countries have a common interest in protecting privacy and individual liberties, and in reconciling fundamental but competing values such as privacy and the free flow of information;
>
> that automatic processing and transborder flows of personal data create new forms of relationships

1. Organization for Economic Cooperation and Development, Guidelines on the Protection of Privacy and Transborder Flows of Personal Data (1980) [*hereinafter* Guidelines], *available* at http://www.uhoh.org/oecd-privacy-personal-data.pdf.

among countries and require the development of compatible rules and practices;

that transborder flows of personal data contribute to economic and social development;

that domestic legislation concerning privacy protection and transborder flows of personal data may hinder such transborder flows.[2]

In the 1990s, the Guidelines were joined by two more agreements from the OECD that demonstrated the continuing evolution of the attitude toward privacy protection. The OECD Guidelines for the Security of Information Systems and Networks,[3] and the OECD Guidelines for Cryptography Policy,[4] signaled a shift in the OECD's thinking. The rise of the Internet meant that international commerce was becoming more important and more democratized as increasing numbers of consumers began dealing directly with businesses in other nations. Yet, at the same time, consumers were also becoming increasingly concerned about the privacy of any personal information they might transmit in the course of such transactions. Maintaining the privacy of personal data was recognized as something

2. Guidelines at p. 13, http://www.uhoh.org/oecd-privacy-personal-data.pdf.

3. Organization for Economic Cooperation and Development, Guidelines for the Security of Information Systems and Networks (1992), *available at* http://www.oecd.org/dataoecd/16/22/15582260.pdf.

4. Organization for Economic Cooperation and Development, Guidelines for Cryptography Policy (1997), *available at* http://www.oecd.org/document/34/0,2340,en_2649_34255_1814690_1_1_1_1,00.html

that encouraged people to use electronic networks thereby increasing transborder dataflows, rather than halting them.

II. NATIONAL LAWS

A. Canada

1. *Canadian constitutional protection*

Canada, like the United States has no explicit right to privacy in its constitution. Section Eight of the Canadian Charter of Rights and Freedoms, however, enacted as part of the Canada Act of 1982, has been interpreted by Canadian courts to guarantee a reasonable right to privacy.[5] Section Eight, which is much like the U.S. Constitution's Fourth Amendment, thus governs any constitutional privacy concerns.

a. *Personal privacy in the public sector*

Canada's Privacy Act governs personal privacy in the public sector. The Act was passed in 1983 to "extend the present laws of Canada that protect the privacy of individuals with respect to personal information about themselves held by a government institution and that provide individuals with a right of access to that information."[6]

Canadian law allows government institutions to collect information only if it relates directly to an

5.   *See* Hunter v. Southam, 2 S.C.R. 145, 159–60 (1984).

6.   Canada Privacy Act (R.S., 1985, c. P–21).

operating program or activity of the institution.[7] With few exceptions, government agencies must inform individuals that their personal information is being collected and the purpose for which it is being collected. Moreover, any information gathered by an institution must be used solely for the purpose for which it was gathered. Personal information collected by the government, in most instances, cannot be disclosed without the permission of the individual who is the subject of the information.

Every Canadian citizen has the right to access the information that is "reasonably retrievable" by the governmental institution storing the information for the purpose of correcting the information if it is inaccurate. Any individual can complain to the Privacy Commissioner if the individual was denied access to his/her information. An individual who is denied access to information has a right to bring suit in the Canadian Federal Court for review of the denial.[8] The Privacy Commissioner also receives and investigates any other complaints submitted under the Privacy Act.

b.   The Privacy Commissioner

The Canadian Privacy Commissioner is a representative who is appointed by the Canadian Federal Cabinet, with the appointment being approved by resolution in the Canadian House of Commons and

7.   Canada Privacy Act at § (4).
8.   Canada Privacy Act at § (41).

Senate.[9] The position was created pursuant to the Privacy Act, but now has significantly broader authority as a result of the enactment of additional privacy legislation discussed below. The Commissioner serves for a seven-year term and can be reappointed.

The Privacy Commissioner, who is considered an agent of Parliament, reports directly to the House and Senate on issues dealing with privacy. The Commissioner is responsible for ensuring that the federal government, as well as the private sector, collect, use, and disclose personal information in a manner that is responsible and consistent with applicable laws and regulations.

The Privacy Commissioner has broad authority within the subject area it has been tasked with overseeing.[10] The Commissioner can initiate audits of an organization's information collection, management, and disclosure practices to determine whether adequate protective measures are in place and to verify that the information is being used in a lawful manner. When conducting an audit, any person with relevant information can be summoned to appear before the Commissioner. The Commissioner also has the power to administer oaths and receive sworn testimony and evidence in quasi-judicial hearings.

9.   Canada Privacy Act at § 53(1).

10.   *See* Office of the Privacy Commissioner, *Resource Centre, A Guide for Individuals, Your Privacy Rights, at* http://www. privcom.gc.ca/information/02_05_d_08_e.asp (last visited Nov. 12, 2007).

Despite the Privacy Commissioner's far-reaching investigatory power, the office lacks the ability to issue orders or impose penalties for any violations. The Commissioner instead usually arrives at decisions calculated to resolve problems through negotiated settlements. If the Commissioner determines that the violation is sufficiently severe, the office can file litigation against the offender in the Federal Court and proceed through the judicial process. As an alternative for disputes that cannot be resolved through a negotiated agreement but are not sufficiently grave to merit the Commissioner pursuing litigation on its own, the Commissioner can, in some situations, provide the results of its investigation to private individuals who have been injured by the privacy breach to facilitate them bringing private litigation against the bad actor.

c. Personal privacy in the private sector

The main legislation governing personal privacy in the Canadian private sector is the Personal Information Protection and Electronic Documents Act (PIPEDA).[11] Beginning with its 1992–93 annual report, the Privacy Commissioner began urging the adoption of legislation extending protection to personal information held by the private sector. Two years later, Canada's Information Highway Advisory Council joined this call. Contemporaneously with these developments, the European Union was start-

11. Canada Personal Information Protection and Electronic Documents Act, (2000, c. 5), P–8.6 ("PIPEDA").

ing to take steps to restrict transmission of its citizens' personal information to parties in non-E.U. nations with inadequate privacy protections, which would have seriously impacted Canadian business.[12] In 1998, the supporting bill for PIPEDA was introduced, ultimately passing in 2000.[13]

Rather than implementing the entire legislation at once, PIPEDA had a tiered implementation schedule. In January of 2001, PIPEDA implementation included all personal information excluding health information held by federally regulated private sector entities. A year later, in January 2002, the act began regulating personal health information. Finally, in January 2004 the act reached full-implementation status. The 2004 implementation encompasses all organizations that commercially collect, use, or disclose personal information.[14]

Personal information under PIPEDA includes "information about an identifiable individual."[15] The name, title, business address, or telephone number of an employee within an "organization," however, is not considered personal information. "Organization" is broadly defined to include associ-

12. The European Union's efforts at privacy protection are discussed in detail in Chapter 4, Part II(B)

13. Office of the Privacy Commissioner, *Privacy Legislation, A guide to the new private sector data protection bill*, at http:// www.privcom.gc.ca/legislation/02_06_02b_e.asp (last visited Nov. 12, 2007).

14. Office of the Privacy Commissioner, *Privacy Legislation, Implementation Schedule*, at http://www.privcom.gc.ca/legislat ion/02_06_02a_e.asp (last visited Nov. 12, 2007).

15. PIPEDA at § 2(1).

ations, partnerships, and unions.[16] PIPEDA does not cover Canadian government institutions that are otherwise subject to the Privacy Act. Information that is collected, used, or disclosed by individuals for personal purposes or for "journalistic, artistic, or literary purposes" is also not included.[17] Provinces may enact their own privacy legislation provided that it meets or exceeds the level of protection afforded by PIPEDA. The provinces of Alberta, British Columbia, Ontario, and Quebec have enacted legislation.[18]

PIPEDA sets forth specific individual rights as well as requiring organizations to follow certain guidelines. PIPEDA gives individuals the right to know why an organization collects, uses, or discloses personal information.[19] PIPEDA also gives individuals the right to expect that organizations collect, use, or disclose personal information reasonably and appropriately and only for the purpose for which the individual has consented. Individuals have the right to know who in the organization is collecting the personal information, and who is responsible for protecting that information. Individuals have the right to expect an organization to implement adequate security measures to protect

16. PIPEDA at § 2(1).

17. PIPEDA at § 4(2).

18. Office of the Privacy Commissioner, *Fact Sheet*, *Questions and Answers regarding the application of PIPEDA, Alberta and British Columbia's Personal Information Protection Acts (PIPAs)*, *at* http://www.privcom.gc.ca/fs-fi/02_05_d_26_e.asp (last visited Nov. 12, 2007).

19. PIPEDA at § 7 and Schedule 1, 4.9.

personal information. Individuals are also entitled to expect that the personal information an organization holds is accurate, complete, and up-to-date.[20] PIPEDA, like the Privacy Act, allows individuals to obtain access to personal information and make corrections if necessary.[21]

Under PIPEDA, organizations which commercially use personal information, or make other non-exempt uses of it, are required to follow ten principles of fair information practices, which are modeled on the OECD Guidelines. The principles are: (1) accountability; (2) identifying purposes; (3) consent; (4) limiting collection; (5) limiting use, disclosure, and retention; (6) accuracy; (7) safeguards; (8) openness; (9) individual access; and (10) challenging compliance.[22] If an organization has safeguards in place to insure compliance with these principles then it is likely fulfilling all its duties under PIPEDA.

PIPEDA requires organizations to obtain consent from the individual, when collecting, using, or disclosing personal information. Organizations must supply an individual with a service or product even if the individual refuses to consent to the collection, use, or disclosure of personal information. Beyond merely collecting information in a lawful fashion, organizations must have personal information poli-

20.   PIPEDA at § 5 and Schedule 1, 4.8.

21.   PIPEDA at § 8.

22.   PIPEDA at Schedule 1.

cies that are clear, understandable, and readily available.[23]

PIPEDA has specific procedures for individuals to make complaints to the Office of the Privacy Commissioner concerning violations of PIPEDA. If the Commissioner determines that certain types of violations have occurred, the complainant will have a cause of action against the violator, which can be pursued in the Federal Court. PIPEDA requires the Commissioner to commence an investigation upon receipt of a properly filed complaint. Once an investigation has been opened, the Commissioner has one year to complete the investigation and issue a written report, although it may be determined in certain situations that a written report is unnecessary.

(i) Trans-border data flows under PIPEDA

As previously mentioned, a significant motivating factor for enacting PIPEDA was to assure the European Union that Canada's privacy laws were strict enough to protect the interests of the citizens of the European Union. Currently, Canada and the European Union allow certain personal data to flow freely to Canada from the European Union, subject to PIPEDA, without additional safeguards.[24] This,

23. PIPEDA at Schedule 1, 4.8.1.

24. European Union Data Protection Working Group—Article 29, Opinion 2/2001 on the Adequacy of the Canadian Personal Information and Electronic Documents Act, Jan. 26, 2001, *available at* http://europa.eu.int/comm/internal_market/en/dataprot/wpdocs/wp39en.htm.

however, does not include data held by national agencies.[25]

The Privacy Commissioner has determined that PIPEDA not only governs the collection, use, and disclosure of personal information within Canada, but it also controls the transmission of personal information internationally pursuant to the federal government's power over international trade and commerce.[26]

The Privacy Commissioner has given some guidelines to individuals wishing to protect their personal information from inappropriate disclosure to foreign parties.[27] Individuals are encouraged to report concerns about the collection or use of their personal information to the Commissioner. Although the Commissioner lacks power to act directly against foreign parties, the Commissioner can raise the issue with the national government of the state where the foreign party is located. Even more powerfully, if a Canadian organization or a multi-national organization with a Canadian presence is

25. Commission Decision of December 20, 2001, Official Journal of the European Communities L 2/13, *available at* http://www.europa.eu.int/comm/internal_market/dataprot/adequacy/canada-faq_en.htm.

26. Office of the Privacy Commissioner, *Fact Sheet*: *Questions and Answers regarding the application of PIPEDA, Alberta and British Columbia's Personal Information Protection Acts (PIPAs), at* http://www.privcom.gc.ca/fs-fi/02_05_d_26_e.asp (last visited Nov. 12, 2007).

27. Office of the Privacy Commissioner, *Fact Sheet: What Canadians Can Do to Protect Their Personal Information Transferred Across Borders*, http://www.privcom.gc.ca/fs-fi/02_05_d_23_e.asp (last visited Nov. 12, 2007).

cooperating with, or otherwise assisting, the foreign party, it can be subject to regular proceedings under the PIPEDA complaint process.

(ii) PIPEDA and the Patriot Act

Following the terrorist attacks of September 11, 2001 the United States Congress passed the USA PATRIOT Act of 2001 ("Patriot Act"). The Patriot Act is discussed at length in Chapter 3, which addresses U.S. privacy law, however, certain of its provisions are relevant to PIPEDA, specifically the Patriot Act's expansion of the U.S. Treasury Secretary's powers to regulate and monitor financial transactions that involve foreign individuals and entities.[28]

Canada is the United States' largest trading partner. As a result, many of the databanks used to store personal information of Canadian residents are located in the United States, thus making them subject to the provisions of the Patriot Act. However, if a U.S.-based company makes a disclosure of a Canadian resident's personal information to U.S. authorities under the Patriot Act without the consent of the individual who is named, this could result in the Canadian organization that originally transferred the information being liable for a breach of PIPEDA unless the disclosure meets an exception in the applicable Canadian law.

One of the exceptions found in PIPEDA is for investigations of criminal activity under the laws of

28.   18 U.S.C. § 5318A(b)(1)(A).

Canada or foreign jurisdictions.[29] Specifically, the statute provides that personal information may be disclosed without the knowledge of the subject where "required to comply with a subpoena or warrant issued or an order made by a court ... with jurisdiction to compel the production of information."[30] It is unclear, however, from the face of the statute whether PIPEDA only allows disclosure under Canadian court orders or if a U.S. court order would apply.

The office of the Privacy Commissioner recognizes this issue and has urged Canadian organizations to take a number of steps that are intended to assist them in avoiding this dilemma.[31] These steps include: (1) informing Canadian residents that their personal information may be transferred to locations in the United States and be subject to search; (2) entering into contracts with United States-based organizations which require them to provide the same level of protection for the personal information of Canadian residents as would be required by PIPEDA; (3) limiting the amount of personal information that is transferred into the United States; and (4) limiting the ability of United States-based organizations to access personal information of Ca-

29. *See* PIPEDA at § 7.

30. Id. § 7(3)(c).

31. Heather Black, Assistant Privacy Commissioner of Canada, Address at the 11th Annual Meeting on Regulatory Compliance for Financial Institutions, *The Latest Developments in Privacy Compliance: PIPEDA Review and the USA PATRIOT Act* (Nov. 18, 2005), *available at* http://www.privcom.gc.ca/speech/2005/sp-d_051118_hb_e.asp (last visited Nov. 12, 2007).

nadian residents stored in Canada. These are only recommendations; therefore if Canadian organizations likely to be transacting business with U.S. organizations must balance the potential risks of violating Canadian privacy legislation against the benefits of working within the United States.

B. European Union

Since the Second World War, Western European nations have shown an increasingly strong commitment to protecting individual privacy. Long before the Internet boom of the 1990s, European countries were focusing on protection of personal privacy by limiting data access. The German state of Hesse, for example, passed the first law granting individuals control of their personal information in 1970.[32] Indeed, the term "data protection" entered the European lexicon from the German word "Datenschutz." Three years later, Sweden was the first country to pass a privacy protection law.[33] While much of the underlying public concern that motivated these early efforts grew from historical concerns about the possible abuses of compilations of personal information, technological developments were the immediate stimulus, as both statutes were enacted in response to proposals to combine separate government archives into computerized databases.

32. Hessisches Datenschutzgesetz, v 7.10.1970, GVBl Hesse I S 625.

33. Datalag (1973:289).

The process of political integration in Europe has advanced considerably since the era of these first attempts at legislating protections for personal information. The governing bodies of the European Union now wield considerably more influence over patterns of economic regulation in the E.U. Members States than the national governments do. While individual member states of the European Union still maintain separate laws addressing privacy issues, the scope of European privacy protection has been driven mainly by the European Union for the past decade or more. The European Union's privacy regime will be reviewed as a "national" policy, notwithstanding its many member states.

1. *The Data Protection Directive*

The mainstay of privacy protection in the European Union arises from Directive 95/46 ("Data Protection Directive").[34] The Data Protection Directive was an outgrowth of the national regulatory schemes promoted by the OECD Guidelines, which had produced a patchwork of different privacy regimes throughout Europe. The Data Protection Directive was designed to harmonize Member States' data protection legislation, thereby reducing obstacles to economic activity within the European Union while preserving (or even enhancing, depending

34.   Council Directive 95/46 of 24 October 1995 on the Protection of Individuals with Regard to the Processing of Personal Data and on the Free Movement of Such Data, 1995 O.J. (L 281) 31 ("Data Protection Directive").

on the preexisting level of national data protection) the privacy rights of individual residents.

The Data Protection Directive encompasses "personal data" of E.U. residents, meaning "information relating to an identified or identifiable natural person,"[35] where that data is processed[36] "wholly or partly by automatic means" and/or where the data will form part of a filing system.[37] A person is "identifiable" if the individual "can be identified, directly or indirectly, in particular by reference to an identification number or to one or more factors specific to [their] physical, physiological, mental, economic, cultural, or social identity."[38] An exception is provided for "purely personal" use by a natural person and for government purposes relating to security, defense, and criminal law.[39]

The laws enacted in accordance with the Data Protection Directive must apply to data "controllers"[40] or "processors"[41] located in a Member State,

35.   Data Protection Directive, art. 2(a).

36.   "Processing of personal data" is defined as any operation pertaining to personal data including "collection, recording, organization, storage, adaptation or alteration, retrieval, consultation, use, disclosure by transmission, dissemination or otherwise making available, alignment or combination, blocking, erasure or destruction." Id. at art. 2(b).

37.   A "filing system" is "any structured set of personal data which are accessible according to specific criteria, whether centralized, decentralized or dispersed on a functional or geographical basis." *Id.* at art.2(c).

38.   Id at art. 2(a).

39.   Id at art. 3(2).

40.   A data "controller" is any "natural or legal person, public authority, agency or any other body which alone or jointly with

a territory subject to a Member State's laws, or located elsewhere but relying on equipment located within a Member State for any purpose other than transmission.[42]

Data must be collected only for "specified, explicit and legitimate purposes," without any further processing that would be "incompatible with those purposes."[43] The data collected must be "adequate, relevant and not excessive" given the purposes for which it was acquired.[44] Data must not only be accurate, but "every reasonable step must be taken" to delete or correct inaccurate and incomplete data. The data must not be "kept in a form which permits identification of data subject" for any longer than is necessary for the original purpose it was collected for, except where Member States provide for safeguards if the data is to be retained for "historical, statistical or scientific purposes." Compliance with these requirements is the responsibility of the data controller.

others determines the purposes and means of the processing of personal data." Id. at art. 2(d).

41.   A data "processor" is any "natural or legal person, public authority, agency or any other body which processes personal data on behalf of the controller." Data Protection Directive, art. 2(e). A data processor may not legitimately process personal data unless instructed by the data controller or otherwise required by law to process the data. *Id.* at art. 16.

42.   Id. at art. 4(1)(a)-(c).

43.   Data Protection Directive, art. 6(1)(b). Processing of previously collected personal data for "historical, statistical or scientific purposes" is permissible with "appropriate safeguards." *Id.*

44.   Id. at art. 6(1)(c).

Absent certain legal circumstances, personal data may only be processed if the subject "has unambiguously given [] consent."[45] Further protections are required for particularly sensitive personal data,[46] which may even override explicit consent by subjects to the use of their personal data.[47] These added protections do not apply where that data is necessary for medical care, law enforcement, or other "reasons of substantial public interest" if an exemption has been provided for by the Member State's data protection legislation.[48] Exceptions based on law enforcement and public interest needs must be notified to the European Commission ("Commission"). If necessary to avoid unreasonable restrictions on free expression, Member States may provide exemptions for journalism, artistic, or literary works.[49]

The data controller or its representative must provide subjects from whom data has been collected with "at least" the identity of the controller and any representatives, the intended purposes for which the data will be processed, and any further relevant information necessary to "guarantee fair

45. Data Protection Directive, art. 7(a)-(f).

46. Referred to as "special categories of data," this includes data "revealing racial or ethnic origin, political opinions, religious or philosophical beliefs, trade-union membership ... [or concerning] health or sex life." Data Protection Directive, art. 8(1).

47. Id. at art. 8(2)(a).

48. Id. at art. 8(3)-(5).

49. Id. at art. 9.

processing" of the subject's data.[50] If the data has not been obtained directly from the subject, the data controller must provide the same information as above to the subject, either when the personal data is initially recorded or no later than when the data is first disclosed to a third party. In the latter case, particularly if the data has been obtained for historical, statistical, or scientific purposes, the controller does not need to provide such notice if doing so would "involve a disproportionate effort," or is otherwise exempted by law, providing that proper safeguards are undertaken.[51]

A data subject must have the right to obtain from the controller confirmation of whether data about the subject is being processed, the purposes of the processing, the types of data involved, and the identities of the data recipients.[52] The subject also has the right to receive communications pertaining to the processing that describe the data "in an intelligible form," the source of the data, and "knowledge of the logic" used in automatic processing of the data, if applicable.[53] The subject has the right to rectify, erase, or block data where processing has

50. Data Protection Directive, art. 10(a)-(c). Other information can include the recipients of the data, whether providing the data is voluntary or mandatory (including the consequences of not providing the data), and the existence of the right to review and correct the data. *Id*. at art. 10(c).

51. Id. at art. 11(2).

52. This right must be able to be exercised at "reasonable intervals and without excessive delay or expense." *Id* at art. 12(a).

53. Id. at art. 12(a).

not been in compliance with the terms of the Data Protection Directive, and of notification to third-party recipients of the data of such corrections or deletions unless doing so would involve a disproportionate effort. Member States, however, have the power to adopt legislation restricting these rights if the limitations are a necessary part of protecting national security, public safety, or law enforcement investigations. Finally, the subject has the right to object "on compelling legitimate grounds" to processing performed on the basis of the public interest exception or the exception provided for processing in the legitimate interest of the controller and/or third parties.[54] If those grounds are found to be justified, the subject has the right to have the processing halted.[55] If the data is to be used for direct marketing purposes, there is an implicit presumption the objection is legitimate and justified.[56]

Data controllers must "implement appropriate technical and organizational measures" for the purpose of protecting personal data from "accidental or unlawful destruction," loss, alteration, disclosure, or theft.[57] The measures must provide a reasonable level of security for the type of data, as determined by the state of the art and cost of implementation,

54.   This is so unless national legislation provides otherwise. Data Protection Directive, art. 14(a).

55.   Id. at art. 14(a).

56.   *See generally* Data Protection Directive, art. 14(b) (bestowing a right to object upon the data subject where the information will be used for direct marketing).

57.   Id. at art. 17(1).

and the risks posed by its processing. The controller is responsible for ensuring that any data processors working on its behalf provide adequate technical and organizational measures to adequately protect the personal data being processed. Agreements between controllers and processors must be by contract or other binding legal act, and the provisions relating to data protection and the protective measures must be in writing or "equivalent form."[58]

The controller or its representative must notify the appropriate national supervisory authority of any intent to carry out a wholly or partially automatic data processing operation.[59] Member States may make exceptions to the notification requirement, or allowances for simplified notice, under certain circumstances. An exception of particular significance is where a data controller, in compliance with national law, appoints a "personal data protection official," who is responsible for independently guaranteeing the internal application of the terms of the Data Protection Directive and keeping a record of processing operations directed by the controller. If notification is required, it must at least include:

58.   Data Protection Directive, art. 17(4). The Data Protection Directive itself does not stipulate what an "equivalent form" would be, indicating that it is left to the Member States to determine that point. For example, Austria does not recognize an "equivalent form," requiring all such contracts to be in writing.

59.   Data Protection Directive, art. 18(1). Member States are required to establish or empower one or more independent public agencies to be responsible for monitoring the implementation of the Data Protection Directive. Id. at art. 28(1).

1. The name and address of the controller and, if appropriate, its representative;

2. The purpose of the processing;

3. A description of the categories of data subjects and the categories of data pertaining to them;

4. The recipients who may receive the data;

5. Proposed transfers to non-Member States; and

6. A general description of the security measures employed to guard the data processing sufficient to allow a preliminary determination of their adequacy.[60]

Member States must also determine which processing operations are likely to pose particular risks to the rights and freedoms of their residents and carry out examinations of these operations prior to their commencement. These examinations are to be carried out by the supervisory authority after notification by the data controller or its data protection official. If the controller or the official cannot decide whether the operation would pose particular risks, the supervisory authority must be consulted. Member States may enact more restrictive pre-implementation notification requirements.

A public record available for inspection by any person must be kept of all processing operations for which the Member State has received notification.[61]

60. Data Protection Directive, art. 19(1)(a)-(f).

61. *See* Data Protection Directive, art. 21(2). This record must contain at least the notification information required by

Data controllers, or another body appointed by the Member State, must also make available to any person, upon request, records of all processing operations other than those for which notice was required. Member States may make an exception for processing done solely for the purpose of keeping a register mandated by law or regulation, and which is intended to provide information to the public, whether generally or for those who can prove a legitimate interest.[62]

In addition to any administrative remedies provided by the supervisory authority, every person is to have access to a judicial remedy for the breach of any rights incorporated in the Member State's data protection legislation. Some Member States have gone even further and provide for criminal penalties for breach of their national data protection legislation in addition to civil penalties. Sweden, for example, allows for a fine and a six month term of imprisonment, with imprisonment up to two years "if the offence is grave." Personal Data Act § 49. Austria provides for a maximum of one year imprisonment "unless the offence shall be subject to a more severe punishment pursuant to another provision." Federal Act Concerning the Protection of Personal Data § 51(1). The injured party is entitled to damages from the controller for loss, unless the controller can prove it is not responsible for the events leading to the loss.

the Data Protection Directive, with the exception of a description of the security measures used to protect the data. *See id.*

   62. Data Protection Directive, art. 21(3).

Of particular significance in the Data Protection Directive are its provisions on extraterritorial application of its requirements. Personal data undergoing processing, or to be processed, may only be transferred to a party in a non-Member State, such as the United States, if the non-Member State "ensures an adequate level of protection." Adequacy of protection is determined by reference to all the circumstances pertaining to a data transfer operation, particularly the nature of the data, the purpose of the proposed processing operation, the duration of the operation, the countries of origin and destination, as well as the laws, professional rules, and security measures employed by the non-Member State. Member States and the Commission must keep each other informed of evidence showing a non-Member State is failing to provide a satisfactory level of security. If the Commission determines that a non-Member State is failing to provide adequate protection for personal data originating from the European Union, then Member States must take measures to block further transfer of the same type of data to the non-Member State in question. Where such a determination has been made, the Commission must enter into negotiations with the non-Member State to remedy the situation.

Member States may, however, provide exceptions to the transfer restrictions on the condition that the data subject has given unambiguous consent to the transfer, or meets other criteria. Member States may also permit transfers to data controllers in non-Member States that have failed to comply legislatively with the Data Protection Directive if the controller itself guarantees adequate safeguards, particularly by contract. Member States must inform the Commission of any authorizations they grant under self-certification criteria, and these may be challenged by any other Member State or the Commission itself. The Commission may also decide that a standard contractual clause provides adequate protection, in which case the Member States must permit data transfers made pursuant to contracts containing this type of clause.

2. Problems implementing the Data Protection Directive

As noted above, the Member States of the European Union enforce the terms of the Data Protection Directive by implementing their own laws—the Directive is not self-executing. Member States were required under the terms of the Directive to have "laws, regulations and administrative provisions" in force no later than three years after the adoption of the directive.[63] Member States were to have had their compliant data protection legislation in place by October 24, 1998. Member States were also allowed to grant an exemption for an additional nine years to manual filing systems. A number of Member States, however, delayed passing the necessary implementing legislation, leading the Commission to file suit in the European Court of Justice in December 1999 against France, Ireland, Germany,

63. Data Protection Directive, art. 32(1).

the Netherlands, and Luxembourg. Even under the pressure of litigation, it was not until July 1, 2003, when Ireland's national data protection legislation became effective that all Member States were compliant.[64]

  Getting all Member States to enact the necessary legislation was by no means the only challenge to implementation. Member States' various approaches to implementing the Directive have resulted in national requirements sufficiently different to mean that compliance with the bare terms of the Directive will not automatically mean a company is in compliance with the laws of any given Member State. The United Kingdom defines "personal data" as information that may be used to identify a living, natural individual.[65] Information concerning deceased individuals, thus, is not ordinarily protected. Austria, on the other hand, protects the information of not just natural persons regardless of their vital status, but legal persons as well.[66]

64.   *See* European Commission, Status of Implementation of Directive 95/46 on the Protection of Individuals with Regard to the Processing of Personal Data, *available at* http://ec.europa.eu/ justice_home/fsj/privacy/law/implementation_en.htm (last visited Jan. 21, 2008). Member States joining the European Union subsequent to the Directive taking effect were obligated to enact compliant legislation as a condition of entry.

65.   Data Protection Act 1998, 1998 Ch. 29, part 1(1).

66.   Federal Act Concerning the Protection of Personal Data, Bundesgesetzblatt I No. 165/1999, § 4(1), (3), *amended by* Bundesgesetzblatt I No. 136/2001, *available at* http://www.ris2.bka. gv.at/Dokumente/Erv/ERV_1999_1_165.pdf.

3. *Updates to the Data Protection Directive*

One of the strong points of the Data Protection Directive is that it is adaptable across a wide range of industries and service providers. The Directive is calculated to avoid technological or economic obsolescence by not depending on the specific details of collection or processing, but rather by focusing on the nature of the data to determine how it should be protected. The Data Protection Directive, did however, focus exclusively on the uses of personal data by "collectors" and "processors." It did not address the question of transmission of data via third parties who served neither as collectors nor processors, but who could potentially compromise the security of the data whether deliberately or inadvertently.

The European Union's response was the E.U. Electronic Communications Directive ("Communications Directive").[67] The Communications Directive creates privacy rules for the telecommunications industry that implement the principles of the Data Protection Directive with respect to communications channels. The Communications Directive speaks specifically to communications privacy in Article 5:

Member States shall ensure the confidentiality of communications and the related traffic data by means of a public communications network and

67. Directive 2002/58/EC of the European Parliament and of the Council of 12 July 2002 Concerning the Processing of Personal Data and the Protection of Privacy in the Electronic Communications Sector, 2002 O.J. (L 201) 37 ("Communications Directive").

publicly available electronic communications services, through national legislation. In particular,
they shall prohibit listening, tapping, storage or
other kinds of interception or surveillance of communications and the related traffic data by persons other than users, without the consent of the
users concerned, except when legally authorized
to do so in accordance with Article 15(1). This
paragraph shall not prevent technical storage
which is necessary for the conveyance of a communication without prejudice to the principle of
confidentiality.[68]

Of note is the mention to Article 15(1) in the
preceding text. Article 15(1) demonstrates the limits
of the strong privacy rights created by the Data
Protection Directive:

Member States may adopt legislative measures to
restrict the scope of the rights and obligations
provided for in Article 5 ... of this Directive
when such restriction constitutes a necessary,
appropriate and proportionate measure within a
democratic society to safeguard national security,
defense, public security, and the prevention, investigation, detection and prosecution of criminal
offences or of unauthorized use of the electronic
communication system, as referred to in Article
13(1) of [the Data Protection Directive]. To this
end, Member States may, *inter alia*, adopt legislative measures providing for the retention of data

68. Communications Directive, art. 5.

for a limited period justified on the grounds laid down in this paragraph.[69]

Article 15(1) of the Communications Directive, when combined with legislation enacted pursuant to Article 13(1) of the Data Protection Directive effectively created an exception with the potential to swallow the rule depending on the actions of the Member States.

Almost immediately after the passage of the Communications Directive, the Member States began enacting national legislation with significant variations in data monitoring and retention requirements for communications providers. In response to the numerous incompatible and in some instances contradictory national legislative schemes, the European Union responded with yet another Directive, this time attempting to set uniform limits on data retention policies.[70]

The preamble clauses of the Data Retention Directive acknowledge the non-uniformity of the Member States' actions, and the technical problems this was causing service providers:

(5) Several Member States have adopted legislation providing for the retention of data by service providers for the prevention, investigation, detec-

69.   Communications Directive, art. 15(1).

70.   Directive 2006/24/EC of the European Parliament and of the Council of 15 March 2006 on the Retention of Data Generated or Processed in Connection with the Provision of Publicly Available Electronic Communications Services or of Public Communications Networks and Amending Directive 2002/58/EC, 2006 O.J. (L 105) 54 ("Data Retention Directive").

tion, and prosecution of criminal offences. Those national provisions vary considerably. (6) The legal and technical differences between national provisions concerning the retention of data for the purpose of prevention, investigation, detection and prosecution of criminal offences present obstacles to the internal market for electronic communications, since service providers are faced with different requirements regarding the types of traffic and location data to be retained and the conditions and periods of retention.[71]

While uniformity may be welcome to some degree, the Data Retention Directive also serves to further legitimize and institutionalize data collection:

(10) On 13 July 2005, the Council reaffirmed in its declaration condemning the terrorist attacks on London the need to adopt common measures on the retention of telecommunications data as soon as possible. (11) Given the importance of traffic and location data for the investigation, detection, and prosecution of criminal offences, as demonstrated by research and the practical experience of several Member States, there is a need to ensure at European level that data that are generated or processed, in the course of the supply of communications services, by providers of publicly available electronic communications services or of a public communications network are retained for a certain period, subject to the conditions provided for in this Directive.[72]

71. Data Retention Directive, Whereas clauses (5), (6).

72. Id. at (10), (11).

The Data Retention Directive in fact not only permits Member States to derogate from the privacy protections of the Data Protection and Electronic Communications Directives, but affirmatively requires the Member States to do so on several points. Member States must enact legislation which compels service providers to retain "data necessary to trace and identify" the source and destination of electronic communications, including the telephone numbers, IP addresses, or other identifiers of both sending and receiving parties. Service providers are also required to preserve information concerning the date, time, and duration of electronic communications as well as the communications protocols used, the transmitting and receiving equipment, and the actual physical location of a mobile device at the time of the communication.[73] Service providers may be required to retain the information for between six months to two years. Member States were given until September 15, 2007 to pass implementing legislation, although they were given the right to exempt certain types of Internet communication from the retention requirements until March 15, 2009.

4. *Safe Harbor*

A key part of the Data Protection Directive is its strong restrictions on the transfer of E.U. residents' data outside of the European Union—recipients of the transferred data must either be subject to na-

73.   Data Retention Directive, art. 5(1)(a)-(f).

tional regulations providing protection equivalent to that of the Directive or otherwise enter into certain contractual arrangements guaranteeing an equivalent level of protection. The United States did not have (and still lacks) a comprehensive privacy protection regime, let alone one that provided equivalent protections to the Data Protection Directive. Some compromise solution had to be reached or E.U.-U.S. trade would be severely impacted. The U.S. Department of Commerce entering into negotiations with the E.U. Commission concerning what steps could be taken to avoid U.S. businesses being summarily cut off from access to E.U. residents' data.

The result of these negotiations is the agreement called the "Safe Harbor." The Safe Harbor, which is administered by the U.S. Department of Commerce, is a self-certification system for U.S. businesses to confirm that they have implemented internal procedures sufficient to ensure E.U. residents' data receives protections equivalent to those required by the Data Protection Directive. The E.U. Commission approved the use of the Safe Harbor in July 2000 pursuant to its authority under Article 25 of the Data Protection Directive to certify non-Member States as being in compliance with the provisions of the Directive.[74] As a result, U.S. businesses that meet the requirements of the

74. See Commission Decision 2000/520/EC of 26 July 2000 Pursuant to Directive 95/46/EC of the European Parliament and of the Council on the Adequacy of the Protection Provided by the Safe Harbor Privacy Principles and Related Frequently Asked Questions Issued by the US Department of Commerce, art. 1(1), 2000 O.J. (L 215) 7, 8.

Safe Harbor may safely receive and process data from E.U. residents. The Safe Harbor itself is analyzed in greater detail in Chapter 4, Part III(A)(2) below concerning transborder data flows.

C. Mexico

1. *Constitutional protection*

The Mexican Constitution contains privacy guarantees similar to the ones found in the Fourth Amendment of the U.S. Constitution. Article 16 of the Mexican Constitution sets up the framework for personal privacy: "No one shall be molested in his person, family, domicile, papers, or possessions except by virtue of a written order of the competent authority stating the legal grounds and justification for the action taken."[75] This is essentially the "right to be let alone;" the Mexican Constitution does not expressly provide protection for personal data.

2. *Statutory protection*

Mexico has numerous statutes that address privacy and data protection. None of these statutes constitute comprehensive data protection in the manner of the European Union's Data Protection Directive. The Mexican approach is very similar to that of the United States: passing laws that cover different sectors of the economy or business prac-

75.   1917 Constitution of Mexico, art. 16 (English translation *available at* http://www.ilstu.edu/class/hist263/docs/1917const.html).

tices. The Federal Consumer Protection Law, for example, gives consumers the right to request their personal information be deleted from direct marketing lists,[76] while the Law of Protection and Defense of the User of Financial Services protects the personal information of individuals engaged in banking or securities transactions.[77] Many of these statutes were updated as part of the passage of the E–Commerce Act in 2000. This legislation updated the language of the Federal Civil Code, the Federal Rules of Civil Procedure, the Commercial Code, and the Federal Consumer Protection Law. This update added language that brought electronic documents, digital signatures, and online activity under the umbrella of legal protection.

3.   *Other organizations & enforcement*

The main focus on data privacy in Mexico centers around the government. The Federal Institute of Access to Public Information is an independent body, which serves to both facilitate citizens' access to information about the internal operations of government and review government activities that impact the privacy interests of Mexican citizens. While there   are   non-governmental   organizations

76.   Ley Federal de Protección al Consumidor [L.F.P.C.] [Federal Consumer Protection Law], Diario Oficial de la Federación, 24 de Diciembre de 1992 (Mex.).

77.   Ley de Protección y Defensa al Usuario de Servicios Financieros [L.P.D.U.S.F.] [Law of Protection and Defense of the User of Financial Services], Diario Oficial de la Federación, 18 de Enero de 1999 (Mex.).

("NGOs") that promote access to public information held by the government, there are no NGOs that focus on privacy rights with respect to individual data held by private entities. Criminal prosecution of companies that violate data privacy laws is taking a higher place in public discourse in Mexico, especially following the discovery of an illegal transfer of personal data to U.S. government agencies, which appears to have been used at least in part by U.S. immigration officials to locate and remove Mexican nationals unlawfully in the United States.

D. Japan

1. *Constitutional protection*

Similar to the U.S. Fourth Amendment, the Japanese Constitution provides the basis of personal privacy (right to be let alone) in Article 35: "The right of all persons to be secure in their homes, papers and effects against entries, searches and seizures shall not be impaired except upon warrant issued for adequate cause and particularly describing the place to be searched and things to be seized...."[78] Article 21 maintains secrecy of communications: "No censorship shall be maintained, nor shall the secrecy of any means of communication be violated."[79] In 2000, the Japanese Diet established a body called the Research Commission on the Constitution to consider possible amendments

78. Constitution of Japan, Kenpo, art. 35(1).

79. Id. art. 21(2).

to the Japanese Constitution. The Research Commission's report was released in 2005 and included a recommendation that an amendment concerning personal privacy be added,[80] but no action on that has yet been taken by the Diet.

2. *Statutory protection*

Personal data collected by the government is regulated by the 1988 Act for the Protection of Computer Processed Personal Data Held by Administrative Organs.[81] This law implements the OECD Guidelines of security, access, and correction, and it also limits subsequent uses of data for purposes other than which the data was originally gathered.

Japan historically has allowed businesses and private organizations to self-regulate the handling of personal information. This began to change in 1997, when the Ministry of International Trade and Industry (MITI) issued a set of guidelines concerning data collections in the private sector.[82] The momentum toward regulating the private sector continued when Japan enacted the Personal Information Protection[83] (PIP) law in May 2003, which took effect

80. Research Commission on the Constitution, *Handbook on the Research Report on the Constitution of Japan*, pt. III, 2(2) (2005), *available at* http://www.sangiin.go.jp/eng/report/ehb/ehb 03_06.htm#0202.

81. Act for the Protection of Computer Processed Personal Data held by Administrative Organs, Act No. 95, Dec. 16, 1988.

82. MITI, *Guidelines Concerning the Protection of Computer Processed Personal Data in the Private Sector*, Mar. 4, 1997.

83. Act on the Protection of Personal Information, Law No. 57, May 30, 2003.

in April 2005. The PIP law extends the notice, security, access, and correction principles to the private sector, protecting information both in electronic and in print form.

3. Other organizations & enforcement

A recent series of high profile database breaches and cases of identity theft have prompted an attitude of increased vigilance on the part of the Japanese government and the private sector. The Ministry of Justice revised its internal regulations to place greater emphasis on prosecuting privacy violations and identity theft. Meanwhile Japanese businesses have moved quickly to adopt the data security management best practices reflected in ISO 27001, with more Japanese businesses being certified as compliant as of December 2006 than the rest of the world combined.[84]

E. Republic of Korea (South Korea)

1. Constitutional protection

The constitution of South Korea contains provisions guaranteeing the traditional "right to be let alone," as well as an express right of privacy. Article 16 states: "All citizens are free from intrusion into their place of residence. In case of search or seizure in a residence, a warrant issued by a judge

84. International Organization for Standardization, *The ISO Survey–2006* 40,41, *available at* http://www.iso.org/iso/survey 2006.pdf.

upon request of a prosecutor has to be presented."[85] Article 17 provides that the "privacy of no citizen may be infringed,"[86] and Article 18 provides secrecy of communication: "The secrecy of correspondence of no citizen may be infringed."[87]

2. *Statutory protection*

South Korea has both comprehensive and sectoral legislation—one act covering the public sphere and many laws covering the private sphere. The public sector is controlled by a comprehensive statutory scheme (the "Public Agencies Act") that implements the OECD Guidelines for the control of personal data by the government.[88] This Act requires government agencies to report lists of databases keeping personal information; a master list of all databases is publicly available. Individuals can access and correct their records in databases held by public agencies.

Personal data in the private sector in South Korea is protected much as it is in the United States: through many laws, each covering different categories of business. These laws include the Protection of Communications Secrets Act, the Telecommunications Business Act, the Framework Act on Electronic Commerce, and the Digital Signatures Act.[89]

85. Constitution of the Republic of Korea, art. 16.

86. Id. at art. 17.

87. Id. at art. 18.

88. 1994 Act on the Protection of Personal Information Maintained by Public Agencies, Act 4734.

89. Act No. 4650; Act No. 4391; Act No. 5834; Act No. 5792.

3. Other organizations & enforcement

The effectiveness of the Public Agencies Act is questionable—the agency that publishes the list of databases is placed in the role of balancing privacy versus administrative efficiency, a role it carries out with no independent supervision. There are stiff penalties—both monetary and imprisonment—for failures of data protection in the private sector. Out of concern about increased incidents of identity theft, the South Korean government has recently proposed to stop using resident registration numbers as an online identification system. In parallel, the Korean Association of Information and Telecommunication developed a privacy "trust mark" which online marketers and websites can display to certify they comply with privacy guidelines.

F. The People's Republic of China ("China")

1. Constitutional protection

The Chinese Constitution has a number provisions dedicated to personal privacy. Article 37 protects individuals from unlawful searches, while Article 39 provides the same protection for private residences. Article 40 expressly protects the privacy of correspondence from both public and private actors, but includes an express reservation of the power "to censor correspondence in accordance with procedures prescribed by law." In addition to this rather significant derogation, the Chinese government has admitted that its domestic law enforcement agencies are not always consistent in applying procedural protections and that any constitutional guarantees may not be applied evenly or systematically.

2. *Statutory protection*

There are Articles of the Chinese criminal code which penalize physical intrusions of privacy, including illegally inspecting mail or entering a private residence,[90] but there is no general law that prohibits personal data collection. The Chinese government is essentially unfettered in its ability to collect, store, and use all manner of personally identifiable data, and service providers are unlimited in their ability to use data related to electronic communications, whether telephonic or Internet.

3. *Other organizations & enforcement*

The Chinese tradition has long been one of keeping close track of its citizens. As far back as the 4th century B.C.E., Chinese provinces kept accurate records of their populations in order to tax and conscript their subjects, and unquestionably, the Chinese legal system has for the past several decades shown little concern for "privacy rights" under any definition one might apply to the term. However, in an implicit recognition of the economic advantages privacy protections can confer, the Chinese government is beginning to research adopting meas-

90. Criminal Law of China, pt. I, ch. IV, arts. 245 & 252 (1997).

ures, including electronic signature certification authorities and database protection standards, in an attempt to increase the level of e-commerce. Several municipalities and provinces have also adopted "Open Government" acts, which allow citizens to check on their personal data stored by the municipal government and request that errors be corrected. Critics, however, have suggested that these experiments at privacy protection are likely to be undermined by broad national security exceptions contained within them.

G. India

1. *Constitutional protection*

Article 21 of the Indian Constitution states, "No person shall be deprived of his life or personal liberty except according to procedure established by law." Although this provision most closely resembles the Fifth Amendment to U.S. Constitution, which is not generally considered a source of privacy rights in U.S. jurisprudence, the Indian Supreme Court found in *Rajgopal v. State of Tamil Nadu* (1994) that the right to privacy is implicitly encompassed within the term "personal liberty."

2. *Statutory protection*

The concept of privacy as the "right to be let alone" is protected in tort and criminal law in India, but there is no general data privacy law. There is some sectoral privacy protection, including the Public Financial Institutions Act of 1993, which mandates confidentiality in bank transactions. The increasing prevalence of business process outsourcing to Indian companies is resulting in high pressure from both E.U. and U.S. firms for India to provide greater protection for personal data.

3. *Other organizations & enforcement*

Indian law enforcement agencies have not prioritized data protection issues. The National Association of Software and Service Companies (NASSCOM), a trade group composed of businesses in the information technology field, is actively engaged in lobbying for more stringent legislation, as well as developing mechanisms for self-regulation in the interim. For example, NASSCOM has established the National Skills Registry, which is a centralized database of information technology workers who have been subject to background checks and whose employment histories have been verified. While the National Skills Registry itself presents challenges to employee privacy (as NASSCOM acknowledges), it serves as an important check on individuals potentially planning on committing serial identity theft or other violations of consumer privacy by moving from job to job.

III. TRANS-BORDER DATA FLOWS AND PRIVACY

With the advent of the Internet, information has been sent across borders in greater volumes and with greater frequency than ever before. This transfer of information is typically referred to as "transborder data flows" or "cross-border data flows." In the context of privacy protection, these transfers pose challenges and opportunities to the public and private sectors.

A. Governmental Developments

Two major inter-governmental attempts have been made to deal with the issue of trans-border data flows: The OECD Guidelines on Privacy, and the E.U./U.S. Safe Harbor.

1. *OECD Privacy Guidelines*

The Organization for Economic Co–Operation and Development ("OECD") is a group of 30 countries committed to the promotion of democratic governance and economic development. As part of these efforts, the members of the OECD collaborate to produce various documents, including model treaties, reports, and recommendations to promote an orderly international system and facilitate trade not just between its members, but between all interested nations.

The Guidelines on the Protection of Privacy and Transborder Flows of Personal Data ("the Guidelines") were approved by the OECD Council on September 23, 1980, for the purpose of harmonizing national data protection legislation and protecting human rights while still facilitating international data transfers.[91] The Guidelines set out eight principles that data protection legislation should follow:

1. Collection Limitation: Personal data should be obtained by lawful means, preferably with the knowledge or consent of the individual who's data is being collected.

2. Data Quality: Controllers of personal data ("data controllers") should strive to maintain records, which are accurate, complete and up-to-date, as well as being relevant to the purposes for which the data is collected.

3. Purpose Specification: Data controllers should disclose the purposes for which personal data will be collected no later than the time of collection, with subsequent use of the data limited to the disclosed purposes or use in a manner not incompatible with the original purposes, although compatible alternative uses should be disclosed when implemented.

4. Use Limitation: Personal data should not be disclosed or used for purposes other than were specified prior to or upon collection unless approved by the individual or to comply with the directions of a legal authority.

5. Security Safeguards: Once collected, if personal data is stored it should be subject to reasonable security precautions.

91. Organization for Economic Co-operation and Development: Council Recommendation Concerning Guidelines Governing the Protection of Privacy and Transborder Flows of Personal Data, OECD Doc. C(80) 58 (Final) (1980), 20 I.L.M. 422 (1981)

6. Openness: Data controllers should provide a readily available means for individuals to determine whether and what type of personal data of theirs is held by the data controller. This should include facilitating the identification of the data controller and the purposes for which the data is being used.

7. Individual Participation: Individuals should have the ability to obtain information from a data controller within a reasonable time regarding any personal data held by the collector and be able to have errors or omissions in the data corrected.

8. Accountability: A means should be provided by which data controllers can be accountable for compliance with the Guidelines' principles.

The Guidelines also set out four recommendations on applying data protection legislation to international transfers of personal data:

1. Nations should consider the implications for other nations when considering domestic processing and export of personal data;

2. Reasonable and appropriate steps should be taken to keep transborder data flows secure yet uninterrupted;

3. Transborder data flows should not be restricted, except where the receiving nation does not comply with the Guidelines or where re-ex-

port of data would defeat the purposes of data protection legislation; and

4. Data protection legislation and related measures should not be enacted that exceed the requirements of protecting the data and have the effect of restricting transborder flows of that data.

As the name suggests, the Guidelines are not binding. While the Guidelines have served as the foundation for other agreements concerning transborder data flows, numerous countries continue to have contrary and incompatible data protection legislation. Subsequent efforts, especially the U.S./E.U. Safe Harbor, have been directed at both harmonization of protection regimes and providing for effective enforcement.

2. *U.S./E.U. Safe Harbor*

Unlike the United States, the European Union has effectively adopted the OECD principles into its law. As discussed in Chapter 4, the European Union has enacted Directive 95/46/EC, commonly called the "Data Protection Directive," modeled on the OECD Guidelines, which required the Member States of the European Union to enact national legislation for the protection of E.U. residents' personal data. The Data Protection Directive included restrictions on the ability of parties inside the European Union to transfer the personal data of E.U. residents to recipients in non-Member States. Given the extremely expansive nature of what constitutes "personal data" subject to protection under the Directive, this posed a serious threat to the viability of inter-U.S./E.U. trade, particularly in services. Shortly after the passage of the Directive, representatives of the U.S. Department of Commerce ("DOC") began negotiating with the E.U. Commission over what steps the United States could take to receive recognition that it was providing sufficient levels of privacy protection for personal data transferred from the European Union.

Although the parties agreed that improvements in data protection were necessary, the DOC and the Commission were divided on the best solution. The DOC concurred with a report by the FTC that found, given the fluid, evolving nature of the "information economy," self-regulation by industry was the superior method by which to achieve maximum protection with minimal constraint on future development.[92] The Commission stood at the opposite extreme, arguing that anything less than comprehensive data protection legislation of the sort Member States were required to enact was insufficient. Through 1998 and into 1999, the DOC submitted multiple proposed self-regulation schemes (referred to as "safe harbors"), all of which were rejected by the E.U. Working Party on the Protection of Individuals with Regard to the Processing of Personal Data (Working Party). The Working Party was established pursuant to Article 29 of the Data Protec-

92.   For the text of the report, *see* FTC, *Self-Regulation and Privacy Online: A Report to Congress* (1999), *available at* http://www.ftc.gov/os/1999/07/privacy99.pdf (last visited Jan. 27, 2008).

tion Directive to give the Commission opinions on the level of data protection both within the European Union and in other nations. As the Working Party stated in its last opinion on the subject, We "deplore[] that most of the comments made in ... previous position papers do not seem to be addressed in the latest version of the US documents."[93]

By the summer of 2000, however, the DOC had worn down the Commission's resistance to permitting some form of self-regulation. With extensive behind the scenes lobbying, and despite the strenuous objections of the Working Party, the Commission issued a decision on July 26, 2000 confirming the adequacy of the draft Safe Harbor proposal submitted by the DOC on July 21 of that year.[94] The decision of the Commission means that national data protection agencies in Member States can only restrict the transmission and processing of personal data by a U.S. business subject to the Safe Harbor under two circumstances.[95] The first is if either the DOC or another authorized U.S. govern-

93. Working Party on the Protection of Individuals with Regard to the Processing of Personal Data, 5146/99/EN/final, at 3 (Dec. 3, 1999) ("December 3 Working Party"), *available at* http://ec.europa.eu/justice_home/fsj/privacy/docs/wpdocs/1999/wp27en.51fpdf (last visited Jan. 27, 2008).

94. Commission Decision 2000/520/EC of 26 July 2000 Pursuant to Directive 95/46/EC of the European Parliament and of the Council on the Adequacy of the Protection Provided by the Safe Harbour Privacy Principles and Related Frequently Asked Questions Issued by the US Department of Commerce, art. 1(1), 2000 O.J. (L 215) 7, 8 ("Decision 2000/520/EC").

95. Decision 2000/520/EC, art. 3.

ment agency notifies the agency that the business breached the terms of the Safe Harbor.[96] The second situation is where there is a likelihood that the Safe Harbor is, or will be, breached.[97] The Commission thus effectively surrendered enforcement of the Data Protection Directive to the DOC as it pertained to businesses within the United States. The decision recognizing the Safe Harbor went into effect on November 1, 2000.

(a) Structure of the Safe Harbor

The Safe Harbor consists primarily of two parts: the Safe Harbor Privacy Principles ("Principles") and the Safe Harbor Frequently Asked Questions ("FAQ"), which offer additional high-level interpretation by the DOC on the meaning of the Principles.[98] Together, the two provide "authoritative guidance" to U.S. organizations that receive personal data from the European Union.[99] Compliance with the Safe Harbor is considered sufficient to meet the requirements of the Data Protection Directive. Issued under the DOC's general power to "foster, promote, and develop international com-

96.   Decision 2000/520/EC, art. 3(1)(a).

97.   Id. at art. 3(1)(b).

98.   *See* Issuance of Safe Harbor Principles and Transmission to European Commission, 65 Fed. Reg. 45,666 (Dep't of Com. July 24, 2000) ("Safe Harbor").

99.   Safe Harbor, 65 Fed. Reg. at 45,666. Only "U.S. organizations" may qualify for inclusion in the Safe Harbor, however what constitutes a "U.S. organization" is not defined. *See id.* at 45,667.

merce," compliance with the Safe Harbor is voluntary and no specific methodology is prescribed.[100] Joining an existing self-regulatory privacy program that complies with the Principles or developing an internal privacy policy that meets the Principles are both acceptable. To fall within the Safe Harbor, these programs or policies must be drafted to make organizations subject to action under Section 5 of the Federal Trade Commission Act concerning unfair or deceptive trade practices. Compliance with the Safe Harbor becomes effective immediately upon self-certifying adherence to the Principles.

(i) The Principles

The Principles cover all "personal data" or "personal information" received by a U.S. organization from the European Union, in any recorded form, which is defined as "data about an identified or identifiable individual that are within the scope of the [Data Protection] Directive."[101] The Principles are based on the OECD Guidelines and are divided into the following seven categories: (1) Notice, (2) Choice, (3) Onward Transfer, (4) Security, (5) Data Integrity, (6) Access, and (7) Enforcement.[102]

Under the principle of "Notice," an organization is obliged to tell individuals about the purposes for which data is to be collected and how that data is to

100.   Safe Harbor, 65 Fed. Reg. at 45,667.

101.   Id. at 45,667.

102.   Id. at 45,667–68.

be used.[103] The organization must also explain how individuals can make complaints or inquiries, the types of third parties to which the data may be disclosed, and the opportunities individuals have to limit such disclosure. The notice must be presented in "clear and conspicuous language" at the time individuals are asked to give personal information or as soon afterwards as feasible, but notice must be given before the organization employs the information for a purpose other than for which it was originally collected or discloses it to a third party. Notice is not required if disclosure or transfer is being made to an agent of the organization, although the Onward Transfer Principle would apply.

In regards to the principle of "Choice," the organization must provide individuals with an opportunity to decide on an "opt-out" basis whether their personal information can be disclosed to a third party or be used for a purpose other than one related to those that have previously been authorized.[104] For "sensitive information,"[105] the individual must affirmatively "opt-in" before that information may be disclosed to third parties or be used for an alternative purpose.

The principle of "Onward Transfer" applies where the original data controller intends to disclose personal information to a third party. All of the following Onward Transfer rules are found in

103. Safe Harbor, 65 Fed. Reg. at 45,667.

104. Id. at 45,667.

105. This is equivalent to the Data Protection Directive's "special categories of data."

the Safe Harbor as reported in the Federal Register.[106] The controller may only disclose personal information to a third party acting as an agent after having determined whether the third party meets the requirements of the Safe Harbor, the Data Protection Directive or another adequate measure of data protection. This provision of the Safe Harbor implies that if the intended recipient is bound by another nation's personal data protection scheme, which has been found acceptable by the Commission, then the requirements of the Onward Transfer principle have been satisfied. Alternatively, the controller may enter into a written agreement with the third party, which guarantees that the recipient of the data will offer at least the same level of data protection as the Safe Harbor. If the original controller makes the determination or otherwise enters into an agreement with the third party, the original controller will not be held at fault if the third party breaches the terms of the Safe Harbor, provided that the original controller did not know and should not have known that the third party would commit the breach.

Under the principle of "Security," data controllers must "take reasonable precautions" to guard against "loss, misuse and unauthorized access, disclosure, alteration and destruction." The "security" principle is the least developed part of the Safe Harbor's Principles, meriting only a single-sentence description. The fifth principle, "Data Integrity," holds that personal data collected must be relevant

106.   Safe Harbor, 65 Fed. Reg. at 45,668.

to its specified purpose. The data controller must not process data "in a way that is incompatible with the purposes for which it has been collected or subsequently authorized by the individual." Controllers are required to take reasonable steps to ensure the integrity of the data.

"Access" is the next principle, stipulating that data subjects must be able to examine personal data concerning them and "be able to correct, amend, or delete" the data if found inaccurate. If the financial and temporal costs to the controller, however, would be disproportionate to the risks posed to the subject's privacy, controllers are not obliged to provide access. Controllers may also withhold personal data where access could threaten the rights of individuals other than the requesting party.

The final principle is "Enforcement." For data protection to be considered effective, data controllers must implement measures to guarantee compliance with the Principles, provide recourse for data subjects whose personal data may have been compromised, and make clear the consequences of failure to comply with the Principles. The measures implemented by the controller must at least include "readily available and affordable independent recourse mechanisms" which will allow a subject's complaint to be investigated and resolved in accordance with the Principles, including damage awards if applicable. There must also be procedures to verify that the controller is in fact complying with the Principles and a commitment to remedy the problems that led to the breach of the Principles.

There must be adequate sanctions to make certain that the controller complies. The FTC and the U.S. Department of Transportation (DOT) are recognized by the European Unions as being competent to investigate complaints of unfair or deceptive practices that are in breach of the Principles.

(ii) The FAQ

The FAQ is divided into fifteen parts, covering the Principles and related issues. The first FAQ asks, "[m]ust an organization always provide explicit (opt-in) choice with respect to sensitive data?"[107] The "opt-in" choice is not required if the data processing operation meets any of six criteria. These include situations where the processing is in the vital interests of the data subject, is necessary for medical treatment, is done by a non-profit organization as part of its mission, involves personal data that has been made public by the subject, is necessary for establishing a legal claim/defense, or where the organization is required to process the information to comply with other statutes or regulations. The second FAQ asks, "do the Safe Harbor Principles apply to personal information gathered, maintained, or disseminated for journalistic purposes?" Due to First Amendment concerns, journalistic interests in data will typically trump privacy interests, although common law privacy torts, contractual obligations, or other regulations of the sort discussed elsewhere in this text may impose inde-

107. Safe Harbor, 65 Fed. Reg. at 45,668. Each of the FAQs are found in this section.

pendent restrictions. Personal information, which has previously published or otherwise made available to the public through another outlet, may be republished without violating the Principles.

The third FAQ asks, "[a]re Internet service providers (ISPs) . . . or other organizations liable under the . . . Principles when on behalf of another organization they merely transmit, route, switch or cache information that may violate their terms?" The answer is no, the Principles do not give rise to any secondary liability where a party merely acts as a conduit for data transmission. The fourth FAQ asks, "[u]nder what circumstances is [the processing of personal data by auditors and investment bankers] permitted by the Notice, Choice, and Access Principles?" Auditors and investment bankers are permitted to process personal data without the data subject's approval only for the duration and to the extent necessary to comply with other legislation or to meet the legitimate needs of the auditor or banker. These needs include verifying compliance with legal obligations and accounting practices, along with transactions concerning mergers, acquisitions, and joint ventures.

The fifth FAQ asks, "[h]ow will companies that commit to cooperate with European Union Data Protection Authorities (DPAs) make those commitments and how will they be implemented?" Data controllers may make these commitments by declaring in their Safe Harbor certification that they will comply with all terms of the Enforcement Principle, cooperate with data protection agencies in investigating and resolving complaints related to the Principles, comply with the advice from the agencies on remedies and compensation, and provide written confirmation of their action to the agencies. The data protection agencies in turn will give their advice through a panel operating at the supranational level within the European Union that will consider both complaints by E.U. residents and submissions by controllers who have joined the Safe Harbor. In the event of a complaint, both the E.U. resident and the U.S. controller will have the opportunity to present their case before the panel, with a non-binding decision to be issued within sixty days where possible. Failure to comply with the panel's decision within twenty-five days of its delivery will result in notification by the panel to the FTC or other federal or state agencies with the power to enforce laws against deceptive trade practices. The panel may also choose to notify the DOC about the controller's failure to meet the terms of the Principles and request that the controller be stricken from the roster of Safe Harbor participants.

The sixth FAQ asks, "[h]ow does an organization self-certify that it adheres to the Safe Harbor Principles?" Certification becomes effective immediately after the following information is submitted:

1. The name of the data controller, mailing address, e-mail address, telephone and fax numbers;

2. A description of the controller's activities with regard to personal data received from the European Union;

3. A description of the controller's privacy poli-
    cy, including where the policy is available for
    public viewing, the date of its implementa-
    tion, a contact for handling Safe Harbor-relat-
    ed issues, the government agency under
    whose authority the controller is subject; any
    privacy programs the controller is part of,
    method of verifying compliance with the Safe
    Harbor, and the mechanism for investigating
    unresolved complaints.[108]

If the controller wants to gain Safe Harbor protection for its E.U.-based human resources information, it may do so only if a government body has
jurisdiction over claims relating to that data. The
controller also must indicate a desire to include
human resources data in its self-certification and
make itself subject to relevant E.U. authorities.

The DOC maintains a list of all data controllers
who have self-certified. The list is updated through
the use of annual statements from controllers certi-
fying that they are still in compliance with the
Principles and noting any changes that have occurred. Data received while a controller is certified
under the Safe Harbor must continue to receive
Safe Harbor protections even if the controller later
leaves the Safe Harbor. Where a data controller
that is currently operating under the Safe Harbor
will be merged into, or taken over by, another
organization which does not enjoy Safe Harbor status, the DOC must be notified in advance as to
whether the new controller will continue the exist-

108.   Safe Harbor, 65 Fed. Reg. at 45,669–70.

ing Safe Harbor protections, make a new self-certification, or provide some other safeguards such as
creating a written guarantee of adherence to the
Principles. If the new controller does not wish to
comply, it must delete all personal data received
under the terms of the Safe Harbor.

A critical point about this process is that it relies
entirely on the honesty of the party making the
certification. As the DOC itself states on the Safe
Harbor website:

> In maintaining the [Safe Harbor] list, the Depart-
> ment of Commerce does not assess and makes no
> representation as to the adequacy of any organi-
> zation's privacy policy or its adherence to that
> policy. Furthermore, the Department of Com-
> merce does not guarantee the accuracy of the list
> and assumes no liability for the erroneous inclu-
> sion, misidentification, omission, or deletion of
> any organization, or any other action related to
> the maintenance of the list.[109]

The seventh FAQ asks, "[h]ow do organizations
provide follow up procedures for verifying [compli-
ance] . . . with the Safe Harbor Principles?"[110] A
data controller may meet the verification requirements of the Enforcement Principle through either
self-assessment or a compliance audit by a third
party. A self-assessment must indicate that the
controller's privacy statement is "accurate, comprehensive, prominently displayed, completely imple-

109.   *See* U.S. Dep't of Com., *Safe Harbor Workbook, available
at* http://www.export.gov/safeharbor/sh_workbook.html.

110.   Safe Harbor, 65 Fed. Reg. at 45,670.

mented and accessible." Furthermore, the self-assessment must show the controller's privacy policy meets the conditions of the Principles, that data subjects are informed as to how they may make complaints, that employees are trained in the privacy policy and are disciplined for failing to follow it, and that there are internal means for "conducting objective reviews of compliance" with the aforementioned requirements. Annually, a corporate officer or other authorized representative of the controller must sign a statement confirming the self-assessment. This document must be kept on file and be made available to individuals upon request or in the event of an investigation concerning whether the company's conduct and certification were proper.

A compliance audit must demonstrate that the controller's privacy policy conforms to the Principles, is being complied with, and that data subjects are told how they may make complaints. There is no prescribed method for how such a review should be conducted. An annual statement confirming that the audit has been satisfactorily completed should be signed by the reviewer or an authorized representative of the controller and made available upon request or in case of investigation.

The eighth FAQ is divided into eleven sub-questions concerning the Access Principle. Summarized briefly, there is not an absolute right of access.[111] Instead, data subjects are limited by questions of "proportionality or reasonableness." The Access

111. *See* Safe Harbor, 65 Fed. Reg. at 45,670–72.

Principle does not require the same degree of thoroughness as a response to a subpoena. Rather, the controller should work to provide only the information specifically requested by the subject. If a request for information is vague or extremely broad, it is appropriate for the controller to ask the subject questions that will help narrow the focus of the request. Importantly, individuals requesting access to their own personal data are under no obligation to justify their petitions. The amount of effort expended by the controller should be dependent upon the significance of the request by the subject. "Confidential commercial information"[112] may be denied to a subject.

"Access" merely means disclosure of information to the subject.[113] The controller does not have to permit literal physical access to databases or other repositories of information. The controller may deny information to a subject where important public interests, such as law enforcement investigations, would be impacted or where other limitations on disclosure, such as professional privilege, would apply. Access may also be refused where the costs or efforts involved would be disproportionate or excessive, although controllers are entitled to charge reasonable fees for providing information to the subject and may limit requests to a certain number of times per period. The burden is on the controller

112.   "Confidential commercial information" is defined as "information which an organization has taken steps to protect from disclosure, where disclosure would help a competitor in the market." Safe Harbor, 65 Fed. Reg. at 45,671.

113.   Id. at 45,671.

to demonstrate why access should be restricted. An example of a legitimate reason for denying access would be where personal data is inextricably bound up with confidential commercial information, such as marketing data. Responses to access requests should be made "within a reasonable time period."[114]

The ninth FAQ concerns human resources information and is divided into four sub-questions.[115] The Safe Harbor covers personal data collected as part of an employment relationship in the EU and transmitted to the United States. A data controller may only disclose such information, or use it for a purpose other than for which it was originally collected, if it conforms to the Notice and Choice Principles. The data collected may be subject to specific national data protection legislation that will impose additional restrictions on its use above and beyond the limitations of the Safe Harbor. Controllers "should make reasonable efforts to accommodate employee privacy preferences," including anonymizing data or otherwise dissociating it from the employee's identity if feasible. Complaints about misuse of E.U. employee data are to be handled according to the national data protection legislation where the employee is located.

The tenth FAQ asks, "[w]hen data is transferred from the [European Union] to the United States only for processing purposes, will a contract be

114.   Safe Harbor, 65 Fed. Reg. at 45,672.

115.   Safe Harbor, 65 Fed. Reg. at 45,672. All references to the ninth and tenth FAQs are found in the Safe Harbor.

required, regardless of participation by the processor in the Safe Harbor?" The answer is yes; however, data controllers are instructed to remember that the contract is intended for their own protection from liability in the event that the data processor mishandles the data. A U.S. processor is not directly responsible for applying the Principles, as they will be encapsulated in the required contract with the E.U. controller. However, processors that are not enrolled in the Safe Harbor may be subject to pre-authorization requirements by the Member States, substantially delaying operations. By joining the Safe Harbor, the processor may enjoy faster approval of such contracts.

The eleventh FAQ asks, "[h]ow should the dispute resolution requirements of the Enforcement Principle be implemented, and how will an organization's persistent failure to comply with the Principles be handled?" A data controller may meet the Enforcement Principle's requirements in any of three ways:

(1) [c]ompliance with private sector developed privacy program that incorporate the Safe Harbor Principles in their rules and that include effective enforcement mechanisms ...; (2) compliance with legal or regulatory supervisory authorities that provide for handling of individual complaints and dispute resolution; or (3) commitment to cooperate with data protection authorities located in the European Union or their authorized representatives.[116]

116.   Safe Harbor, 65 Fed. Reg. at 45,673.

Controllers should encourage data subjects to raise concerns with them before proceeding to contact other enforcement bodies. The enforcement process should function with great independence from the controller or processor, as demonstrated by such matters as "transparent composition and financing or a proven track record."

Any remedies provided must have the effect of reversing or correcting the breach of the Principles vis-à-vis the data subject and ensure that future processing will be in compliance. A range of penalties would best serve private sector regulatory bodies so that they may respond with some finesse based on how egregious the breach is. A private sector regulatory body must alert the appropriate government agency if a controller subject to the Safe Harbor refuses to comply with its rulings. The FTC will review referrals by such regulatory bodies and E.U. Member States to determine whether a controller has violated Section 5 of the FTC Act concerning unfair or deceptive trade practices.[117] These reviews are to be made on a priority basis. If the FTC determines a violation has occurred, it may obtain an administrative cease-and-desist order addressing the bad conduct or file a compliant with a federal district court. As discussed above in Chapter 3, Part II(E)(1), the FTC may assess its own penalties. The FTC is required to notify the DOC of any action it takes to penalize a failure to comply with the Safe Harbor's Principles.

117. Safe Harbor, 65 Fed. Reg. at 45,673.

If a data controller "persistently fails to comply with the Principles," then it is no longer entitled to the benefits of the Safe Harbor.[118] "Persistent failure to comply" results when a controller refuses to obey a final determination by any private sector regulatory body or a government agency or where such an organization has found that the controller has failed to comply with the Principles so frequently that its claim of compliance is no longer credible. The DOC must be notified by the controller about the finding, and failure to do so may be punishable under the Fraud and False Statements Act, 18 U.S.C. § 1001. After receiving notice of a persistent failure to comply, the DOC must grant the controller thirty days to respond, after which, assuming the matter is not resolved satisfactorily, the controller will be cited on the Safe Harbor list for persistent failure to comply and be stripped of Safe Harbor benefits. A controller that has received a citation and later seeks enrollment in another private sector regulatory body must provide that body with a complete accounting of its previous participation in the Safe Harbor. The exact dynamics of the enforcement of the Safe Harbor remain unclear. In over seven years of operation, no entity registered with the Safe Harbor has been subject to an enforcement action or otherwise cited for failure to comply.

The twelfth FAQ asks, "[d]oes the Choice Principle permit an individual to exercise choice only at the beginning of a relationship or at any time?" A

118.   Safe Harbor, 65 Fed. Reg. at 45,674.

data subject should have the right to opt out of having her data used for direct marketing at any time, subject to reasonable limits related to processing. A controller may also request information to confirm the identity of the subject before permitting the subject to opt out. If it is not feasible to contact subjects before using their data for direct mailings, the mailing itself should offer them a means to opt out of future mailings.

The thirteenth FAQ asks, "[w]hen can ... travel information, such as frequent flyer or hotel reservation information ... , be transferred to organizations located outside the [European Union]?" If a data controller has joined the Safe Harbor such data may be automatically transferred, subject only to specific national data protection legislation. If the controller has not joined the Safe Harbor, then the transfer must be "necessary to provide the services requested by the consumer or to fulfill the terms of an agreement" or, alternatively, the transfer can be made if the data subject/traveler has given unambiguous consent. An example of a transfer "necessary to provide the services requested by the consumer," would be participation in a frequent flyer program.

The fourteenth FAQ deals with medical privacy concerns and is divided into seven sub-questions.[119] Medical data gathered from individual E.U. residents is subject to the national data protection legislation of the Member State where they reside and becomes subject to the Principles when trans-

119.   Safe Harbor, 65 Fed. Reg. at 45,674–75.

mitted to the United States. To minimize the likelihood of breaching the Safe Harbor, data controllers are instructed to anonymize personal data concerning medical care/conditions when possible. Where the data has been gathered as part of a particular medical research project, the Notice and Choice Principles must be met before the data is employed in a different research project. Since future lines of research are not always predictable, a general clause stating that the personal data collected from the subject may be used in other forms of research is acceptable unless the purposes of the new research project prove inconsistent with the original purpose.[120]

Finally, the fifteenth FAQ asks, "[i]s it necessary to apply the Notice, Choice and Onward Transfer Principles to public record information or publicly available information?"[121] The answer is no, so long as the public data is not combined with personal data and there are no restrictions imposed by specific national data protection legislation. Data controllers suffer no liability under the Principles if they obtain data from published sources, but if controllers intentionally publish personal data for the purpose of removing it from the scope of the Safe Harbor, they will lose their Safe Harbor certification.

120.   Safe Harbor, 65 Fed. Reg. at 45,674.

121.   Id. at 45,675.

(b) The Safe Harbor's Scope

The Safe Harbor is a completely voluntary self-regulatory program, thus no entity is legally required to join it under U.S. law. Because of the scope of the Data Protection Directive any business that has contact with E.U. residents on anything other than an anonymous cash-only basis, has effectively collected some form of personal data and thus would be subject to the Data Protection Directive. In the realm of e-commerce, any organization that operates a Web site and collects information from websurfers for commercial purposes, including serving advertising to them, will be at risk of violating the Directive if an E.U. resident should happen to visit the site. On the other hand, the Safe Harbor is limited to only those entities that are subject to FTC or DOC regulatory jurisdiction, since they are the only two U.S. administrative agencies recognized to enforce it. Certain types of businesses, including telecommunications common carriers or insurance companies are ineligible and must pursue alternative means of complying with the Data Protection Directive.[122]

3. Regulation of airline passenger data

Following the terrorist attacks of September 11, 2001, the Aviation and Transportation Security Act ("ATSA") was passed by Congress.[123] ATSA re-

122. *See* U.S. Dep't of Com., *Safe Harbor Workbook, available at* http://www.export.gov/safeharbor/sh_workbook.html (last visited Jan. 28, 2008) (identifying types of businesses not subject to FTC or DOT authority).

123. Pub. L. No. 107–71, 115 Stat. 597 (2001) (codified as amended in scattered sections of Title 49, U.S.C.).

quired the Department of Homeland Security ("DHS") to promulgate regulations to be followed by airlines for international flights landing at U.S. airports. Among the regulations implemented by DHS is 19 C.F.R. § 122.49a to d, collectively referred to as the "Passenger Manifest provision."

The Passenger Manifest provision requires that an airline provide to the U.S. Commissioner of Customs, or other designee, a passenger and crew manifest for any international flight bound for the United States prior to the departure of the flight. As part of this manifest, airlines are required to provide the full names of passengers, date of birth, sex, nation of citizenship and residence, passport information, and other personal data. Airlines that fail to provide the information required face fines or the possibility of losing landing rights at all of the United States' airports.

The adoption of the Passenger Manifest provision immediately caused tension with the European Union, as it set up a sharp conflict with the E.U. Data Protection Directive's restrictions on the collection and use of E.U. residents' personal information. In 2003, as the DHS pressed forward with plans to begin enforcement of the Passenger Manifest provision, the E.U. Parliament passed a resolution denouncing both the scope of the data collected and the apparent inadequacy of protection against misuse of personal information once received by U.S. authorities.[124] Airlines operating flights between

124. European Parliament Resolution on Transfer of Personal Data by Airlines to the US Immigration Service, 2003 O.J. (C

points in the United States and the European Union were naturally put in the awkward position of deciding whether to disclose passenger information and face fines or even criminal penalties from E.U. Member States, or to withhold the information and face fines in the United States and possible revocation of their landing rights.

The conflict seemed to be resolved in May of 2004 when the United States and the E.U. Commission and Council reached agreements, which made the sharing of passenger information subject to usage limitations and retention policies.[125] Yet still dissatisfied with the level of protection afforded E.U. residents' personal data, the E.U. Parliament sued the Commission and the Council in a proceeding before the European Court of Justice arguing that the agreements were in conflict with the Data Protection Directive, and beyond the scope of authority conferred on the Commission to negotiate agreements with other nations concerning the handling of personal data. The Court of Justice agreed with the Parliament's analysis and annulled the agreements in a 2006 ruling.[126]

61), 381 (2003), *available at* http://europa.eu/bulletin/en/200310/p 103041.htm.

125.   Commission Decision 2004/535/EC of 14 May 2004 on the adequate protection of personal data contained in the Passenger Name Record of air passengers transferred to the United States Bureau of Customs and Border Protection (O.J. 2004 L 235, p. 11).

126.   Joined Cases C–317/04 and C–318/04, European Parliament v. Council of the European Union, O.J. C 178 (May 30, 2006).

The Court of Justice decision compelled the United States and E.U. Council to negotiate further and establish a new agreement governing the transfer of airline passenger information. Adopted July 23, 2007, the new agreement permits DHS to collect personal information pursuant to the Passenger Manifest provision, but places greater restrictions on its ability to use or retain such information beyond an initial screening of passenger identities.[127] The E.U. Parliament registered an objection to the agreement before it even took effect, but through early 2008, the Parliament had not commenced litigation to try and set it aside.[128]

B.   Business Developments

1.   *Outsourcing*

Outsourcing may be defined as a the transfer of responsibility for execution of a business activity from one organization to an external service provider which assumes a primary role in performing the activity and returns a value-added product or service. Historically, outsourcing was primarily associated with manufactured products, but with declin-

127.   Agreement between the European Union and the United States of America on the processing and transfer of Passenger Name Record (PNR) data by air carriers to the United States Department of Homeland Security (DHS) (2007 PNR Agreement), O.J. L 204/18.

128.   European Parliament Resolution on the Passenger Name Records (PNR) Agreement with the United States of America, Bulletin EU 7/8–2007: 1.10.18 (2007), *available at* http://europa.eu/bulletin/en/200707/p110018.htm.

ing communication costs and the ability to easily transmit documents at near instantaneous speeds, services are increasingly subject to outsourcing as well. Outsourcing services on an international basis has become particularly attractive given "transportation" costs are almost non-existent, thus profit margins realized from wage differentials can be even greater than for manufactured products.

While outsourcing is, all things being equal, generally a good strategy for increasing profits in those service sectors that can be performed remotely, it also poses significant privacy challenges. Many of the services businesses consider outsourcing, including medical transcription, payroll record management, or insurance claim processing, implicate personal information of customers or employees. Compounding this situation further is that, given the increasingly multinational nature of many businesses, personal information (both customer and employee) may have been collected in multiple nations and be subject to different privacy protection regimes. This poses the possibility of a business inadvertently committing violations of numerous laws. For example, if an E.U. resident purchases shares listed on the Toronto Stock Exchange through the Canadian branch of a U.S.-headquartered brokerage house, and the brokerage house transmits the information concerning that transaction to an outside vendor in India for processing, it is possible the brokerage house has almost simultaneously violated (a) the E.U. Member State's national data protection legislation enacted pursuant to the Data Protection Directive, (b) PIPEDA; and (c) the Gramm–Leach–Bliley Act.[129] Strategies for dealing with this challenge break down into four principle approaches.

The first is the "ostrich" approach. Companies using this approach, assuming they are even fully aware of the intricacies of the statutes and regulations affecting their collection, use, or retransmission of personal information, ignore the problems they are facing and simply proceed with their activities. Although no systematic study has been made of business strategies for coping with the challenge of international transfers of personal information, what evidence exists suggests this approach is the most popular. By way of example, although the U.S./E.U. Safe Harbor has been open for registration for over seven years, fewer than 1,400 businesses are currently enrolled in it. While this approach may seem surprising in light of the general reputation of businesses being cautious with regard to liability exposure, it is a rational approach in the short term. Enforcement of privacy laws in the context of international transactions has been virtually non-existent, except in cases of serious criminal conduct. The cost of compliance, thus, can be significantly greater than the costs of non-compliance when the latter is adjusted for the very low risk of being held accountable for violations. Anecdotal accounts suggest that many European corporate enti-

129. In this example, the U.S./E.U. Safe Harbor is not implicated because the customer's transaction would be regulated by the SEC rather than the FTC and thus be outside the Safe Harbor's scope.

ties actually take this approach, retain appropriate privacy counsel, and ultimately pay whatever fines are assessed. How viable this approach will remain in the long run is questionable though, as agencies within the European Union have been pressing to bring test cases to deter precisely this sort of attitude.

A second approach has been termed the "Just in Time" approach. Companies using this approach deal with privacy issues in outsourcing as problems are brought to their attention. A typical example of this sort of approach arises when a Canadian customer informs a U.S.-based vendor that it will require compliance with PIPEDA from the vendor before continuing to do business. This approach allows companies to deal with challenges on a more manageable level, but at the risk of creating contradictory or incomplete internal processes. The vendor in the example above, after making the requested changes, would still be at risk of violating the Data Protection Directive if it was also collecting personal information from E.U. customers, since PIPEDA compliance by a U.S. business has no impact on the legality of transfers between the European Union and the United States.

The third approach sometimes called the "E.U. Gambit," has companies simply complying with the Data Protection Directive, relying on the fact that there is substantial overlap between the Directive and most other data protection regimes. While of course this strategy is effective when dealing with parties located in E.U. Member States, it is still an incomplete approach.[130] National variations still result in compliance gaps and, when the onward transfer restrictions of the Data Protection Directive are factored in, a business relaying personal information from E.U. residents to a third party in another country might still be violating the Directive even if its internal compliance is sufficient.

The final approach is the "audit" strategy. Under this approach, companies conduct audits on their privacy compliance. The audits analyze three things: (1) the privacy protection regime in each jurisdiction where the company collects or processes personal information; (2) the categories of personal information the company collects; and (3) the internal procedures the company employs for handling the information and the procedures its outsourcing vendors use in handling transferred information. The purpose of the audit approach is to permit a company to segregate personal information by its point of origin and treat each category of information with the necessary level of care to comply with the law of the country of origin. This approach can be characterized as a "best practice" and, while undoubtedly the least compatible with the *laissez-faire* principles underlying outsourcing, widespread

130.   It bears mention that even in that instance the strategy is not completely safe. As discussed in Chapter 4, Part III(A)(2) concerning the Data Protection Directive and the Safe Harbor, each E.U. Member State has enacted its own variant of the Directive and compliance with the bare terms of the Directive without Safe Harbor certification or being subject to PIPEDA (or equivalent legislation approved by the E.U. Commission) will be insufficient.

voluntary implementation may be the most effective means to head off more restrictive regulation.

2. Data havens

One of the latest developments affecting privacy concerns is the "data haven." Data havens are either complex internet structures, or even entire political entities, which are intended to serve as a "safe haven" from the regulatory authority of another jurisdiction. Data havens serve to put online gambling, pornography, copyright infringement, and political speech, outside the reach of local or national regulation. Data havens usually take two forms: centralized and decentralized. Both types of data haven are heavily reliant on the rise of inexpensive international communications and widely available Internet access. The most famous centralized data haven is HavenCo. One of the many decentralized data havens is Freenet.

(a) HavenCo

HavenCo was established in May of 2000 on the self-styled Principality of Sealand. HavenCo has been described as "the world's first truly offshore, almost-anything-goes electronic data haven—a place that occupies a tantalizing gray zone between what's legal and what's ... possible."[131] The Principality of Sealand is located in international waters off the southeast coast of Great Britain, in the

131. Simson Garfinkel, *Welcome to Sealand, Now Bugger Off*, WIRED, July 2000, at 230.

North Sea. Originally named Fort Rough Towers, Sealand was constructed as an anti-aircraft platform for the defense of the British coast against German air raids during World War II. After the end of the war, British troops were sent home and Fort Rough Towers lay abandoned until September 2, 1967, when a former English army major occupied the artificial island with his family. After an extensive legal battle over ownership of the property, the British courts concluded they lacked jurisdiction outside British territorial boundaries and declined to exercise authority over the dispute. The British government since that time has not attempted to intervene in Sealand's affairs, thus leading to what Sealand's government characterizes as recognition as an independent state, although no national government officially recognizes it. Sealand subsequently created the business HavenCo to manage Sealand's Local Internet Registry and information systems.

HavenCo does not sell data haven services on a "retail" level, but rather operates servers and other large-scale computer and network connectivity facilities, which it leases to third-party businesses and organizations to provide a secure location for the storage of sensitive data. HavenCo is subject to Sealand's laws, which, with regard to illicit materials, including child pornography or copyright piracy, substantially mirror those of the United Kingdom and the European Union. Its services cannot be formally used in an unlawful manner. What is significant in regard to privacy concerns is that Sealand does not permit outside access to its territory except under tightly controlled circumstances.[132] This means that the data of HavenCo customers is, theoretically at least, beyond the reach of legal process by other sovereigns unless Sealand concludes that a failure to cooperate would jeopardize its security.

This latter point is the greatest flaw in the concept of centralized data havens—the security of information held by them is ultimately dependent on the goodwill of the operator and its calculation that it is more advantageous to protect the privacy of users than to compromise its reputation. While there are no confirmed instances of Sealand compelling HavenCo to hand over user information to other parties, this sort of uncertainty has contributed to the popularity of decentralized data havens, particularly those built on an "open source" basis, where even the original creators lack control over their operations.

(b) Freenet

Freenet is one of many popular decentralized data havens developed in recent years. Freenet is software that permits its users to obtain information by encrypting and routing the information in a manner calculated to conceal the sender and recipient, as well as the actual contents of the communication. Users of Freenet become part of the data haven by

132. Principality Notice: Persons seeking general visits or residence, PN 036/07 (May 1, 2007).

downloading the appropriate software application and committing a portion of their hard drive and bandwidth to be available to other users. Other users may then upload and download data from the Freenet portion of the user's drive.

While this is similar to the general structure of traditional peer-to-peer file sharing systems, Freenet differs in several important aspects for purposes of shielding its users' privacy. In addition to "anonymizing" features, users have no control over what files are stored on their computers by Freenet, and also no knowledge as to what specific information is being saved in the Freenet portion of their drive. All files are stored and transmitted in encrypted formats. The Freenet folder on a user's computer is effectively a "black box;" and, depending on the amount of space allocated on the drive, it could contain anything from digital photos and music to copies of entire operating systems.

CHAPTER FIVE

CURRENT PRIVACY CHALLENGES, DEVELOPING TECHNOLOGIES & FUTURE TRENDS

With the quickening pace of technological development, any attempt to divide challenges to privacy into concrete categories of present, imminent, and remote-but-approaching, threats, is by its very nature an exercise in artifice. However, there are certain issues that are clearly more manifest than others. This chapter explores these ongoing and upcoming challenges and contemplates what lies ahead in the field of privacy law.

I. CURRENT PRIVACY CHALLENGES

A. Identity Theft

Identity theft occurs when someone poses as another person by using that person's personal information without his or her permission. Although the term "identity theft" was coined relatively recently, the concept of impersonating an individual to realize undeserved gain has existed since ancient times, being reflected in such sources as the biblical account of Jacob impersonating his brother Esau to gain their dying father's blessing. What has made identity theft an increasing problem is the ease with which it can now be committed on a massive scale due to technological changes. Identity theft once required such risky acts as physically stealing a limited number of paper records or actually entering a financial institution in person to complete a transaction with forged documents. Today it can be accomplished remotely and with little risk of apprehension. Complaints filed with the FTC concerning identity theft rose from 31,117 in 2000, to 256,000 in 2005. Furthermore, while identity theft is usually thought of as a crime perpetrated against individuals, it is also an increasing problem for corporations and other organizations.

The difficulty of actually finding and prosecuting identity thieves (who are commonly located in a different country than their victims or are judgment proof), in recent years, has led to litigation against institutions from which the personal information used to commit identity theft was stolen. The central theory behind this litigation is one of shifting "externalities," *i.e.*, costs, to the party best able to bear them. Institutions, particularly those operating domestically in the United States, traditionally had little financial incentive to protect customer or employee information since the theft of information had minimal impact on the institution that actually had the information stolen. It was the customer or employee who usually suffered the greatest injury, along with third parties deceived by the identity thief. However, the institutions that hold personal information are, of course, the parties most able to protect the information. Consequently, litigation against institutions for failure to adequately protect personal information is arguably one of the most dynamic areas of privacy law to develop in recent years.

1. Causes of action for identity theft

(a) Negligence

The most common type of action brought in litigation resulting from identity theft is a negligence claim. The tort of negligence requires a breach of duty, which causes, both actually and proximately, an injury to the party whom the duty was owed. Identity theft negligence claims typically are predicated on one or both of two duties. The first duty is to take precautionary measures to protect the plaintiff's personal information, while the second is to eliminate or correct any incorrect information that has already been attributed to the plaintiff. Courts have found that this duty may arise even in situations where the individual whose personal information is held by the institution is not a customer, employee, or other category of person whom one might expect to be owed a duty.

Remsburg v. Docusearch, 816 A.2d 1001 (N.H. 2003), was a seminal case concerning negligence claims based on a failure to take adequate precautions in the handling of personal information. In *Remsberg*, a stalker employed the help of a company called Docusearch to locate a woman with whom he had become obsessed. The stalker obtained several pieces of personal information concerning the woman from Docusearch, including her Social Security number and work address. Docusearch itself had obtained the information from other sources or from the woman herself under false pretenses. Shortly after receiving the information, the stalker drove to the woman's place of employment and killed her.

The victim's estate sued Docusearch on several theories of liability, including negligence. The New Hampshire Supreme Court found that, given the serious and pervasive threat of stalking and identity theft, "the risk of criminal misconduct is sufficiently foreseeable so that an investigator has a duty to exercise reasonable care in disclosing a third person's personal information to a client." *Remsburg*, 816 A.2d at 1008. A claim for negligence could be based on the unauthorized disclosure of another party's personal information.

(b) Privacy torts

A second theory of liability analyzed in *Remsburg* was whether Docusearch's conduct and that of contractors in its employ could constitute the commission of the tort of intrusion, *i.e.*, an invasion of the victim's privacy interests in a manner as to be offensive to persons of ordinary sensibilities. *See* 816 A.2d at 1008. The New Hampshire Supreme Court concluded that a person could have a protectable privacy interest in a Social Security number, but that the question of whether any particular use or distribution of the number without the permission or knowledge of the number's holder was a sufficiently egregious violation of the victim's privacy interests to be actionable would be a question of fact. The court, however, rejected the argument that the plaintiff could have a claim based on the disclosure of the victim's place of employment because, while individuals could reasonably expect their Social Security numbers to be kept private, places of employment are usually public in nature and thus the victim could not reasonably assume that information was private.

An alternative privacy tort that has been pled with some success in the context of identity theft, even in the absence of specific evidence that identity theft has occurred, is that of public disclosure of private facts. In *Shqeirat v. United States Airways Group*, 515 F. Supp. 2d 984 (D. Minn. 2007), a plaintiff included a claim for disclosure in a lawsuit against the Minneapolis Metropolitan Airport Commission. Following an altercation at the Minneapolis airport, the Commission published a police report containing the plaintiff's Social Security number on its official website. *See id.* at 998. The Commission did not dispute that it had made the plaintiff's Social Security number publicly available, but instead moved to dismiss on the grounds that the plaintiff had not sufficiently pled an injury. The United States District Court for the District of Minnesota, applying Minnesota tort law, found that the emotional distress resulting from the threat of identity theft could constitute a sufficient injury to support a claim for disclosure and denied the motion to dismiss.

(c) Infliction of emotional distress

Several courts have entertained claims for infliction of emotional distress as a result of identity theft, but there are as yet no reported instances of a plaintiff having successfully brought such a claim.[1] The difficulty of establishing the elements of intentional infliction of emotional distress in an identity theft situation is the reason these claims have failed so far. In most jurisdictions, a plaintiff must prove that the defendant acted with malice, ill will, or in an extremely outrageous manner and that an actual physical injury, or apprehension of physical harm, resulted. Because identity theft is usually not accompanied by these facts, the claims are typically struck on a motion to dismiss or a motion for summary judgment. This theory of liability still bears mention, however, as none of the courts to consider the issue have suggested such claims are barred *per se*.

(d) Constitutional rights

In the specific context of government handling of personal information, courts have recognized that the threat of identity theft occasioned by govern-

1. *See, e.g.*, Polzer v. TRW, Inc., 682 N.Y.S.2d 194 (N.Y. App. Div 1998); Jones v. Alltel Ohio Ltd. P'ship, 06 CV 02332, 2007 WL 1731321 (N.D. Ohio June 14, 2007).

mental infringement of privacy rights can support a claim under 42 U.S.C. § 1983. In *Tomblin v. Trevino*, No. SA01CA1160–OG, 2003 WL 24125145 (W.D. Tex. Feb. 19, 2003), a plaintiff argued that a local police force's practice of collecting Social Security numbers during routine traffic stops was a Fourth Amendment violation. Noting that the use of Social Security numbers was regulated by statute and that dissemination of an individual's Social Security number posed a significant threat of identity theft, the court concluded that an individual could have a reasonable expectation of privacy in the number. A government actor would require a justifiable basis for collecting information, given the Fourth Amendment privacy interest attached to a Social Security number. Based on testimony from the local police chief and the officer involved in the traffic stop, the court concluded that there was not a sufficiently strong government interest to justify collecting the information in the circumstance of an ordinary traffic stop.

2. Remedies for identity theft

(a) Damages

Although some courts have permitted plaintiffs to proceed with claims arising from identity theft, even in the absence of specific damages resulting from the theft itself, *see*, *e.g.*, *Shqeirat*, 515 F. Supp. 2d at 998 (permitting disclosure claim based on injury in form of fear of identity theft), it appears that the vast majority of claims are dismissed or disposed of by summary judgment due to an inability by the plaintiffs to demonstrate an actual injury. *See Pisciotta v. Old Nat'l Bancorp*, 499 F.3d 629, 635, 639 (7th Cir. 2007) (discussing lack of precedence for finding a mere risk of identity theft to be a compensable injury). For a successful claim, a plaintiff must prove that the breach of duty by the defendant resulted in both an exposure of personal information, and that the exposure resulted in a use of the personal information in a manner that caused an injury. This effectively means that most large-scale incidents in which the security of personal information is compromised will not be compensable because it is quite rare that a specific injury can be traced to the breach.

(b) Restitution

Actual damages resulting from identity theft are difficult to prove and even if demonstrated, often do not fully compensate victims for costs incurred in correcting the damage to their credit and financial standing. A number of states, therefore, have enacted statutes that require identity thieves to pay restitution to their victims. "Restitution" in this context refers to costs incurred by identity theft victims which are the consequence of the theft, but which do not result directly from the theft. In Delaware, for example, identity thieves may be ordered to pay a victim's lost wages and reasonable attorney fees incurred as a result of the theft.[2]

2. 11 DEL. CODE § 854(e).

Maryland also allows reasonable attorney fees, costs for clearing the victim's credit history, and costs incurred to satisfy debts, judgments, or liens against the victim that resulted from the defendant's actions.[3]

B. Pretexting

"Pretexting" is the act of creating and utilizing an invented scenario (the pretext) to persuade a target to give information or perform an action. Typically, pretexting is more than a simple lie, but usually involves prior research and the use of pieces of known information to establish legitimacy in the mind of the target, so as to increase the likelihood that he or she will reveal the sought after information. Like identity theft, pretexting is not in and of itself a new phenomenon. Mythology is replete with tales of characters gaining information on the weaknesses of others by posing as an innocent third party. Technology has simply made pretexting far more feasible because of the ease by which it can be remotely accomplished.

Pretexting has been addressed through two major pieces of legislation. Under the GLB,[4] it is illegal to use forged or stolen documents or false statements to obtain customer information from a financial institution or directly from a customer of a financial institution. The GLB Act also criminalizes the same conduct by intermediaries. Congress recently passed

3. Md. Crim. L. Code Ann. § 8–301(g).

4. 15 U.S.C. §§ 6801 to 6809.

the Telephone Records and Privacy Protection Act ("TRPPA") in reaction to the revelation that the management of Hewlett–Packard had employed private investigators who used pretexting to obtain the telephone records of board members and members of the media as part of efforts by Hewlett–Packard's management to investigate leaks of internal discussions.[5] The TRPPA specifically criminalizes making false or fraudulent statements to a telephone service provider or providing false or fraudulent documents to a telephone service provider in an attempt to gain a third party's telephone records.

C. Phishing

"Phishing" is a broad term covering any sort of internet fraud scheme designed to trick the recipient into revealing credit card account information, passwords, Social Security numbers, and other personal information to individuals who intend to use them for fraudulent purposes. Phishing typically involves communications (particularly e-mails) made to appear as if they have come from a reputable source, whether a government agency, such as the IRS, or a commercial source, like the victim's bank. The communications often instruct the recipient to verify or update account information by requesting a reply to the e-mail with updated information, or by providing the recipient with a link to a website where the new information may be entered. Regardless of type, phishing schemes are

5. Pub. L. No. 109–476, 120 Stat. 3568 (Jan. 12, 2007).

typically dealt with via traditional laws governing fraud or criminal impersonation. The most commonly encountered types of phishing schemes include:

False e-mail messages: The message appears to be from a company that the target does business with, warning that they need to verify account information, and if the information is not provided the account will be suspended. Customers of eBay and Paypal are two of the most targeted groups for this type of phishing scheme, but the approach can be applied to the customers of any business. Although many companies now specifically warn customers that they do not request personal information via e-mails, this remains the most popular variety of phishing scheme, likely because it is the most simple to execute. Many companies now have phishing watch groups that monitor this area, and upon discovery, immediately notify the ISP where the e-mail originated, as well as any appropriate law enforcement.

False escrow sites: This occurs when items are put up for sale at a legitimate online auction to lure the target into making payments to a fake escrow site rather than through the auction provider's regular payment channel. This scheme is more time consuming and elaborate than a simple e-mail, but it has the potential to collect more information, particularly if the phisher actually sends the merchandise that was ordered so that the target does not associate a later instance of fraud with the transaction where the personal information was collected.

False charities: The fraudster in this type of phishing scheme poses as a charity and asks for direct monetary donations. These schemes most commonly flourish in the wake of major disasters and around holidays when people are likely to be in a particularly generous spirit. While seemingly the most foolproof scheme, since the targets are usually not expecting to receive anything in return, genuine charities vigorously search for evidence of such activities and typically are better able to pressure law enforcement agencies to conduct investigations of suspected charity fraud. The substantially higher risk of law enforcement becoming involved causes this type of phishing scheme to remain less popular with fraudsters.

False websites: This scheme uses websites made to look similar to legitimate sites or having web addresses that are sufficiently similar to popular sites that they may be accidentally reached by mistyping an address. In a few particularly extreme cases, phishers have hacked the websites of legitimate enterprises and reconfigured them so that visitors are redirected to the phishers' false websites. In any of these variants, the websites will typically contain false login screens designed to convince visitors to type in their usernames and passwords. The website may also attempt to download spyware onto the target's computer, whether covertly or by representing that the target needs to download a particular software application to use the site. This type of phishing scheme is often paired with the use of false e-mails to drive traffic to the site, and can include a "man in the middle" attack which intercepts login information entered into a legitimate website after passing through the phisher's false site.

II. DEVELOPING TECHNOLOGIES

Beyond making traditional challenges to privacy more prevalent, technology is also creating entirely new challenges. Justice Brandeis foresaw this possibility eighty years ago in his dissent from *Olmstead v. United States*:

> The progress of science in furnishing the government with means of espionage is not likely to stop with wire tapping. Ways may some day be developed by which the government, without removing papers from secret drawers, can reproduce them in court, and by which it will be enabled to expose to a jury the most intimate occurrences of the home. Advances in the psychic and related sciences may bring means of exploring unexpressed beliefs, thoughts and emotions.

277 U.S. at 474 (Brandeis, J. dissenting). While Brandeis was warning solely against the actions of law enforcement agencies, the same forces which drive the continuously declining cost and increasing ease of use that applies to consumer goods, also applies to technologies which can impact individual privacy. While government actors will likely always remain the largest single threat to privacy interests,

technology has "democratized" surveillance in manners never before seen, and which will likely continue to accelerate in the future.

A. Keystroke Logging

1. *Technological overview*

The practice of keystroke logging or "keylogging" broadly refers to monitoring, collecting, and transmitting the keystrokes a user sends to a computer through the keyboard. There are three general types of keylogging devices: (1) software; (2) hardware physically connected between the keystroke input device and computer; and (3) wireless devices.

Software-based keyloggers send user information back to the surveilling party over the Internet or other network connection. Most typically, keylogging software is installed on a computer through spyware that has been inadvertently downloaded. The software often collects not just keystroke information, but also the infected user's IP address and other information. Depending on their sophistication, software keyloggers can be detected by antivirus software or other types of software designed to monitor malicious programming. Software keyloggers, even if successfully installed, can also potentially be foiled by the infected user's firewall program.

Hardware-based keyloggers are devices that may be inserted into the keyboard socket in the back of the computer or can be planted within the keyboard case itself. Hardware-based keyloggers benefit from the ability to store massive amounts of information, upwards of 2 million keystrokes for the most powerful units. Physical keyloggers also have the advantage of being undetectable by antivirus programs or similar software. However, these types of keyloggers must be planted by physically accessing the machine and can be visibly spotted by a user or IT maintenance personnel, therefore these devices are not a preferred technique for malicious parties. Employers most commonly install hardware-based keyloggers to monitor employees' computer use.

2. *Privacy implications*

Keylogging can theoretically compromise any type of data that is entered via a keyboard, whether it is a user login, a credit card number, or detailed health information. The principal limitation on the technology, whether software or hardware-based, is that the context of the keystrokes may not be deducible without other information. Despite this limitation, at least one-third of computer crimes are attributed to keylogging of some sort. As consumers become more comfortable using computers to pass private information to banks, bill-paying services, and online stores, the chances for malicious use of keylogging software only increases.

The use of keylogging for purposes of government surveillance has also recently come under significant scrutiny. *United States v. Scarfo*, 180 F. Supp. 2d 572 (D.N.J. 2001) represents the leading federal case dealing with the intersection of the personal right of privacy under the Fourth Amendment, and the use of keylogging software to collect evidence in support of a criminal prosecution.

Scarfo and an associate were under investigation by the FBI for allegedly running an illegal gambling and loansharking operation. Pursuant to federal warrants, FBI agents entered Scarfo's office to search for evidence related to illegal gambling and loan sharking. The search revealed a personal computer suspected to contain crucial evidence of the crimes, but the needed files were protected by encryption software. The FBI later received additional warrants, returned to Scarfo's business, and installed keylogging software on the computer. The software allowed the FBI to capture the passphrase to the encrypted file, and subsequently decrypt incriminating evidence after executing a third set of warrants to retrieve the computer. The evidence was deemed sufficient to indict Scarfo on charges for gambling and loansharking.

Scarfo challenged the use of keylogging software and moved to suppress evidence on three theories, with two implicating the personal right of privacy, specifically: (1) that use of keylogging was a violation of the Fourth Amendment's prohibition on general warrants; and (2) the keylogging software was an unlawful interception of a wire communications in violation of Federal law.[6] The court found Scarfo's arguments unpersuasive.

6.   Scarfo, 180 F. Supp. 2d at 576.

Scarfo's argument concerning general warrants was that the keylogger did not just capture the keystrokes of the passphrase to decrypt the files the FBI was seeking to access, but also all other keystrokes entered on the computer during the time the software was operating. The court acknowledged that the Fourth Amendment prohibits general search warrants. The Fourth Amendment requires the language of the warrant to describe with "particularity ... the area and items to be searched and/or seized."[7] The fact that the keylogging software recorded keystrokes other than the keystrokes needed to unlock the encrypted file was of no consequence. It is acceptable during a search for law enforcement agents to review material, later deemed innocuous, to determine whether the object should be seized.

The keylogging software was installed on a computer which connected to the Internet via a modem. This led to Scarfo's argument that the evidence was collected "in violation of the wiretap statute (18 U.S.C. § 2510) by recording keystrokes of e-mail or other communications made over a telephone or cable line while the modem operated."[8] The court rejected this argument for a reason unique to the FBI's keylogging software: the software did not simultaneously collect and transmit keystrokes. Presumably aware of the risk of a wiretap challenge, the "F.B.I. configured the [software] to avoid

7. *Id.* at 577 (citing Torres v. McLaughlin, 163 F.3d 169, 173 (3d Cir. 1998)).

8. *Id.* at 581

intercepting electronic communications typed on the keyboard and simultaneously transmitting in real time via the communication ports."[9] The court concluded that no constitutional or statutory bar existed to the use of evidence collected as a result of the keylogger's activity.

B. Online Profiling
1. *Technological overview*

Online profiling is a nebulous concept subject to many differing definitions. In essence, online profiling is the idea that each time users access online content they create a "digital fingerprint." This "fingerprint" consists of any sort of information that can be considered "personally identifiable," including IP addresses, user names, credit card numbers, physical addresses, etc. Over time, and in aggregate, these digital fingerprints, which can be created consciously through these activities as registering an account with a website and without being aware of the transmission of IP addresses, are combined to construct detailed profiles of users' activities. This information can be packaged and sold or licensed between Internet advertisers and retailers.

Each time a user connects to the Internet, a series of events are set in motion allowing profiling data to be collected. Most methods of connecting to the Internet rely on a process that assigns the user an Internet Protocol ("IP") address. From the IP address, an online profiler is usually able to obtain

9. *Id.* at 581–82.

the domain name associated with the users' Internet service provider ("ISP") or the organization providing the Internet connection. The web browser used also provides significant profiling data to websites for collection purposes. A web browser's "header" often contains not only the user's IP address, but also the time, pages, and images downloaded, the referring website, form data entered by the user during that browsing session, and any "cookie" data relevant to sites previously visited. "Cookie" files are stored on a user's computer to collect website specific information, *e.g.*, registration information, user preferences, sites previously visited, customer codes, etc. Technology inherent to, and embedded in, a web browser also facilitates profile data collection. All of this information can theoretically be concealed or otherwise screened by users, but in practice, most users do not take such precautions.

Any data that a user actively and voluntarily provides to a website is further fodder for profiling activity. Web-based forms, registration, and input allow data to be directly transferred to the sponsoring website. Responses to e-mail marketing and advertising campaigns are tracked, not only to gauge success of the campaign, but also to identify the respondent and track their consumption preferences.

2. *Privacy implications*

At its most innocuous level, online profiling is a benefit for Internet users. It facilitates targeted advertisements for products that the user is more likely to be interested in, tailors results from search engines to highlight results which fit a user's past preferences, and otherwise enhances a user's interaction with websites. Yet online profiling can also be used to learn information that users may generally prefer to keep private, including political or religious views, sexual interests, or medical conditions. Most parties engaged in on-line profiling do not attempt to be selective in the information they gather about users. Indeed, being selective would in large part defeat the purpose of on-line profiling: attempting to extrapolate the user's interests from many disparate pieces of information.

The principal objection to online profiling is the seemingly clandestine nature of the data collection. Although it is now common knowledge that it is possible to monitor users' on-line activities, users are rarely aware of which parties are monitoring their activities, how extensive or limited that monitoring may be, and to what use the collected information will be put. Compounding this problem further is that many websites, particularly commercial sites, are now so heavily dependent on collecting user information that users who have made efforts to anonymize their browsing habits may find the sites unusable. Even sophisticated users often find that they have to compromise on the degree of privacy protection they employ while websurfing.

Attempts to find legal solutions to this issue have been disjointed, but the possibility of some sort of regulation has motivated a number of businesses with strong online presences to form the Network Advertising Initiative ("NAI") to push self-regulatory solutions to avoid more rigid government oversight. The NAI describes itself as a "cooperative of online marketing and analytics companies committed to building consumer awareness and establishing responsible business and data management practices and standards."[10] Central to the NAI's self-regulatory scheme is consumer education and choice. Online advertisers who adhere to the NAI principles through the Online Privacy Alliance ("OPA") Privacy Policy Guidelines for Personally Identifiable Information, must agree that they:

[1] will not use sensitive personally identifiable data for online preference marketing;

[2] will not, without prior affirmative consent ("opt-in"), merge personally identifiable information with information previously collected as non-personally identifiable information;

[3] will provide consumers with robust notice and choice regarding the merger of personally identifiable information with non-personally identifiable information collected on a going forward basis for online preference marketing;

[4] will not use personally identifiable information ("PII") consisting of PII collected offline merged with PII collected online for online preference marketing unless the consumer has been

10. Network Advertising Initiative, *About Us*, *available at* http://www.networkadvertising.org/about.

afforded robust notice and choice about such merger before it occurs; and

[5]   will require Web publishers with which they have contractual relationships to provide notice and choice regarding the collection of non-personally identifiable information for online preference marketing.[11]

The NAI principles have been lauded by the FTC,[12] and represent the current industry standard for privacy protection online outside of specifically regulated fields such as businesses regulated pursuant to the Gramm–Leach–Bliley Act.

C. Radio Frequency Information Device ("RFID")

1. *Technological overview*

A Radio Frequency Information Device ("RFID") is a system that identifies objects, collects data, and transmits information about the object through a "tag." RFIDs consist of three components: a chip, antenna, and a reader. The chip is typically programmed with relatively simple information, including a specific alphanumeric string of characters. The antenna transmits information from the chip to

11.   NETWORK ADVERTISING INITIATIVE, SELF-REGULATORY PRINCIPLES FOR ONLINE PREFERENCE MARKETING BY NETWORK ADVERTISERS § I.B to F, *available at* http://www.networkadvertising.org/pdfs/NAI_principles.pdf.

12.   *See* Federal Trade Commission, *Federal Trade Commission Issues Report on Online Profiling*, July 27, 2000, *available at* http://www.ftc.gov/opa/2000/07/onlineprofiling.shtm.

the reader via radio waves. When the reader comes in close enough proximity to the chip, signals transfer between the two. RFIDs are either active or passive. Passive RFIDs stay inactive until a reader scans the tag. Active RFIDs have energy sources built in, allowing active transmission of information without the need of a reader to initiate the action. The latest generations of the devices, called "extended capability" RFIDs, include the ability to be read at longer distances (up to 50 meters), operate in more extreme environmental conditions, and to be paired with microprocessors on a single chip, enabling much more comprehensive monitoring of the object the RFID is attached to.

The principal purpose of RFIDs is to allow a user to track objects that have been "chipped" or "tagged." In a typical application, the user encodes each RFID chip with an alphanumeric string and then in a separate database the user creates a description of the object that corresponds to that particular alphanumeric string. Each time the "tagged" object is scanned, that alphanumeric string can be relayed from the reader to the database, allowing the user to determine the location of the object at the time of the scan. Depending on the degree of detail in the underlying database, and how distributed its RFID readers are, a user can potentially form a very detailed overview of the object's movements.

2. *Privacy implications*

RFIDs, in of themselves, pose no privacy issues. An RFID chip cannot record information about its surroundings and they typically are not encoded with information that is of use without also having access to an accompanying database providing the information associated with the object to which the chip was attached. The principal privacy concern raised by RFIDs is that they can potentially allow users to track the movement of individuals by tracking the movement of objects in their possession. This concern has been particularly raised in the context of RFID chips being embedded in government identification cards, passports, license plates, or similar items. If one assumes a sufficiently distributed network of RFID readers, it would be feasible to monitor the location of the individual who is associated with the identification card, assuming that it remains at all times in the possession of the owner. Currently, this type of network is speculative, although many nations are introducing RFIDs as part of passport control stations at ports of entry.

Currently, no federal law directly regulates the use of RFIDs. However, New Hampshire, North Dakota, Utah, Virginia, Wisconsin, and Wyoming have passed state legislation restricting the use of RFIDs, with several other states debating legislation.[13] To avoid further regulation, a number of

13. *See* H.R. 203, 159th Gen. Ct., Reg. Sess. (N.H. 2005); S.L. 2007, ch. 122, § 1 (N.D. 2007); H.R. 185, 2005 Leg., Reg. Sess.

industries connected to the manufacture and use of RFIDs have formed EPCglobal, an organization intended to promote the development of industry standards for self-regulation on the use of RFIDs in consumer products. As part of this effort, EPCglobal has developed guidelines to help deal with RFID privacy concerns. The guidelines call for products containing RFIDs to be labeled, the RFID tags to be capable of being disabled or discarded, information about RFIDs to be readily available to the consumer, and for any personal information collected in conjunction with the use of RFIDs to be handled in a manner complying with any applicable laws.[14] The EU is also currently studying RFID technology, and expects to have regulations for its use and an RFID Directive.

D. Online Social Networks ("OSNs")

1. *Technological overview*

Online Social Networks ("OSNs"), also referred to as "social networking sites," are transforming the way individuals interact. The term OSN encompasses any sort of computer network, although most OSNs are Internet-based, that is designed to facilitate personal interaction between its users. While computer users have been able to interact with each

(Utah 2005); S. 148, 2004 Gen. Assem., Reg. Sess. (Va. 2004); Assem. 290, 97th Leg., Reg. Sess. (Wis. 2006); H.R. 258, 58th Leg., Reg. Sess. (Wyo. 2005).

14. EPCglobal, *EPCglobal Guidelines on EPC for Consumer Products, available at* http://www.epcglobalinc.org/public/ppsc_guide/.

other via networked computers or over modems for decades, improvements in bandwidth and user-friendly software have revolutionized the ease and flexibility with which users can share information.

While there are literally hundreds of OSNs world-wide, catering to both general interest users and specialized communities, the largest OSN remains the well-known MySpace. Launched in February 1999, MySpace's membership base reached over 100 million individuals in a mere seven years. MySpace is centered around the concept of user-created on-line profiles, which can include embedded text, photographs, music, and videos. After creating a profile, users can enter into "communities" with other users of the service. Through MySpace communities, individuals can exchange information with other users. While MySpace offers some privacy protection, the degree ultimately realized depends largely on the user. Users can make their information available only to other users designated as "friends" by activating privacy settings built into the software. The alternative is a public profile, which is, as the name implies, open to anyone who visits the site, regardless of whether they are MySpace members. MySpace's user policy prohibits members from posting certain types of personal information; however, enforcement of this policy is heavily dependent on users reporting violations.

LinkedIn, a career and professional networking OSN, faces some of the same privacy issues that MySpace does, but in a different context. Unlike

MySpace, which is a general interest OSN, Linked-In is specifically intended to help professionals make business contacts, whether for potential clients, employers, or employees. When a person joins LinkedIn, they create a profile or resume summarizing professional accomplishments, interests, and educational background. After creating their profiles, users can search for other users by name, e-mail address, company name, industry, or educational institution, and ask to be added to that user's list of "connections."

Similar to MySpace, a user who asks to be part of another user's list of connections must be confirmed by the invitee before being added to the list of connections. A higher level of privacy is provided to LinkedIn users because a user seeking to become part of another users list of connections must provide the e-mail address and name of the person they wish to connect with. If accepted, both connected users may view the users contained in each other's respective list of connections. The actual amount of privacy realized by a user of LinkedIn depends on the amount of information placed on the site. A user can place as little or as much information about their professional background and, for that matter, personal interests, as they like, including preferred websites. This information is searchable by other registered users on the site. Moreover, LinkedIn profiles appear when doing a general search for a particular person using any of the major Internet search engines.

2. *Privacy implications*

The potential privacy issues in using OSNs divide into two principal categories: lack of sophistication on the part of users and vulnerabilities in the OSN software itself. With regard to user sophistication, anecdotal evidence suggests that many users of OSNs are unaware of the ease with which other individuals may access personal information placed on the sites. Although no systematic survey appears to have been made of OSN users regarding their familiarity with the amount of privacy particular OSNs afford,[15] news accounts of employers, business competitors, and other parties retrieving embarrassing information from OSN services are a routine occurrence. A survey of employers in 2007 showed that 45% reported conducting some form of online research concerning job applicants, with 63% of those who conducted such research choosing not to hire the job applicant based in part on the results of that research.[16] While users may feel their privacy has been violated in some manner by these searches, the solution to this problem will lie mainly in the realm of experience and education. OSNs, by their very nature, are intended to permit people to

15. Rick Smith, director of career development at Bradley University in Illinois, has estimated based on informal inquiries that less than half of college students, prime users of OSNs, were aware that potential employers may attempt to review their OSN profiles. Mike Maciag, *Be Careful What You Put On Your Web Site*, JOURNAL STAR, Mar. 4, 2008, 2008 WLNR 4301435.

16. Maciag, supra note 15.

find other people and review personal information they have placed on the sites. Attempts to make OSNs truly "private" are inconsistent with their primary purpose.

Technical vulnerabilities in OSN software mostly involve flaws that facilitate identity theft and phishing issues similar to those discussed in Sections I.A and C above. Many OSNs allow users to embed files and even so-called "widgets" or "applets," software that runs a separate application within a web browser. These items are usually innocuous, consisting of videos, music, or simple computer games. Embedded software can, however, harvest information from the user's browser (lists of sites visited, stored usernames, passwords, etc.) and, in extreme cases, plant spyware on the user's computer, permitting wholesale theft of personal information.

Regulation of privacy issues in the context of OSNs has been limited to concerns about the potential for children using such sites to be harassed or otherwise improperly contacted by adults. This issue gained widespread attention in June 2006, when a 16–year-old girl flew from the United States to Jordan in order to meet a 20–year-old man she met through MySpace after having tricked her parents into getting her a passport.[17] Although no criminal charges were filed in that incident, it did lead to greater scrutiny concerning individuals using OSNs, particularly MySpace, and their motivations. Based on allegations that registered sex of-

17. Alison Hoover, *Keeping MySpace Safe*, WASHINGTON TIMES, A2, June 28, 2006, 2006 WLNR 11202308.

fenders might attempt to use such sites to contact children, a number of state attorneys general opened investigations into what efforts were being made by OSN providers to avoid that problem. On January 14, 2008, the parent company of MySpace entered into an agreement with the attorneys general of 49 states to make a number of changes to how the profiles of minors are displayed and accessed.[18] Whether this sort of negotiated self-regulation becomes a model for other OSNs remains to be seen.

E. Global Navigation Satellite Systems

1. *Technological overview*

The term "global navigation satellite system" refers to any system that relies on a network of orbiting satellites to determine the geographic position of a radio beacon. The only fully deployed global navigation satellite system at present is the U.S. Global Positioning System ("GPS"), but several other such systems are under development.[19] The GPS is composed of twenty-four satellites that each orbit the Earth twice daily. The orbits of the satellites are structured so that four satellites are above

18. *See Joint Statement on Key Principles of Social Networking Sites Safety, available at* http://ago.mo.gov/newsreleases/2008/pdf/MySpace–JointStatement0108.pdf.

19. These other systems include the Russian GLONASS (scheduled to become fully operational in 2009); the E.U. Galileo system (scheduled to become fully operational in 2013); and the proposed Chinese COMPASS and Indian IRNSS.

the horizon relative to any point on Earth at any given time. Each GPS satellite has an atomic clock, and continually transmits a signal containing the current time at the start of the message and information concerning its location in the orbital pattern. A GPS receiver intercepts the satellites' signals. The receiver computes the difference in time between when each signal was transmitted and when it arrived, allowing it to extrapolate the receiver's position relative to each of the satellites. Collating this information from all the satellites allows the receiver to determine its latitude, longitude, and altitude.

GPS receivers can be very compact. Commercially available GPS processing chips as small as 7 millimeters by 6 millimeters have been developed, although display screens, user interfaces, and other features that make the GPS receiver's information usable to human operators inevitably make the devices larger. Once limited to military and high-value commercial use, it has become routine for GPS receivers to be installed in automobiles, cellular phones, and other consumer electronics. The main limitations on the use of GPS receivers is that they are susceptible to having the signal disrupted on a local level by electromagnetic interference or physical obstacles, and they must have a power source to be able to process signal data from the GPS satellites.

2. *Privacy implications*

The major privacy concern with GPS receivers is that, when paired with a computer capable of recording GPS position information, they are capable of producing extremely accurate records of the movement of a vehicle or individual carrying the device. While the privacy implications of the use of GPS have been litigated in both the criminal and civil context, courts have thus far not found that the technology violates any recognized privacy rights, whether constitutional or at common law.

The common thread in these cases is a reliance on the United States Supreme Court's ruling in *United States v. Knotts*, 460 U.S. 276 (1983). *Knotts* predated public access to GPS (although military applications of the system were already being made), and instead concerned the use of a radio tracking device installed on a drum of chemicals as part of a police sting operation. The Supreme Court found that no Fourth Amendment violation resulted from the tracking because a "person traveling in an automobile on public thoroughfares has no reasonable expectation of privacy in his movements from one place to another." 460 U.S. at 281. Subsequent cases concerning GPS tracking have applied the reasoning of *Knotts* to both criminal and civil cases to find that the use of GPS did not present actionable privacy concerns.[20] Recently, however, the Seventh Circuit, in rejecting a privacy challenge, did

20. *See, e.g.*, United States v. Garcia, 474 F.3d 994, 996–98 (7th Cir. 2007) (finding no Fourth Amendment violation where

acknowledge that the proliferation of GPS receivers might eventually present a problem. Judge Posner, writing for the court, concluded his opinion by stating:

> [W]hile the defendant's efforts to distinguish the GPS case [from earlier cases applying other technologies] ... are futile, we repeat our earlier point that there is a difference ... between all three of those situations on the one hand and following suspects around in a car on the other. The new technologies enable, as the old (because of expense) do not, wholesale surveillance. One can imagine the police affixing GPS tracking devices to thousands of cars at random, recovering the devices, and using digital search techniques to identify suspicious driving patterns. One can even imagine a law requiring all new cars to come equipped with the device so that the government can keep track of all vehicular movement in the United States. It would be premature to rule that such a program of mass surveillance could not possibly raise a question under the Fourth Amendment—that it could not be a search because it would merely be an efficient alternative to hiring another 10 million police officers to tail every vehicle on the nation's roads.

* * *

GPS receiver was placed on vehicle by law enforcement agents); Elgin v. St. Louis Coca–Cola Bottling Co., Case No. 4:05CV970–DJS, 2005 WL 3050633, *3 (E.D. Mo. Nov. 14, 2005) (rejecting claim for tort of intrusion based on placement of GPS receiver on vehicle by employer).

Technological progress poses a threat to privacy by enabling an extent of surveillance that in earlier times would have been prohibitively expensive. Whether and what kind of restrictions should, in the name of the Constitution, be placed on such surveillance when used in routine criminal enforcement are momentous issues that fortunately we need not try to resolve in this case. So far as appears, the police of Polk County (a rural county in northwestern Wisconsin), where the events of this case unfolded, are not engaged in mass surveillance. They do GPS tracking only when they have a suspect in their sights. They had, of course, abundant grounds for suspecting the defendant. Should government someday decide to institute programs of mass surveillance of vehicular movements, it will be time enough to decide whether the Fourth Amendment should be interpreted to treat such surveillance as a search.

Garcia, 474 F.3d at 998 (citations omitted).

F. Biotechnology
1. *Technological overview*

Biotechnology has made historic leaps in the past several decades, resulting in both promising benefits and unanswered questions. It seems only a few years ago that scientists undertook to *map* the human genome—now scientists hope to *manipulate* the human genome, among other things. New technologies in biochemistry, genetics, and molecular biology have enlightened our understanding of the underlying causes of disease, have enabled the discovery of new pharmaceuticals that specifically target disease, and have offered hopes of detecting and preventing disease even before patients become symptomatic.

These new innovations, and the research methods giving rise to them, have led to several diverse privacy concerns. First, much of the biotech research currently conducted requires human tissues, cells, or embryonic materials. This fact, paired with the enormous financial stakes involved, has led to questions over the privacy and ownership rights of tissue donors. Second, advances in biotechnology have enabled the advent of personalized medicine, which seeks to diagnose and treat patients based on their particular genetic make-ups. This individualistic treatment rouses concerns over how personal genetic information will be gathered, stored, and transmitted. Third, with the increasing availability and specificity of genetic disease screening and diagnosis, privacy issues arise over potential discrimination by employers and insurance companies based on genetic predispositions or pre-symptomatic genetic diagnosis. Fourth, with the advent of new methods for genetic disease detection, government surveillance and reporting may increasingly rely on individualist genetic data, rather than on group statistical data, resulting in still other concerns over privacy.

2. Human Tissues and Cells in Research and Commerce

Biotech research and development currently relies heavily on human tissues, cells, and embryonic materials. As a result, there is an increasingly lucrative market in human biological materials. Both of these phenomena implicate privacy concerns.

(a) Rights of tissue donors

Ultimately, as one commentator noted, our bodies are "the source of all we feel and think" and our treatment of them "must incorporate the dignity and sanctity of the body as the source of all we experience."[21] Indeed, one court noted, in considering a patient's right to refuse medical treatment, that "[e]very human being of adult years and sound mind has a right to determine what shall be done with his own body...."[22] As a result of this intimate connection, the donors of biological materials have a special interest in how their tissues are used. Privacy concerns are implicated by various actions of third parties in this area, including: (1) unauthorized use of biological materials in research; (2) unauthorized sale of biological materials after donation; and (3) profits inuring to third parties rather than to donors, but based on donor samples.

The California Supreme Court, *en banc* in *Moore v. Regents of the University of California*, considered

21. Elizabeth E. Appel Blue, Article, *Redefining Stewardship over Body Parts*, 21 J.L & HEALTH 75, 114 (2008).

22. Bouvia v. Superior Court, 225 Cal.Rptr. 297, 302 (1986).

the legal rights of tissue donors when researchers made unauthorized use of their biological materials. 793 P.2d 479 (Cal. 1990). John Moore ("Moore") had been treated for many years at the University of California at Los Angeles Medical Center ("UCLA Medical Center") for a unique type of leukemia. He later learned that his doctor had developed and patented an extremely valuable cell line by utilizing his cells—without his knowledge or consent. Moore subsequently sued for damages alleging conversion and basing "ownership" of his biological materials on principles of privacy rights.

The *Moore* court concluded that Moore's doctor breached his fiduciary duties by failing to disclose his financial and research interests prior to obtaining Moore's informed consent. The court, however, declined to find the Regents, researchers, and commercial genetics corporations liable on Moore's theory of conversion because of its stifling effect on research. Although the court recognized the lower court's concern that "[a] patient must have the ultimate power to control what becomes of his or her tissues [and] [t]o hold otherwise would open the door to a massive invasion of human privacy and dignity in the name of medical progress," the court declined to find a donor property interest in the materials and held that privacy concerns could be adequately addressed by doctor-patient fiduciary duties and informed consent. *Id.* at 491.

Subsequent courts have also declined to find property ownership rights in body parts, following

Moore.[23] On the other hand, courts have shown a willingness to find property rights in regenerative biological materials, including blood, plasma, and sperm cells—even allowing sale of these materials.[24] Commentators have proposed alternate legal theories to protect the privacy and personal interests of donors, including heightened regulation, trust law and privacy law principles.

(b) Special considerations regarding human embryos

Courts have dealt with reproductive tissues, especially embryos, differently than other biological materials. The Supreme Court's decision in *Roe v. Wade* provides the primary basis for this differential treatment. In *Roe v. Wade*, the Supreme Court recognized a right to procreate, or not, that was inherent to the right of privacy protected by the Fourteenth Amendment. 410 U.S. 113, 153 (1973). Proponents for special treatment of reproductive tissues rely on the privacy rights of the gamete providers, or "parents," for support, but courts remain split.

In *Davis v. Davis*, the Tennessee Supreme Court considered whether the husband or the wife was entitled to "custody" of preembryos that were cryo-

23. *See* Washington Univ. v. Catalona, 437 F. Supp. 2d 985 (E.D. Mo. 2006); Greenberg v. Miami Children's Hospital Research Inst., 264 F. Supp. 2d 1064 (S.D. Fla. 2003).

24. Green v. Commissioner, 74 T.C. 1229, 1980 WL 4486 (1980); Hecht v. Superior Court, 20 Cal.Rptr.2d 275 (Cal. Ct. App. 1993).

genically preserved during the marriage. 842 S.W.2d 588 (Tenn. 1992). The court held that "preembryos are not, strictly speaking, either 'persons' or 'property,' but occupy an interim category that entitles them to special respect because of their potential for human life." *Id.* at 597. The court further held that both gamete providers had equal decision-making authority regarding the disposition of the preembryos and proceeded to balance the individual privacy interests involved, specifically the rights to procreation and to avoid procreation. The wife sought only to donate the preembryos and not to become impregnated and the husband was vehemently opposed to the donation. Thus, the court held that the husband's interest prevailed—at least absent prior agreement to the contrary.

In *Kass v. Kass*, the Court of Appeals of New York considered a near identical issue, but held that the wife's right of privacy was not implicated prior to implantation. 696 N.E.2d 174, 179–80 (N.Y. 1998). The court declined to decide whether the prezygotes were entitled to "special respect" as recognized in *Davis*, and rather than weighing the privacy interests of the gamete providers, held that the consent agreement entered into with the fertility clinic controlled the disposition of the pre-zygotes.

(c) Special considerations regarding human reproductive tissues

Quite distinct privacy concerns arise in the area of sperm and egg cell, or gamete, donation. Donors and recipients are often complete strangers, but the private information of the donor is highly valuable to the recipient. Worldwide, the sale of gametes has become increasingly lucrative, and the private donor information linked to the gametes drives the value of individual gametes.[25] This donor information traditionally includes: (1) a complete medical and genetic history; (2) general information regarding age, weight, height, educational background, sexual activity, and drug usage; and (3) personal information regarding religion, hobbies, talents, and physical features (including a photograph)—even so far as disclosing "what would send [one] ... to an ATM at three in the morning."[26] Most, if not all, of this information is available for perusal by potential recipients who subscribe to a gamete broker's services.

Unfortunately, the international sale of gametes is virtually unregulated and U.S. regulations focus primarily on gamete collection and screening by sperm and egg banks, neglecting regulations regarding the collection, transfer, and protection of personal donor information.[27] As brokers who deal in gametes do not fall neatly under the HIPAA definition of "covered entities," their duties regarding the protection of donor information are questionable. One commentator proposes a regulatory scheme

25. *See* Sunni Yuen, Comment, *An Information Privacy Approach to Regulating the Middlemen in the Lucrative Gametes Market*, 29 U. Pa. J. Int'l L. 527, 528–29 (Winter 2007).

26. *Id.* at 535–36, 540.

27. *See* 21 C.F.R. § 1271.1 (2007).

for protecting donor information administered by the Federal Food and Drug Administration ("FDA"), which currently regulates sperm and egg banks.

3. *Personalized Medicine*

Personalized Medicine ("PM") refers to the individualized diagnosis and treatment of disease based on one's particular genetic makeup.[28] PM thus involves both genomics, the mapping and study individual genotypes, and pharmacogenomics, the tailoring of pharmaceuticals to particular genotypes. PM appears to be the wave of the future. Dr. Elias Zerhouni, Director of the National Institutes of Health ("NIH"),,stated in congressional testimony that we "can now clearly envision an era when the treatment paradigm of medicine will increasingly become more *predictive, personalized and preemptive.*"[29]

Scientists are becoming more and more aware that the particular genetic makeup of patients and their diseases is directly related to whether and how well they will respond to treatment. The genetic profiling of breast cancer patients, for example, reveals that between seven and ten percent of wom-

28. Gary E. Marchant, *Personalized Medicine and the Law*, 44 ARIZ. ATT'Y 12 (Oct. 2007).

29. *Testimony Before the House Subcommittee on Labor, HHS, Education Appropriations*, 109th Cong. (April 6, 2006) (statement of Dr. Elias Zerhouni, NIH Director) (emphasis added), *available at* http://olpa.od.nih.gov/hearings/109/session2/testimonies/overview.asp.

en are unable to metabolize the cancer drug tamoxifen. Genetic testing is thus necessary before the drug is prescribed. Genetic disease profiling also reveals that only tumors exhibiting an over-expression of the HER2 gene are responsive to the drug trastuzumab.

PM represents a powerful tool for the diagnosis, prevention, and treatment of disease, but commentators raise major privacy concerns. There are questions about the regulatory oversight of genetic testing. Any laboratory currently may offer genetic testing without government approval and, although the FDA recently proposed a rule for expanding its approval requirements, it was met with considerable opposition, and subsequently revised in 2007. Commentators also raise questions as to how individual genetic information will be collected, maintained, and transmitted.

4. Insurance and Employment Discrimination

The advent of personalized medicine and genetic testing have led to concerns over whether this information may be used by employers or insurance companies to discriminate against tested individuals.

One 1989 study, conducted by the Congressional Office of Technology Assessment ("COTA"), found that forty-two percent of employers considered the health-insurance risks of job applicants relevant to their employment decisions.[30] In 1989, nearly four percent of the companies surveyed already used some type of genetic screening. Another commentator cited a study in which "twenty-five percent of Fortune 500 companies [admitted] that they have used DNA testing to weed out job applicants with a certain disposition for genetic diseases."[31] With the increasing costs of healthcare insurance, more employers may be inclined to base employment decisions on genetic profiling, to the detriment and discrimination of high-risk applicants.

In addition to potential employment discrimination based on genetic profiling, insurance companies may also utilize genetic information to exclude individuals or to charge higher rates for insurance. A non-profit bioethics organization, the Council for Responsible Genetics, documents individual cases of genetic discrimination by insurance companies and others.[32] One commentator, however, notes that insurance companies are under a duty of care by virtue of the insurance relationship, which prohibits them from acting primarily on the basis of self-interest.[33] In some respects, this duty extends even

30. *See* Paul Steven Miller, Article, *Is There a Pink Slip in My Genes? Genetic Discrimination in the Workplace*, 3 J. HEALTH CARE L. & POL'Y 225, 236 (2000).

31. Aaron P. Stevens, Note, *Arresting Crime: Expanding the Scope of DNA Databases in America*, 79 TEX. L. REV. 921, 933 (2001).

32. *Genetic Discrimination: A Position Paper Presented by the Council for Responsible Genetics* (Jan. 2001), *available at* http://www.gene-watch.org/programs/privacy/genetic-disc-position.html.

33. Sonia M. Suter, *Disentangling Privacy from Property: Toward a Deeper Understanding of Genetic Privacy*, 72 GEO. WASH. L. REV. 737, 794 (2004).

to insurance applicants. Even so, an early 1995 study conducted by Georgetown University indicated that eighty-five percent of persons surveyed were concerned about discrimination by employers or insurers using their genetic information. This same study found that seventeen percent of those surveyed had not revealed known genetic information to their employers or insurance companies as a result of these fears.

In response, many states have passed legislation prohibiting the discriminatory use of genetic information by employers and insurers, but these laws are by and large ineffective. It is hoped that the proposed GINA legislation will alleviate many of the privacy concerns regarding discrimination based on genetic profiling.

5. *Government Surveillance and Reporting*

Privacy law not only protects the ability to make personal choices, which was the aspect of privacy protected by the Supreme Court in *Roe v. Wade*, but must protect the very core of each human's existence. As genetic knowledge expands in breadth and depth, it approaches the very basics of each human. Increased governmental surveillance into our genetic information is especially alarming.

The government has increasingly relied on individually-identified health information to monitor public health—whereas traditionally, group statistical data was collected. This tendency by the government to rely more and more on individualist health data is even more alarming when the data collected is genetic data.

In 1977, the Supreme Court in *Whalen v. Roe* outlined the basic principles for balancing privacy with the police power when maintaining individual public health data. This decision indicates that the government will be granted significant leeway in fashioning reporting schemes that promote or protect public health—even when reporting may involve personal genetic information. One commentator notes, however, that surveillance programs should balance public health concerns with individual privacy and confidentiality rights.[34]

III.   FUTURE TRENDS

Judge Posner's words in *Garcia* are a fitting lead-in to the final part of this Nutshell: "It would be premature to rule that ... a program of mass surveillance could not possibly raise a question under the Fourth Amendment.... Should government someday decide to institute programs of mass surveillance of vehicular movements, it will be time enough to decide whether the Fourth Amendment should be interpreted to treat such surveillance as a search." Over the next ten to twenty years, Judge Posner's prognostication will be put to the test as continuing improvements in computing power com-

34.   Michael A. Stoto, *Public Health Surveillance in the Twenty–First Century: Achieving Population Health Goals While Protecting Individual's Privacy and Confidentiality*, 96 Geo. L.J. 703, 717 (2008).

bined with the proliferation of Internet-capable wireless devices will cause many of the technologies discussed above to become ever cheaper and more widely distributed. In turn, as ever-greater volumes of information are collected, whether by fair or foul means, data mining from that information will become an increasingly powerful tool for both monitoring and manipulating individuals. The following topics provide a few examples of the future technological challenges that privacy will face.

Ubiquitous Observation: The term "ubiquitous observation" has been coined to describe programs that focus on prolonged surveillance of individuals and geographic areas. The starting point of ubiquitous observation begins with broad area surveillance as well as "birth-to-death" tracking and identification of critical targets. This ever-present observation is facilitated using both existing technologies and anticipated near-future improvements in them. Many of the technologies required for ubiquitous observation, *e.g.*, wireless microcameras, facial recognition software, RFID-enabled identification cards, "always on" GPS receivers in cell phones and automobiles, are already available on the consumer market. The key to moving from these many scattered components to an integrated surveillance system will be improvements in networking and data management so that information from many thousands of separate collection points can be collated and searched within a reasonable time frame. Ubiquitous observation will effectively be Jeremy Bentham's Panopticon made real, except that instead of consisting of a single building, it will exist as an overlay on cityscapes.

No full-scale ubiquitous observation system is yet in use, but the United Kingdom is rapidly progressing in that direction through the deployment of increasingly sophisticated networks of closed-circuit television cameras and listening devices. The U.S. military is experimenting with developing these systems for purposes of using them in Iraq and Afghanistan to identify and intercept small groups of insurgents, car bombers, snipers, and other enemy forces that might evade more traditional observation techniques.

Data Strip Mining: The concept of data mining has existed for decades, but was primarily limited to searching for patterns in one database at a time and then cross-referencing results. As a result of improvements in computer networking and processing power, it will become increasingly feasible, particularly for government actors who can compel access to otherwise proprietary databases by law, to consolidate and scrutinize personal information from numerous different sources, allowing a previously unrivaled degree of analysis. Critics have dubbed these efforts "data strip mining" to denote the broad nature of such programs.

In the United States two abortive attempts have been made at establishing data strip mining programs. The Total Information Awareness (TIA) Program was launched shortly after the September 11, 2001 terrorist attacks, and was designed to combine information from disparate sources and then, using computer algorithms, filter the information and search for "suspicious" behavior. After considerable negative media coverage of the project, Congress, in 2003, terminated funding for the TIA Program. A new data strip mining program, the Multistate Anti–Terrorism Information Exchange (MATRIX) was initiated. MATRIX was designed to combine and share government and private-sector data about individuals. The MATRIX database contained more than 20 billion records from private sources. The information included criminal histories, driver's license data, vehicle registration records, and public data record entries. Out of privacy concerns, Congress cancelled funding for the project and in 2005 MATRIX was shut down. While no publicly acknowledged data strip mining program is in effect at this time, the eventual implementation of this kind of program appears to be inevitable. The only issue will be whether Congress has the political will to actually control the program.

Targeted Real–Time Advertising: Less pernicious, but certainly more obtrusive, is the concept of targeted real-time advertising. Targeted real-time advertising personalizes video and audio advertising to patrons in much the same way as online profiling allows web advertisers to customize advertising to each individual. Tokyo's Ginza shopping district represents a pioneering effort at deploying such systems. The district contains 10,000 embedded RFIDs in stores, restaurants, and other commercial outlets, which transmit information to shoppers via earphones and a small portable video screen. The information relayed to the shopper automatically changes as the shopper moves from one store or location to another. Developments including video monitors which can display different images depending on viewing angle and narrowcast speakers, particularly if paired with an RFID-enabled identification card and a database assembled from shopping habits derived from customer "loyalty cards," would permit the creation of advertising kiosks that deliver personalized messages to each viewer.

Genetic Testing: Genetic testing is the process of testing an individual's DNA to determine vulnerability to certain diseases and conditions. Genetic testing raises privacy concerns in two principal areas: employment and medical insurance. In the employment context, businesses, looking to maximize profits and productivity, may look to genetic predispositions in making hiring determinations. Proponents and detractors of genetic testing in the workplace are engaged in a debate over whether the information derived from genetic testing is comparable to traditional forms of health information. Currently, there is no federal law on the subject. Some states, however, protect individuals from discrimination based on genetic testing.

The debate over genetic testing in the context of medical insurance pits the interest of insurance companies to avoid insuring individuals with elevated health risks against the individuals' interest in obtaining affordable coverage. At present, it seems the latter interest is prevailing since over half of states have passed legislation prohibiting insurers from engaging in genetic testing to determine coverage. Yet this may change over the coming years as genetic testing becomes more affordable and covers an ever-greater number of possible conditions. Relatively few individuals currently go to the trouble of having themselves tested for genetic conditions for purposes of attempting to take advantage of their insurer. As the cost of this testing drops into the low three figures range, however, the temptation to attempt to "game the system" by purchasing insurance coverage on favorable terms when an individual knows that an elevated risk of a particular condition exists. As this practice becomes widespread it will undoubtedly affect insurers' bottom lines. If that begins to be a problem, insurance companies may pursue more favorable federal regulation to preempt state laws.

Dickens once wrote: "It was the best of times, it was the worst of times...." In these times of rapid technological developments, we hope society will have the political will to shape and guide technology, while protecting privacy.

*

INDEX

343

†